The Complete Manual for
Young Sportsmen

The Complete Manual for
Young Sportsmen

The Original Handbook for Hunting, Fishing, and Game

Frank Forester

Foreword by Nick Lyons

CLYDESDALE

First published in 1857 by Stringer & Townsend

First Clydesdale Press Edition, 2019

Foreword © 2019 by Nick Lyons

Clydesdale books may be purchased in bulk at special discounts for sales promotion, corporate gifts, fund-raising, or educational purposes. Special editions can also be created to specifications. For details, contact the Special Sales Department, Skyhorse Publishing, 307 West 36th Street, 11th Floor, New York, NY 10018 or info@skyhorsepublishing.com.

Clydesdale Press™ is a pending trademark of Skyhorse Publishing, Inc.®, a Delaware corporation.

Visit our website at www.skyhorsepublishing.com.

10 9 8 7 6 5 4 3 2 1

Library of Congress Cataloging-in-Publication Data is available on file.

Print ISBN: 978-1-945186-71-4
eISBN: 978-1-945186-76-9

Printed in the United States of America

TABLE OF CONTENTS

Game Fish and the Best Modes of Fishing Them

LIST OF ILLUSTRATIONS

*Originally Designed or Adapted and
Drawn on Wood by Author*

FOREWORD

WHAT a fascinating and worthwhile pleasure it is for a passionate young or adult fisherman or hunter to glimpse the sporting world of more than a century and a half ago. Technology has thrust us so far forward that the tools of sport—the gun, the rod, the reel, the flies and lures—are almost unrecognizable from those used in the 1850s, let alone the customs and practices. Customs have changed radically too—and conservation, because of threatened species and their environments, has become one of our primary concerns. *The Complete Manual for Young Sportsmen* was first published in 1852, and republished in 1873, in the present edition, twenty years after its author died.

Frank Forester, the pen name of Henry William Herbert (1807-1858), was a man of many parts. He was born in London, the oldest son of the Dean of Manchester, and came to America in 1831. With a classical education at Eton, he was well enough versed in both Latin and Greek to teach both in New York City. He translated French novels, wrote a variety of entries for a prominent encyclopedia, wrote eight novels himself and half a dozen biographies, and—under his pen name—published popular articles and books on hunting, fishing, and horsemanship, including this long manual, in twenty-five years. And he illustrated many of his books. He took his own life at 51, in 1858.

Much of what he wrote about sport, because so very much has changed, is impractical, irrelevant, even outrageous. But not all. We are mesmerized by this book partly for the reasons we love an early Sears Roebuck or Montgomery Ward catalog; we love the nostalgia that wraps itself around guns, rods, and lures available at eye-opening prices and the fact that we'll never know how they were used. But we're especially interested by the older practices and the good number of continuities that still obtain. Here's Forester in his chapter "The Gun, and How to Choose It:"

"First the gun must be a good one in itself, well built of good materials, strong, sound, and safe, by the excellence of finish, which also produce efficient carrying of its charge, rapid firing, and clean killing."

Though too abstract, the principles remain valuable and even contemporary.

Forester is very good on guns and field sports, which

he loved, and he often offers sound practical advice that remains pertinent:

> ". . . the gun must particularly suit the individual owner . . . and no man can any more shoot well with a gun that does not come readily to his shoulder and fairly to his eye, than he can be at ease in a suit two sizes under his fit, or walk a footrace in boots that pinch him."

He offers us a broad vision of what guns were then available, from the shotgun to the minié rifle to Sharps, and is severe and uncompromising on matters of safety, carelessness, and care of equipment. Always he is patient in distinguishing what his favorites are, and what is more a matter of taste and not what he would insist upon. He is especially careful on the matter of learning to shoot and quotes at length from "Oakleigh's Shooting Code" or another authority when he deems something has been said as well as it could be said.

Much of what he tells us about dogs—setters, pointers, spaniels, retrievers, hounds—and dog training or care is most interesting for the way it was done then. We don't whip dogs these days, but they did then. Some advice is simple and quite viable today: "Never lose one's temper."

Game was more plentiful and diverse then, and too often the hunter lacked any sense of conservation. Forester shot golden plover, sandpipers, along with woodcock, grouse, and waterfowl. He reports that Audubon once killed 127 snipes, "three barrels" worth. He announced, without explanation, and much before the turkey "revolution" occurred, that "turkey hunting is not a sport."

Forester grants fishing less than one quarter of his book. It clearly interested him much less than hunting and though he claims that what he offers will "contain all that is needful in theory and practice for the instruction of the young angler," it clearly doesn't. So much is different. *Salmo fontinalis*, the beautiful brook trout, is the only trout present and the ways we fish for brown, rainbow, and cutthroat trout today are vastly more complex and interesting. He sets out to cover all forms of fishing, fresh and salt water, and too often his treatment here is thin.

Most interesting, I think, are his views of fly rods made of ash, hickory, lancewood, and whole bamboo cane. But there's a very early mention of fly rods being constructed from "rent and glued bamboo," forerunners of the fine split bamboo rods we treasure today. It's fascinating to hear what flies were used in the mid-nineteenth century, the nature of the early hooks, the natural materials used in fly construction. Fly fishing, called "whipping," has come the greatest possible distance since then and not out of nostalgia alone but to appreciate how much twentieth and twenty-first century innovation has advanced the practice of the sport, the book is invaluable. Of course, we're interested in the baits they used, too: salmon-roe paste, shrimp paste, parts of fish, live fish, grubs, caterpillars, live mayflies and stone flies, and, of course, good old garden worms. What good fun and how instructive it is for the curious sportsman of today, to know what his world was then.

The Complete Manual for the Young Sportsman has much about what sport so many years ago was—how it was practiced, and with what weapons and rods. There is much to learn and enjoy in this journey back—and much to admire about how fortunate we are to have such good sport today.

—Nick Lyons

Manual FOR Young Sportsmen.

INTRODUCTION.

It is not known, probably not now to be discovered, at what period in the history of man, the pursuit of wild animals—which was originally undertaken by the semi-barbarous tribes as a means of procuring animal food, or for protection against formidable *carnivora*, which threatened either their own existence or that of their flocks and herds, as they gradually adopted stationary homes and pastoral habits—began to be regarded as a sport. But from a very remote period of antiquity such has undoubtedly been the case; and so universally diffused in all countries, so generally implanted in all hearts, does this passion now exist, that we may assume it as certain, that so soon as hunting ceased to be a laborious and painful necessity, obligatory on the nomadic tribes for the support of life, it came to be followed as a sport, to be the delight of the warrior nobles, and, as game gradually became scarce and rare, to be regarded as the privileged prerogative of the crown.

In the Bible, it is true, there is little mention of hunting, either as a method of procuring meat, or as a pursuit of pleasure. Nimrod, the son of Cush, we are told, indeed, was a mighty hunter before the Lord, but the probability of the case would point to him as a destroyer of savage beasts, like Hercules and Theseus in Hellenic fable, rather than as one,

> With hound and horn his way who took
> To drive the fallow deer;

even if we do not regard him, in the wider light, as a hunter not of quadrupeds but of men, by the chase of whom "he began to be a mighty one in the earth."

Esau, again, we read of, somewhat as an exception among the pastoral people, over whom he was born a leader—although, partly in consequence of his addiction to this pursuit, which with him clearly must have been a sport rather than an occupation, he lost his hereditary title—in the light, probably, of the first authenticated hunter of the deer. There are, however, many natural reasons, among which not the least is the sterile, rocky and rugged face of the country which they inhabited, why the children of Israel should never have acquired a taste for, or proficiency in, field sports. The horse, whose pliable pasterns and delicate hoofs were ill adapted to the craggy hill-sides and rocky roads of Palestine, was prohibited by the great legislator of the people of the Lord; and his place was filled by the stiff-jointed, stubborn, long-enduring ass, between whom and the chase there is the least imaginable connection. To the Israelites, as to many oriental peoples, the dog was an unclean animal; his name a reproach, and himself, instead of the best servant and domestic friend of man, the very outcast and *pariah* of creation. Lastly, owing to the strictness of the Levitical prohibitions, many of the chief animals of the chase, as the hare, the coney, the wild boar, and not a few of the choicest game birds, were forbidden as articles of food to the chosen people. The means, and inducements, to carry on hunting to any profitable or pleasurable extent, seem, therefore, to have been, alike, wanting to the Israelites; nor, under these circumstances, can it be a matter of surprise that it was little, if at all, practised among them.

In the other great kingdoms of the East, however, from the earliest ages, hunting and hawking were practised on the largest and most royal style by the monarch® and their chosen nobles.

The noble sculptures recently disinterred at Khorsabad, in the vicinity of Mosul, and the ruins of Nineveh, contemporaneous with the events described in Holy Writ, abound in delineations of this regal mimicry of war. The histories of the Median, Persian, and Assyrian empires are filled with allusions to the eager spirit of sportsmanship with which the chase was prosecuted at a time, when, "to speak the truth, to ride, and to shoot" were esteemed the brightest educational gems in a Persian prince's diadem. We learn from Xenophon, soldier, hunter, philosopher, historian, that wherever, on the line of the long march of the Ten-thousand from Sardis up to Babylon, there was found a royal residence, it was accompanied by a great pleasure park and preserve of wild animals, some of them the savage *carnivora*, which Cyrus, he says, hunted on horseback, when he desired to take exercise. It is remarkable, moreover, that the name *papádeisos*—by no means a word of common occurrence in the Greek language, nor, so far as I remember, ever used of any enclosed ground within the confines of Greece proper, which is invariably applied to these pleasure parks maintained for hunting purposes—is identical with the word Paradise, otherwise rendered Garden of Eden, in its primary terrestrial signification, which we have transferred to the seat of celestial beatitude and repose hereafter.

The Greek and Roman writers, both in verse and prose, abound with allusions to this heroic pursuit and passion, which is attributed especially to their most favorite and famous demigods. The legends of the Nemean lion, the Caledonian boar, the tragical hunting of Acteon, the tales of Cephalus and Procris, of the wild Thessalian Centaurs, who nursed the martial vigor of the young Achilles on the marrow of hunted bears and lions; of Phoedra, Atalanta, Adonis the beloved of Venus, and above all Diana, the huntress queen, with her attendant train of nymphs, are familiar to all, and point evidently to a period, when, in the intervals of war and warlike forays, the chase was the daily delight and occupation of the patriarchal hero-kings and their rude aristocracies, who held their ancient sway over the scattered Argive or Ionic tribes, from sandy Pylos and the blue waves of the Mediterranean waters to the broad plains of Thessaly and the far hills,

> That loot along Epirus' valleys,
> Where freedom still at moments rallies
> And pays in blood oppression's ills.

In like manner, those great world-conquerors, the Romans—though, after they had attained to greatness, and become, for the most part, city-dwellers, they were too much occupied in the forum or the field, too busy in the struggle for existence, or in the pursuit of empire, to give much time to mere amusements, however manly or martial in their tendencies—always continued in some degree to hold the sports of the field in esteem and honor; and no young man was thought much the worse, if he did at times neglect forensic duties and the "long business of his clients," to couch him in the open field "beneath the frigid Jupiter," awaiting the first gleam of the wintry dawn, when he might hope

"latitantem excipere aprum fruticeto."[1]

It was not, however, until the advent of the Northern deluge of invaders, Scythians, Huns, Scandinavians, Teutons, Norsemen, that the hunting mania took permanent possession of the popular heart, in every land which yielded to the sway of those warrior and hunter races.

And to this day, wherever a drop is to be found of that fierce Northern blood surviving in the people's veins, there you will find, and in no other land, the passion for the chase alive and dominant.

In southern Europe, in the nations which speak the soft bastard Latin, in Italy, Spain, Portugal, the shores and isles of the Mediterranean, there is no hunter-spirit in the people; and even where the chase has been attempted, as a regal pastime, by the rulers and the princes of the lands, it has fallen dull and ineffectual, a mere mimicry and *simulacrum* of the genuine sport, and no more like the real hunts-up, "than I to Hercules."

In the Teutonic wolds and woodlands, on the contrary, on the bleak mountain-tops and misty moors of Scotia, in the deep green morasses of Hibernia, in the

1 "To receive upon his spear the lurking wild hoar, when it rushes from the thicket."—*Hor.*

rejoicing valleys, over the breezy downs, in the time-honored forests of old England, among the perpetual snows of the frore and frozen Alps, upon the broad and burnt karroos of soul horn Africa, among Australian gum-trees or Canadian pine-woods; from the ghauts, from the grand peaks of the Himalayas, to the stern flanks of the Rocky Mountains and the skirts of the American salt desert, how genuinely, how spontaneously burns the hunter ardor of the Norse populations.

So long as Britain remained provincial, the inhabitants having become almost entirely Romanized, during four centuries of subjugation, the chase, if it were followed at all, was but a desultory, casual and unsystematic pastime; but so soon as the Saxons obtained a foothold on the soil, hunting with well-trained hounds, and the pursuit of fowls, "along the atmosphere," by means of reclaimed falcons, became at once a science, a systematized royal recreation, and in the end, as it has continued to this day, wherever the Saxon and Norman strains of blood are extant, a popular passion.

During the reigns of the Saxon monarchs, to such an extent was this sport carried by the nobles, that "the sportsmen in the train of the great were so onerous on lands, as to make the exemption of their visit a valuable privilege; hence a king liberates some lands from those who carry with them hawks or falcons, horses or dogs."[2] At the same time, so general had the taste become, that statutes were framed, and even the church interposed its censures, to prevent its abuse or misapplication. "Hunting[3] was forbidden by Canute on a Sunday. Every man was allowed to hunt in the woods, and in the fields that were his own, but not to interfere with the king's hunting." The increase and prevalence of this recreation

2   History of the Anglo Saxons.—*Sharon Turner*, 3, 38.
3   Ibid. 3, 37.

may be judged of, by the fact, that the "Saxon Boniface[4] prohibited his monks from hunting in the woods with dogs, and from having hawks and falcons." Even that weak, impassive, priest-ridden, half-monk king, Edward the Confessor, had "one earthly enjoyment in which he chiefly delighted, which was hunting with fleet hounds, whose opening in the woods he used with pleasure to encourage; and again, with the pouncing of birds, whose nature it is to prey on their kindred species. In these exercises, after hearing divine service in the morning, he employed himself whole days.[5]

Up to this time it would appear that game laws, such as they were, had been enacted only with reference to the maintenance of the liberties of all persons, the conservation of good order and decorum, and the prevention of violations of the Sabbath; not as yet with any bias to the preservation of game, much less to interference with the natural rights of classes.

With the Norman conquest, however, while the passion for the chase received a vast farther impetus; while as a science, under the gentle terms of venerie and woodcraft, it was materially advanced; while in its appliances of all sorts, imported Andalusian coursers, partaking largely of the desert blood, which has since rendered the English horse so famous, imported hounds from Pomerania, Albania, Germany, imported falcons from Norway, Iceland, and the Hebrides, it was carried forward to a systematic completeness unheard of before, it was fenced in, as a royal and aristocratic privilege, with forest laws so cruel, so arbitrary and so stringent, as rendered the life of a red-deer, or even the egg of a swan, a heron, a bittern, or a long-winged hawk, more valuable than the blood of a low-born man; and finally it drove

4   Ibid. 3, 38.
5   William of Malmesbury's Chronicle of the Kings of England.—Book II. Chap. 13, p. 217, Bolin's edition.

a large proportion of the rural, Saxon populace, into outlawry and direct rebellion, under chiefs who have acquired immortality, like Robin Hood and his merrymen, through the medium of those contemporaneous ballads, which sound so truly in unison to the chords of the popular heart.

Parcelled out, as greater and lesser fiefs, to the high Barons of the realm, and again by them to their knightly vassals, as were all the lands of England, as fast as they were overrun and conquered by the equestrian army of the Norman William and his successors; the sole right of following and taking game in the field, the forest, the morass, of keeping animals or implements of the chase, was vested firstly in the king, and secondly in the holder of feudal and manorial tenures; without the smallest reference to the ownership or cultivation of the soil.

By degrees the stringency and the cruelty of these statutes were remitted; and it is a curious fact, that the cooperation of the Barons in securing the liberties of the English people, as against the encroachment of the crown, was induced mainly by their desire to abridge the royal prerogative in the matter of the forest laws.

From this period, and the state of things then existing unquestionably, dates the hunting spirit of the English gentleman; his addiction to field sports, in utter disregard of climate, country, toil, hardship or exposure; his jealousy concerning manorial rights and the preservation of his game; qualities and ideas, which he carries with him into whatever quarter of the globe he migrates, whether to the snows of Canada, the unwatered barrens of Australia, the pestilential brakes of Africa, or the tiger-haunted jungles of Hindostan,

Coelum non animum mutans si trans mare currat;—

qualities and ideas, to which, though at times, perhaps, pushed to extremes and degenerating into something of license, he yet owes much of his excellence; and for which his country has a right to be proud and thankful, in that she may rely on him to *rough it,* as the noble of no other land can do, in the hour of toil and trouble.

And this brings me to the gist and bearing of this my introduction. When first it was my fortune to become a dweller on the Atlantic seaboard of the United States, to be a lover of field-sports, was in some sort to be tabooed, as a species of moral and social pariah—the word *sportsman* was understood to mean, not him who rises with the dawn, to inhale the pure breeze of the uplands or the salt gale of the great south bay, in innocent and invigorating pursuit of the wild-game of the forest or the ocean wave; but him who by the light of the flaring gas-lamp watches, flushed and feverish, through the livelong night, until the morning star, to pluck his human pigeon over the greenfield of the faro table. The well-to-do merchant foreboded no good of the younger man, who borrowed twenty-four hours in a month from business and Wall Street, for a day's snipe-shooting at Pine Brook, or a day's fowling at Jem Smith's. The lawyer, who, by chance, loved such sports, took them on the sly—packed up his gun and shooting toggery in his carpet-bag, and stole across the Fulton ferry in full court-fig, having the dread before his eyes, of becoming, thenceforth, a briefless barrister, should but one of his clients begin even to suspect that he knew the butt end of a Manton from its muzzle, much less could stop a cock in a July brake, or land a four-pounder, without a gaff, on a single gut.

It is a fact undeniable, and there be many yet alive, beside myself, who know it, that, when T. Cypress, jun., was inditing those exquisite bits of natural and sporting humorism, his Fire-island-ana, and other similar morsels of unsurpassed simplicity and art, which and which *alone* have made his name to be remembered; it was under the strictest seal of secrecy that he communicated his productions to the favored few, who were allowed to introduce them to the world,—it was in fear and trembling, in some sort, that he saw himself in print J and with a firm conviction that, if it should be once discovered, that he, a practising counsellor of high standing in New York, was actually guilty of the authorship of *genre* sketches, on sporting subjects, second, if second only— as I think not second, but superior—to Elia Lamb's best Essays, "Othello's occupation" were done for ever. That to be an author first, and then a lover of field-sports, must be the "deep damnation" of any New York lawyer, though he were a Blackstone himself, and a Coke upon him.

At that time no man, however fine a scholar, however brilliant an artist, was held altogether reputable as an associate, or entirely right in his mind, if he were not wholly and solely devoted to *business;* and the only business, which was esteemed business, in the eyes of the wise men of Gotham, was that of making and hoarding money.

In many respects matters have mended since that time. It has been discovered that there are other uses for money besides hoarding it; that a merchant may be just as much Sir Oracle on Change, and that a lawyer may hold fully as able an argument before a Supreme Court, though he be able to read a French novel, to enjoy an Italian Opera, or to have an opinion of his own concerning the merits of Maud or Hiawatha; that a native poet is not, necessarily, an idle fellow, fit for nothing rational or useful; nor a profound historian a sad misapplier of his time and talents; though still, be it said with all humility, the last-named laborers in the vineyard are far from holding the same place in society here, which they do, and ought to do, every where else.

Still, while it must be admitted that some species

of mental culture and improvement, which were, but a few years since, held to disqualify a man for success and usefulness in life, are now tolerated, and even admitted, if they do not prevent the main end of money-making; it cannot be denied, that all bodily recreations, all athletic relaxations of the mind by alternation of physical efforts, all tastes and tendencies toward field-sports are as much or more discountenanced by the grave men of cities, and less practised by the gay young men of society, than they have been at any time before.

With the former, it is regarded as pretty much the same, whether the young man, who has his way to make in the world by a trade, an art, or a profession, borrow a few hours or days from the counter, the studio, or the closet, to unbend the overstretched bow of his intellect by that needful exercise of the body, without which the mind cannot be preserved sound; or to waste them in morning practisings of polkas with fast girls, or in nocturnal battles against the Tiger with fast men.

And as to the latter, one need no more than look at the bleared eyes, sallow half-valanced faces, dwindled limbs, undeveloped frames, and rickety gait of the rising generation of those, who, by virtue of their natural advantages of wealth and position, ought to be the flower of the land, to see that they are utterly degenerate both in vigor of mind and stamina of body, and to prognosticate them, if they wed—as doubtless they will wed—like to like, with the fast, precocious, weedy beauties of the polka-nursery, as

—*mox daturos*
Progenien vitiosiorem[6]

6   Soon about to produce a progeny yet more defective.—*Hor.*

Of late, I have observed with pleasure, that many of the best and clearest intellects in America have perceived the necessity of calling public attention strongly to this peculiar feature of the American character and constitution. One of the most eloquent, perhaps, the most finished of American orators, has dwelt impressively on the fact, that the headlong race and struggle, the earnest, life-enduring and life-consuming contest, for advancement, for wealth, for preeminence, for power; beginning before the gristle of youth is hardened into the bone of manhood and ending only in the grave, is, in far too many instances, never relaxed for a moment, to enable the competitor to seek those changes and diversions from unremitting care and travail, which are as necessary to restore the tone of the mind, as are repose and sustenance to recruit the forces of the body.

Even from the pulpit, the true sense of the word *recreation,* which men are wont to use frivolously as equivalent to pleasurable excitement, has been pointed out—much doubtless to the wonderment of those ascetic geniuses, who have set up their witness against all amusement—as if it were at best idle and unprofitable, if not sinful in itself, apart from its consequences.

Much exercised, one can understand these Pharisees to find themselves in the spirit, on discovering that this re-creation, as they are wont to style it in their nasal self-sanctification, is so called, because it has the acknowledged potency, indeed, to *re*-create; or make anew from the beginning, and restore to all its pristine elasticity, lost and worn out by overcarefulness concerning the things of to-day, the mind, which has been actually *unmade* by preternatural tension.

That relaxation of the overtasked mind is necessary even to the maintenance, much more to the improvement of its powers, has never at any period of the world been doubted or disputed.

Neqne semper arcum
Tendit Apollo—[7]

has at all times been a proverb with the most Draconian of pedagogues; and never surely was there a time, when its value is so appreciable, as this age of high pressure, when every thing,—education, business, politics, all that concerns or interests mankind, is forced ahead without stay or stop, whether for consideration or repentance, as if by steam and electricity.

And if it be admitted, as I think it will not be denied, that never was it more needful for the advantage, moral and physical, of all classes, that some comprehensive plan of rational diversion and relaxation from incessant labor and anxiety should be devised and recommended—it will scarcely, I think, be questioned or disputed, that never was there more need that some measure of manliness should he infused into the amusements of the youth of the so-styled upper classes—the *jeunesse doree*—of the Atlantic cities, some touch of manhood inoculated into the ingenuous youths themselves.

It is worthy of remark that whatever faults, whatever weaknesses, follies, deficiencies or vices, may be justly laid to the charge of the English gentry and nobility, want of manliness, of pluck to do or to endure, is not of them.

Of European armies alone the English is officered, from its subalterns to its commanders-in-chief, by the gentry. In France, the nobility have long ceased to be the nobility of the sword; the splendid hosts of the French are officered entirely by th*e juste milieu*. While all other aristocracies are wholly effete, effeminate, evirated, field sports have preserved the English gentleman strong, at least, of body, capable to walk, to ride, to endure cold,

7   Nor does Apollo always bend his bow.—*Hor.*

heat, hunger, weariness, wounds as well—he could not do it better—as the meanest of his fellow-countrymen or fellow-soldiers.

Lamentable as has been the misconduct of the war, disgraceful as the incapacity of the leaders of the war, infamous, I had almost said treasonable, as the apathy and nepotism of the home government, no word of blame has found utterance concerning the pluck, the stamina, the endurance, the devotion of the highly-born, softly-nurtured, noble subalterns of the English army.

They died in their stirrups in that appalling charge at Balaclava, avenging themselves by tenfold slaughter of their outnumbering foes—they rotted piecemeal in those charnel trenches—they weltered in mute agony, in that dreadful ditch of the Redan, compelling their comrades in anguish to like silence by the wonderful example of their young constancy.

Heaven knows I wish to draw no invidious distinctions, or to institute odious comparisons, but I must be permitted to doubt whether the Schottishing flower of young York, who would shrink dismayed from the verge of snipe-bog, and faint at the idea of a ten hours' July tramp over the Drowned Lands after woodcock, would have shone with much splendor in that hand-to-hand affair, in the Valley of Death, or have come with the vivacity of the Polka out of the semi-liquid, semi-frozen mud of those disastrous trenches.

Seriously speaking, I believe that over earnestness in the pursuit of gain on the one hand, and over frivolity in the pursuit of pleasure on the other, are two of the besetting vices of the age; and I farther believe, that a little more charity and less austerity on the part of the old, and a great deal more manhood and less Miss Nancyishness on the part of the young men of our Atlantic cities, are desiderata much to be desired.

For both complaints I would seriously recommend, as a physician no less of the mind than of the body, moderate doses of field sports, to be systematically taken, as the disciples of æsculapius have it, *pro re natâ.*

As I have, however, little faith in the docility, obedience or teachability of the old men, it is principally to the young men, and more especially to the young men of pleasant rural villages, of flourishing inland cities, and of the beautiful free country itself, from the pine forests and clear trout-streams of the farthest East, to the boundless prairies and towering crags of the farthermost West, that I commend this my complete manual of field sports. And this I will promise them, that, if they will follow my precepts in the letter and in the spirit, although I may fail to turn them out very Nimrods and perfect Izaak Waltons, I will at least put them in the way of acquiring what is known, as the *mens sana in corpore sano*—in other words a good appetite, a good digestion, a good constitution; the use of their limbs for the purposes to which the God of nature intended them, "the slumbers light, that fly the approach of morn;" the consciousness of living innocently before God and manfully among men, and the certainty of dying, when the time of death shall come, as it behooves men to die, not misers or monkeys.

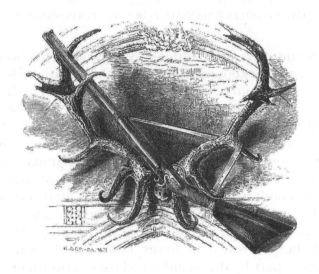

THE GUN, AND HOW TO CHOOSE IT.

In the United States and British Provinces of North America, as a general rule, shooting with the shot gun or the rifle, must he regarded as the head and front of Field Sports; and not, as is the case in Europe, second, as a tamer and far less exciting pursuit, to the glorious excitement of the chase.

In the northern States of the Union and the British Provinces, the extreme severity of the winters rendering the country too hard to be run over by hounds or ridden over on horses, except during a few weeks in the autumn, and a few more in the first opening of the spring, as well as the difficulty of the almost unjumpable timber fences, nearly debar the possibility of fox or deer-hunting with complete packs and mounted hunters. Nor, were it otherwise, is it probable that this sport could ever become very general or popular, owing to the dislike of farmers to have their fields crossed, and their fences broken down, by a rout of hard-riding Nimrods.

Some years since, indeed, two packs of fox-hounds were regularly kept up in full English sporting style, the one at Washington, in the District of Columbia, by the gentlemen of the British legation, while Sir Richard Vaughan was at the head of it, the other at Montreal by the British residents and the officers of the garrison. They languished, however, in an uncongenial clime, and year by year were less and less strenuously supported, until both have, I believe, fallen into total abeyance.

In the southern States, where the seasons are not so unpropitious to the sport, where the properties are much larger, vested in fewer hands, and owned for the most part by the wealthier classes, who themselves constitute the sporting population, as in Maryland and Virginia, foxhunting is still carried on, to some extent, by the planters; though with none of that accuracy of detail and completeness of appointment which attach to it, and render it so magnificent, both as a spectacle and a sport, in England; and, it is believed, with decreasing spirit and smaller favor, even in the imperfect manner which there obtains.

In the Carolinas, Georgia, and some of the southwestern States, deer-hunting on horseback with packs of hounds prevails; but even there the shot gun is the *modus operandi,* and the object of the hunter is to get a killing shot, not to ride across the open to a long and slashing run, and to be in at the death, when the quarry is pulled down by the pack at the end of a gallant chase. Bears are also hunted in the same style with packs of bloodhounds in Louisiana, Mississippi and Arkansas, but there the rifle does the execution, and the slaughter of the game by that instrument, not the rapture of the pursuit, is the end and aim of the pursuer.

The only sport which bears any considerable analogy to hunting, as it is practised in Great Britain, is the coursing of the stag or elk with greyhounds, as it is, within the last few years, beginning to be considerably practised in some of the western prairie States; for in that, as in the English chase, the pursuit of animal by animal, the hunters and the hunted both, for the most part in full view, and the keeping them in sight by the speed of horses and by skill and daring in equestrianism, are the sources of enjoyment and the ultimatum to be obtained.

Still, this phase of the sport being yet, as it were, in its infancy, few hounds of the peculiar race requisite being thus far introduced, and the pursuit itself rather exceptional than of common practice, it must be admitted that hunting, in the European, and more particularly British sense of the word, is not an American field sport. The pursuit of the larger animals of game, where they exist, as the deer, the bear, the elk, the moose, the cariboo, and perhaps I may add, the turkey; although it is usually known in common parlance as hunting, is not properly such, but comes under one of three heads,—"stalking," which is here generally termed still-hunting, where the animal is followed by his sign, left on the soil, or on the trees and coppice which he may have frayed, by the aid of the eye and experience in woodcraft and the habits of the quarry alone, without the assistance of hounds— "stable-stand," where the sportsman, taking his station at the intersection of deer-paths, at a haunted salt-lick, or at a well-ascertained watering place, awaits the voluntary advent of the animal, when he shall be impelled to move by the solicitation of his own instincts—or, lastly, "dog-draw," where, posting himself, as before, in such place as he judges likely to be passed by the fugitive, the shooter expects its coming when driven by slow hounds, who have drawn for it, and aroused it from its lair, under the guidance of his servants or companions.

The last terms "dog-draw" and "stable-stand," have long ceased to be sporting words in England, those methods of taking game having long fallen into disuse as sport; and the latter being practised rarely by the park-keeper, only in killing the half-tame fallow deer for the table—an animal, which is no more looked to for sport, or regarded as a beast of chase, than a south-down sheep, or a fatted calf.

They were, however, common in the olden time, when a large portion of Great Britain was still covered with the natural forest, in which the wild animals roamed nearly unmolested, preserved by rigorous forest statutes, and obtainable only as game for the table, by shooting them, in one of the two methods described, with the cross-bow, which then played, though less effectually, the part of the unerring rifle.

Shooting is, therefore, as I have said, with one arm or other, the head and front of all American field sports; since but one species, the fox, and that only in one or two States, and in them but partially and exceptionally, is pursued and killed for sport, without the use of firearms. While every other animal, which we follow for the excitement of the pursuit, or for the sake of its flesh on the table, from the gigantic moose and formidable grizzly bear to the crouching hare, from the heaven-soaring swan or hawnking wild-goose to the "twiddling" snipe, is brought to bag by means of the rifle, the fowling-piece, or the ducking-gun; and to his thorough acquaintance, and masterly performance, with one or all of these, in his own line, the rank of the sportsman must be mainly attributed, and his claim to preeminence ascribed.

I say, *mainly* attributable; because, although there are many other qualifications which go to constitute the accomplished sportsman, and without which, though he be the best and surest marksman that ever drew a trigger or squinted over a brown barrel, he has no right to arrogate to himself the title of a true sportsman, it is on this that he must rely.

These qualifications may be named generally, as the art of breaking dogs, of managing them in sickness or in health, in the kennel or in the field—the perfect acquaintance with the habits, food, feeding-grounds, breeding seasons, migrations and haunts or habitations of those animals, whether of fur or feather, which are the objects of his pursuit; and, beyond these, the possession of general information as to all the ruses, stratagems, and resources adopted in, and adapted to, the life of a hunter, which assist him not only in his first object, the overcoming or circumventing the victim on which he is intent, but on providing for the well-being and comfort, the subsisting and conditioning, both in and after the chase, in the forest or on the prairie, of himself and his companions, brute or human, quadruped or biped.

Still, essential as all these things are to the character of the real and thoroughbred forester, they are all of no avail, unless he be skilful, prompt, swift, steady, deliberate and sure with the shot-gun or the rifle, at all shots, running, flying, bounding, crossing him to the right or left, going from him, coming toward him, or at rest.

For of what use shall it be to him, though he have the finest, the most thoroughbred, the best-broken, the stanchest and fleetest dogs; though he bring them into the field in the best condition of stoutness and of nose; though he be so well acquainted with the propensities and natural history of the game he may be in search of, that he know almost as it were instinctively, at each season of the year, or at each hour of the day, on what ground to look for it, where, almost to a certainty, to find it, how to mark it down, whither to follow it up, how to bring his dogs upon its scent, to the best advantage; if when it he found, or flushed upon the wing, or started from its covert, he cannot bring it down from its flight, or stop it from its course in full career.

I have known many men in my life, both on this side

and the other of the Atlantic, who have kept dogs which they could not hunt, horses which they could not ride, guns out of which they could not shoot; lovers, or at least, pretended lovers of a sport, which they assuredly could not pursue to any profit, nor, so far as I can imagine, to any possible pleasure; who have yet fancied themselves, and even been called by others—who knew even less about it than they did themselves—sportsmen. But, though I may have been willing to give them credit as good fellows and promoters of sport for the benefit of others, I never could be induced to prostitute, by bestowing it on such as they, the noble appellation in which all, who have the right to bear it, rejoice with so legitimate a pride and pleasure.

This being admitted, therefore, it will necessarily follow that the first thing to be done by the person aspiring to be a sportsman is, to provide himself with a good and effective weapon, and next, to obtain proficiency, in the highest degree possible, in its use.

To both these ends, therefore, I shall devote a few pages of instruction, founded on long experience, and tested to my own satisfaction, at least, by the only sure proof of practice.

I shall begin by assuming, what it needs no argument to establish, that for game-shooting of smaller animals on the field, there is but one weapon; the double-barrelled percussion shot gun. For the most inveterate supporters of the old flash-in-the-pan, flint-and-steel system have long ago been compelled to abandon their prejudices on the subject, and to conform to the progressive improvement of the arm, or to fall behind the genius of the age.

It cannot be, perhaps, denied that, in point of force and range, the flint and steel had some advantage over the percussion fowling-piece; for the charge being more slowly, was more thoroughly ignited, so that nearly every grain of powder in the load was burned before the shot was expelled from the barrel; whereas it is now not by any means uncommon to find—as one may clearly observe by firing a gun over new-fallen snow—at least one half of the quantity driven out of the barrel, unconsumed, and of course useless.

The other advantages of quickness, certainty of discharge, sureness in all weather, in fogs or rain, or at sea, accuracy of aim, absence of smoke from the priming which often, especially in damp days, prevented a second shot, and instantaneousness of explosion, so vastly counterbalance the only existing drawback, that no man in his senses would think of using a flint-and-steel gun, when another could be procured.

Even in military service, where the obstinacy of routine and the economy of governments always cause improvements to be most slowly adopted, and old exploded systems to be most pertinaciously upheld, the percussion system has every where been adopted; and in view of this and the other improvements, as to range and accuracy, in the new arms, it is not too much to say that any body of men armed with the old soldier's musket, the far-famed brown Bess, of the commencement of the present century, must be annihilated in spite of all advantages of courage, strength or discipline, if opposed to troops armed with percussion and breechloading *minie*-rifles, which do not miss fire once in fifty shots, and carry as many hundreds of yards, with accuracy, as their predecessors did paces.

No one, again, it is presumed, who can afford the price of a double gun, would be content to shoot with a single, unless for ducking, where weight length and bore of such magnitude are required, as to render two barrels unhandy if not absolutely unmanageable; since a fair shot will kill at least a third more game in a day's shooting, beside doing it in far more beautiful and artistic style with a double than with a single fowling-piece.

The prettiest thing in the art of shooting, and that which is the result of the highest skill and practice, so that it may be regarded as nearly the perfection of sportsmanship, is the killing double-shots accurately, cleanly, and in fine dashing style; and I have never, certainly, seen a person, who had any real claim to be considered a crack-shot, or a fine working sportsman, who used a single barrel, after he had attained years of maturity, and had become a master of his craft.

For boys, just beginning to acquire the art of shooting, single guns are, in some respects, preferable, because they can be manufactured of sufficient strength, bore, and solidity, to shoot well at fair distances, yet sufficiently light to be managed by juvenile limbs; where a double gun not too heavy to be brought up to the shoulder cleverly by a boy, must be either a mere plaything and pop-gun, or, if of sufficient calibre and length to be at all effective, must be so lightly put together and so deficient in metal, as to be absolutely dangerous. It is, moreover, perhaps a trifle more difficult to learn to take aim over a single barrel, the double hammers tending, in some degree, to guide the eye along the elevation, so that when the young sportsman is promoted to the height of his ambition, the possession of a double-barrel, he will readily come into its use, and find it, apart from its superior weight, the easier of the two to direct rapidly and effectively toward its object.

There is, moreover, clearly, less danger of accident, which is a matter calling for much attention from beginners, where there is only a single trigger to be drawn and a single explosion to be guarded against. A very effective gun of fourteen gauge and twenty-eight inches, with a bar lock, capable of doing its work cleanly and well at forty yards, can be turned out, not to exceed five pounds in weight, at a reasonable price. Whereas a double-barrel of the same weight could not be manufactured of any thing like responsible materials, strength and solidity, of a calibre to exceed eighteen or twenty, with a length of two feet; a very useless and inefficient tool, incapable of operating, with any certainty, beyond twenty-five or thirty yards; and one necessarily useless for any purpose, after its owner shall have acquired power to wield the weapon of a man; whereas the single piece of the same weight would always retain its utility, and be a handy and serviceable gun for ordinary purposes.

The first thing desirable, then, for every sportsman, I hold to be, to furnish himself with the best and most available gun, as an instrument, suited to the purpose for which he requires it, at a price suited to his means.

First, the gun must be a good one in itself, well built, of good materials, strong, sound, and safe by the excellence of metal and superiority of finish, which also produce efficient carrying of its charge, rapid firing, and clean killing.

Secondly, the gun must particularly suit the individual owner; for one gun will no more suit all men, than one coat will fit all wearers; and no man can any more shoot well with a gun that does not come readily to his shoulder and fairly to his eye, than he can be at ease in a coat two sizes under his fit, or walk a foot-race in boots that pinch him. According to the length of the shooter's arms and neck, must be the length and curvature of the stock, from the heel-plate to the breech; and that which constitutes a perfect *fit*, if I may use the word in reference to a gun, is this—that its weight being in duo proportion to the size, strength, and comfort of the shooter, when it is raised deliberately to the shoulder, the right hand grasping the gripe, with its fore-finger on the trigger, and the left hand supporting the barrels immediately in front of the trigger guard, it shall come so justly and handily to the face, that, the cheek being naturally lowered, without consideration or adjustment, the eye may clear the level of the breech, and at once find the sight at the end of the barrels, precisely on its own level. If the eye, above the breech, find any part of the barrel in view between itself and the sight, the stock is certainly too straight; and possibly too short also. If the sight appear sunk below the breech, and it be necessary to advance the left hand, and so elevate the muzzle, in order to bring it into the plane of vision, the stock is certainly too crooked, and not improbably too long. If, on the other hand, the eye palpably over-ranges the breech, or fails to reach it when the head is naturally couched to the aim, the stock is, in the first place, manifestly too short, in the second, as much too long.

An ordinary shot will, by no possibility, shoot decently well with a gun defective on either side. A very crack shot, indeed, perfectly deliberate, and carrying all his experience and practice continually in his mind, will, after a few shots, probably, so adapt his aim, by elevating his line of sight, or by depressing the muzzle of his piece, as to kill his shots; but he will never do so in his usually beautiful, sharp, clean, unhesitating style— for the posture of his head will necessarily be forced and unnatural; the gun will, as necessarily, not hold its correct natural position and purchase against the hollow of his shoulders; and, furthermore, the shooter will be obliged constantly to adjust his aim and search about for his object; instead of finding it precisely in its proper relative position to his eye, as soon as the butt touches his shoulder.

This fitness of a gun to the shooter, can only be ascertained by himself, how little soever he may know about a gun; and he must not think of selecting a friend, how competent a judge of fire-arms soever, to choose for him, in this particular; though, in all other regards, he will be unwise, indeed, if he do not obtain and defer to judgment.

Whether the gun comes truly to his shoulder and eye, he must try himself, and he may easily do it—thus:

Let him, wearing any easily-fitting coat, accustomed to his shape, and buttoned at the throat, place himself in a natural position, having the left foot advanced about eighteen inches; let him seize the gripe of the gun, as I have described above, with the right hand, having its forefinger on the trigger; let him place the left hand edgewise, under the barrel, immediately in front of the trigger guard, with which his palm will be in contact; and keeping his muzzle directly in front of him and his butt below his right elbow, hold his right hand close to his hip. Thus, let him raise the piece, steadily and deliberately, so that the heelplate shall be brought evenly and firmly in contact with the hollow of the shoulder, and bend his head naturally, without any effort or attempt at adjustment, to the cheek- piece of the stock. Then, if the gun suit the holder, the eye will find itself accurately laid on the level of the breech, and the sight will meet its first glance, as if it rose from the base, instead of the muzzle of the gun; for the whole length of the elevated rib, along which the eye ranges, being exactly on the plane of the breech, howsoever elevated or depressed, will be as completely unseen as if it had no existence.

Consequently, when a deliberate point-blank aim is taken at a lifeless or motionless object, all, of which the eye will be conscious, is the breech of the piece, with the metallic sight rising above it, and set off by the substance of the mark aimed at, as if by a background immediately in contact with it.

If this be not the case, without a second adjustment of the aim, after the gun shall be brought to the face— much more if it cannot be made to be the case at all, owing to an incorrigible variance of its build to the formation of the shooter—the gun may be thrown aside; and farther trials resorted to, until a piece be found possessing the necessary length and curvature of the stock.

In addition to this, the pull on the trigger necessary to the release of the tumbler, should be tested, and ascertained to be agreeable to the finger and nerve of the intended purchaser.

The way of ascertaining the exact force requisite to discharge the gun, is to hold it muzzle upward at full cock, when the weight attached to the trigger, which will cause the hammer to fall, is the measure of power needful.

This power is very variable. In bad, ill-finished, ill-filed and insufficiently burnished locks, it is *ex necessitate* great. In coarse military weapons, intended for the use of men with hard, heavy hands, insensitive, nervous systems, and dull natures, as ordinary fighting men, the pull is intentionally made heavy; in order to counteract the occurrence of accidental discharges. The power required for the drawing the trigger of an old-fashioned soldier's musket varies from fourteen to sixteen pounds. That for the firing of the most highly finished and best London made fowling-piece is from four to four and a half pounds; that of a hair-trigger about one to one and a half pounds.

Common Birmingham, or German guns, are exceedingly various in this respect, ranging from two to ten or twelve pounds power.

Now, it must be remembered, that, while too heavy a pull annoys the firer, frustrates his aim, and, in nine cases out of ten, causes him to overshoot his mark; too light a pull is dangerous, since a lock which works so easily as at two pounds pressure, or under, is liable to be put in motion by an unconscious touch, or even by a jar from a touch or fall. In common, low-priced guns, such easiness is invariably owing to weakness and deficiency, and always augurs danger.

To the beginner, this attention to the pull is comparatively a matter of indifference; since his unmade finger readily forms and adapts itself to any pull. Still, it is advisable that he should early accustom himself to the true pull, which he must one day adopt. At first, it is well to use rather a hard-going gun, say of four or five pounds pressure, but no higher. It is easy to come down from a heavy to a light pull, but almost impossible to make the other exchange.

The best shot, who was ever born, and who had been accustomed for half a life to triggers of four pounds power, would not be able, after daily practice for six months, to shoot, up to his own force, with triggers of eight or ten pounds. Both triggers of a double gun should, moreover, yield to precisely the same pressure; and, if a man desire to shoot equally and evenly, all his guns, pistols, and rifles should go accurately to the same pull, even his heavy ducking guns—stancheon or punt guns alone excepted, which for reasons hereafter to be stated require a hard and heavy hand: hair-triggers, for all field purposes, I utterly eschew. If a rifleman cannot shoot close enough with a four pound pull, he will not do so with a hair-trigger.

More shots in the field are missed by too rapid, than by too slow firing. Nervousness and excitement are, nine times out of ten, the cause of missing; and, whether on the duelling ground, or in the sporting field, the bravest and coolest man will be a shade more hasty and excited, than in the shooting gallery or the target ground. Therefore, no hair-triggers for me!

Now, then, it has been shown briefly, and I trust comprehensively, above, how to choose a gun in reference solely to its peculiar fitness and adaptation of form, length, weight, manageableness, &c., to the individual purchaser, wholly apart from its intrinsic goodness of metal, workmanship, finish or effectiveness. If it be of such weight that he can handle it readily and rapidly, and can carry it without fatigue during a long and hot day's shooting— if it come up truly and quickly to his eye—if its trigger yield to a pull which requires no jerk or effort, in the first instance, the gun may be said to suit the person.

Of its intrinsic value much more remains to be said. I do not by any means propose, in this place, to follow the example of many of my predecessors in the composition of works of this order, an example I think "more honored in the breach than the observance," in attempting an elaborate description of the various kinds of metal, the varieties of workmanship, much less the manifold processes used in, or applied to, the manufacture of fowling-pieces; or in pretending to disclose all the various tricks of the trade, and to show how the latter may be certainly detected by the purchaser.

Were I to undertake the first, I should, in all probability, show myself incapable of the task; for few amateurs, even of those the best informed, are competent to describe, perhaps to comprehend, the materials and mechanism of a first-rate gun; although they may he perfectly capable of deciding on the quality of the gun when manufactured. If I should succeed in explaining these matters correctly it is still very certain that the best of such explanations convey but a limited degree of information to readers, and necessarily fail of enabling them to judge for themselves. I know few cases in which the old saying, "that a little knowledge is a dangerous thing," is more justly evinced than this. A little knowledge will probably suffice to render the possessor of it satisfied of his own ability to choose for himself; and, rejecting the aid of experience, he will probably get cheated for his pains.

It is, in fact, a very difficult task for any person, from inspection, to detect with absolute certainty the nature of the metal of which the barrels are composed. In old times horseshoe-nails, wrought into wire or ribbon form, and welded together, were the basis of what were then the best barrels, known as stub-twist. The use of horse-nails has latterly decreased, owing to the deterioration of the iron used in their formation; and old carriage springs of wrought steel, mixed with Wednesbury iron, which is generally used and known in the trade as stub-iron, are now principally adopted for the manufacture of the best, ordinary twisted barrels. "Gunmakers themselves," says an accurate and able English writer on field-sports, Stonehenge, in his manual of British Rural Sports, "are often deceived; and therefore it is reasonable to suppose that no inspection, which an amateur can make, will detect the defect in the quality of the iron or workmanship. No one should buy a cheap gun, who values his life or limbs; at all events, he should be careful to have the recommendation of some one who really understands his business, before he trusts to one."

It is my own opinion, that the only way by which one can be morally certain—physically one can *not* be certain of the quality of a gun—is by dealing with a house of established character and reputation, who have therefore credit to lose and name to sustain. And by the word *house,* be it understood, I mean gunsmiths or gunmakers, and not *importing-hardware-man's* house. From the former, if he state frankly the manner of gun he desires, the price to which he means to go, and leave himself to the just dealing of the firm, the purchaser will probably, in nine cases out of ten, be fairly dealt with and well-suited. From the latter, do what he may, he never will, and never can, obtain a safe or decent piece; because such men do not themselves know any thing about the quality or character of the guns they are selling, merely purchasing them in the lump, by invoice, according to sample, to sell again singly at ten dollars, or at fifty, or at a hundred, each, including all the intermediate prices; all being guns precisely of the same intrinsic worth, but valued at more or less, according as they are filed down, French varnished, damascened by aid of acids, tricked out, with German silver, and fitted up complete with velvet-lined cases and all appurtenances and means to boot, from the wholesale furnishing shops of Birmingham, and its vicinity.

A good judge of a gun, by careful examination of all its parts; of its finish, engraving, the filing, buffing, and working of its looks, and by testing its firing, will be able to pronounce, with something nearly approaching to certainty, on the value of a fine gun; and, from its value and its finish, to satisfy himself whether it be or be not turned out of the shop of the builder whose name it professes to bear; since, be it known, the names of makers of guns are forged much more easily, much more frequently, and with much less risk of detection, or of punishment if detected, than are those of the makers of securities and powers of attorney.

I have certainly seen many hundreds of guns, unquestionably short of three English pounds sterling value, to the original Birmingham wholesale manufacturer, bearing the names of Richards, Lancaster, Moore, and Joe Manton, sold in the United States, and shown by the purchasers as authentic productions of those makers, at prices varying from 50 to 150 dollars; for no one of which would I have given a ten-dollar bill—and this in the teeth of the fact, which every one knows, or might know, if he chose to learn, that not one of those makers ever sold a gun at home, for much less than twice the largest sum mentioned.

Now, having satisfied himself, by examination of the finish, and by fixing the actual value of the gun, that it is the work of such and such a maker—which, if much acquainted with the work of eminent makers, he will do the more readily, that all of these have in some sort a peculiar style and character of their own—an amateur may at once rest content, that the workmanship is not out of proportion to the goodness of the material; and, in short, that the weapon is, what it assumes to be, first-rate.

For instance, an amateur, who is a tolerable judge, can easily recognize a lock of the first and finest quality, and distinguish between it and one even slightly inferior, on a very cursory examination. So he can judge, also, positively of the finish, fitting, and mechanism of every part of the stock, there being nothing in the whole gun wherein the hand of the master more clearly renders itself visible. Now, if the locks and stock be manifestly of first-rate quality and workmanship, if they show in those niceties, for which every judge knows where to look, the skill of the cunning craftsman, the *appearance* of the barrels outwardly corresponding to the details of the rest, the purchaser need not fear but that there is "that within that passeth show"—for it is not the habit, nor would it be worth the while of any workman to bestow labor of the most costly description, that which is the best paid, and to be procured with the most difficulty at any terms, on materials intrinsically valueless.

Again, it is only gunmakers of the superlative class, who can command or furnish such work; and their character and interest must alike prohibit them from the practice of low rascality, which must be ultimately, and, to themselves ruinously, detected. Thus, undoubtedly, many an old sportsman of intelligence and observation, who has had the advantage of long experience of the works of a number of distinguished gunmakers, who has compared them with one another, and contrasted them against the highly-finished pretending shams of the furnishing shops, and the mere rubbish of the Birmingham, German, and Belgian wholesale manufactories, will readily decide on the value of a gun in all respects, including the quality of the metal, and the unseen workmanship of the barrels. In the latter respect, however, his opinion will be induced mainly by analogous reasoning, and not by indirect scientific judgment; though, of course, he will, even in this respect, fully appreciate the difference between fine, common, and very inferior work.

As to what is the best quality of modern barrels, the difference of opinion is so great, that it may almost be said that no two sportsmen are of the same mind. Every species of barrel, cast-steel, laminated steel, damascus-twist, stub-twist, has its admirers and defamers; all of whom are charged by their adversaries with deciding, and many of whom probably do decide in many cases, as much from prejudice, as from sound judgment. Many believe exclusively in laminated steel barrels; others hold them to be utterly valueless and dangerous. Some adhere to the stub-and-twist; while others, again, admitting that these were of old the best of all, assert that, the stub-nail iron, having lost its original high quality, the new substitutes have outstripped them. In the same manner some persons prefer fine wire-twist, some damascus-twist, and so on.

I do not pretend to say that I have not my own opinions, though I do not wish to set up for infallibility, or to assert that I have no possible bias, although assuredly I am not aware of any; and, for such opinions as I have, I can in some sort assign a reason.

My own preference is, I confess, for the stub-twist barrels, now as of old, as the strongest, safest, and, above all, the least easy in which to be deceived; and if it be admitted that the modern stub-iron is inferior in toughness to the old horse-nail stuff—which, however,

I cannot hold to be sufficiently proved—I still consider it, when of the best quality, to be of superior tenacity, and consequently a safer *metal*, than even the best laminated steel. I am aware that this opinion of mine is diametrically opposed to that of the advocates of the steel barrels, and that tables and scales of tenacity and endurance, as proved by experiment, have been published, leading to a different conclusion; but it is well known that great changes take place in the crystallization of metals and the arrangement of their component particles, long after they have become perfectly cool, and indeed long after they have been in *use*, which, according to one theory, causes these changes. These changes, it is admitted, when they occur, render the metal vastly more brittle than it was in the first form, and consequently dangerous.

Now I am *not* satisfied that the trials, on which the alleged comparative tenacity of laminated steel is assumed, have been carried far enough, in relation to time; and I am all but entirely convinced, that dangerous cases of bursting have been more frequent, and, when they have occurred, more complete and terrible, in the laminated steel barrels of the highest quality and price, than in any other description of barrels of equal supposed and guaranteed quality. I am certain it is more difficult to judge by their exterior appearance of what they are made, than it is of any other work.

The latter objection, also, militates strongly against the damascene-twist barrels, which may be, and are so exactly imitated by means of etching with acid, and high-finishing afterward, that it will puzzle the best amateur to pronounce positively which is the real and which is the imitated article.

It is further alleged, that in twisting and re-twisting the metallic threads to the degree necessary to produce the beautiful wavy appearance, which procures for this

species of work the name of damascus—as if it were analogous to the celebrated method of scymitar-making,
now lost, *which it is known not to be*—the tenacity of the
separate fibres is destroyed. This question I leave to the
expert, not being sufficiently informed to venture an
opinion. The fact, however, that there is an apparently
reasonable doubt existing among those best capable of
speaking to the book, as to the toughness and tenacity
of the component parts of these two species of metal,
and as danger is inextricably connected with error, I
judge it best to hold to the safe side; the rather, that no
one will deny imposition to be both easier, and of more
common occurrence in these, than in any other form
of barrels.

It tells, also, disadvantageously for the damascened
twist, that one rarely, if ever, sees one by any of the great
London or, even Birmingham houses. I am certain
that I have *never* seen a damascus-twist gun by Purday,
Manton, Moore, Lancaster, or—I think—Westley
Richards; though I will not say that none such exist.
Their rarity, however, goes to indicate that they are not
approved by those makers. Laminated steel guns I have
certainly seen of rare beauty and finish, and of excellent
performance, by many makers of high standing and reputation; as Greener, Ellis, Dean and Adams, and others;
still, in truth, I can only say I do not like them—

timeo Danaos et dona ferentes.

I have seen Belgian guns, the best, I think, of all
the Belgian work I have met, of the damascened twist,
which, to a sound and safe appearance, have united
good performance, and have stood well in service. But I
have never seen any foreign European work, which for

performance in the field and in long endurance can compare with the best English. Le Page, of Paris, turns out, unquestionably, the best French work. I have seen little Belgian, and no German work, I mean on fowling-pieces, not rifles or pistols, which I would care to own.

In reference to laminated steel and damascus-twist barrels, I will state here one fact, which may be of use to novices, and on the correctness of which they may rely. Exceedingly cheap guns of both these descriptions, are to be found in every hardware and every gunsmith's shop. These are, *invariably*, shams of the worst and most atrocious kind—infinitely worse than the common rubbish, for the most part, which professes to be little more than rubbish; since the very catchpenny frippery and fretwork are merely put on to cover flaws and conceal the real fibre of the metal. There *never was such a thing* made in the world, as a low-priced, damascened twist or laminated steel barrel. The labor necessary to produce them *real*, causes them of necessity to be dear. Therefore, if a cheap one be offered to the merest tyro, let him instantly reject it, without a second glance; and as he values his life, let him not fire it off.

I do not, of course, mean to say that every cheap gun must necessarily burst; but I do say that, against each one, severally, the odds are heavy that it will, at some time or other, apart from any carelessness of the shooter, fail in some part of its mechanism; and then, woe to the holder. No length of acquaintance with such a gun, no goodness of its performance—and I have seen some for which I would not have given a dollar, and which I would not have fired for a hundred, shoot more than passably— can justify the slightest confidence in it. On the contrary, the more times one may have fired it with impunity, so much the greater are the odds against him that he will do so again; as any one would say of a person who should undertake to draw the fusee of a live shell with his teeth, or to lie down on a railroad track before the engine, in the expectation of being picked up safely by the cow-catcher.

By the word *low-priced* guns, I mean, as a general rule, in reference to buying a safe and serviceable piece, anything like *new,* with two barrels and the smallest show of exterior ornament, cheaper than fifty dollars.

Of the mere rubbish of the German, and nameless English wholesale-murder-manufactories, sold at prices varying from three to twenty dollars, it is almost useless to write; since it is scarcely to be supposed that any one, who reads, ever thinks of buying such. They are mere cast-iron, in all parts, except the lock-springs, and I should about as soon fire one with a reasonable charge, as I would hold a hand-grenade in my fingers until it should explode.

My opinion, preference and recommendation, therefore, are decidedly in favor of the best English stub-and-twist barrels that can be obtained for the price the individual sportsman can command; of which I shall speak anon. It may be presumed, I suppose, that every person who has the taste and means to follow field-sports at all, intends to follow them to the best of his ability, and to fit himself out with the best appliances and outfit his circumstances will command. Not because I take it for granted, with old Izaak Walton and some modern enthusiasts, that a sportsman is of necessity a larger-hearted and freer-handed fellow than his neighbor—for I must acknowledge to having been cognizant, in my day, of some very bitter screws among sportsmen, though, on the whole, I think they may claim to be above average—but because it is manifestly for their interest and their pleasure, for once, in their case synonymous, to be so.

I shall, therefore, proceed to speak of the work produced by different makers, of different localities; first, in their relative scale of excellence; second, in their relative scale of price. Lastly, I shall state my own views as to the comparative ratio of excellence and price combined; and the method of purchasing suitably to comparative pockets. It must be remembered, that, in all this, I profess only to give my own opinions, not to claim for them infallibility, or even superiority to the opinions of others. I have had some experience, and some opportunities of judging, and according to these, I have formed conclusions which I believe—as most men do of their own conclusions—to be correct and sound. These I proceed to give, sometimes with reasons in brief, sometimes, where to reason would be too long, simply as conclusions, for the benefit of those who have either formed no opinions at all, or hold them in abeyance, subject to farther experience.

I wish to interfere with no man's notions, which are his own peculiar property; and with no man's legitimate business—the sale of condemned and perilous fire-arms I do not esteem a legitimate business—and this I think it well here to state, because, some years since, I was assailed in a most ungentlemanly and unjust manner by anonymous scribblers, in various journals—most of them directly set on by persons who were interested in the sale of articles to which I did not choose to award praise; some doubtless actuated by mere prejudice in favor of some old gun of their own, and consequently of its maker—for presuming to recommend certain guns, made by a certain maker, all of which, by the way, have given the highest satisfaction to their purchasers, and for recording my preference of London to provincial English makers.

This preference, I again beg most distinctly, and if possible, more distinctly than before, to record. And I am fully aware and confident that no sportsman, who ever owned a first-class gun, made by a first-class

London maker, ever did or ever will exchange it for any other gun in the world. And that no sportsman, who has examined and tried the two articles, and whose pocket will afford the expense of the London maker's gun, will ever order one from the best provincial.

The reason of this superiority of the London makers, is easy to be discovered. London concentrates the largest number of the wealthiest men and the best sportsmen and judges, consequently of the largest and best *buyers* in the kingdom, probably in the world—men who will have nothing but what is the best, and will have the best, whatever it may cost.

Therefore, the most ambitious, enterprising, intelligent, best, master-gunmakers make London their head-quarters; they, finding that nothing but the best work will do, and that for it they can realize the best prices, must have the best workmen to execute that work, and, to have the men, must pay the best prices, and do so.

Hence the most intelligent and best mechanics are constantly drawn from the provinces to the metropolis; and so soon as any one becomes known as a fine craftsman in any division of the work, he is sought for, and knowing that he can command larger wages in London, beside a wider sphere of fame, than he can in his province, at once moves thither; for it needs not to premise that no man works for small wages, who can command large, for the same amount of labor.

Hence, London work is necessarily, naturally, and by admission of the most competent judges, the best; and comparatively, that of the highest reputed and highest priced London makers is the best of London work. For, although we may say fashion has much to do with it, very few men of the very richest—unless they chance to be natural fools—will prefer giving sixty to forty guineas for any article of purchase, unless they honestly believe the sixty-guinea article to be intrinsically worth its value above that which they can buy for forty.

Generally, it may be assumed that the sixty-guinea maker pays higher wages than his competitor who sells for forty. It may be answered the price is sustained by the name. Be it so; the name must have been originally gained by something beyond luck—for luck never made a fowling-piece; and by that something which gained it, the name must be sustained. That something is superior workmanship—in all such houses the best of material may be assumed—and I believe fully that the workmanship of the highest priced is superior to that of the lower priced London maker, in full proportion to the superiority of his charges; and I believe the same thing to be yet more clearly the case, as between the London and the provincial maker.

I perceive that this opinion is not likely to be the popular one, for there are of course fifty men, especially in this country, who will buy a Westley Richards gun for two hundred dollars, where there is one who will buy a London gun for twice that sum. And as every man who owns a gun, believes it, and is prepared to maintain it, to be the best gun in the world; therefore there are always fifty *best* Westley Richards guns, where there is one *best* London gun. Again, every gunmaker so soon as he ascertains that his customer will go as high as the price of a Westley Richards', but cannot be possibly induced to rise to a London value, assures him, in the most positive manner, that Westley Richards' guns are in every respect equal to Purday's, or whose you will; and that the difference is mere fancy and fashion. It is true that, so soon as he has gone out of the shop with his bit of Birmingham, the seller will laugh at what he has just been saying with the man who happens to be buying copper caps for the London gun, which he imported the other day on his own hook. But then the buyer of the bit of Birmingham does not hear the laugh.

Therefore, dear reader, I believe the best gun is that which you can buy of the best London maker, for something between fifty and sixty pounds sterling; from two hundred and fifty to three hundred dollars, including case and appurtenances, made to your own order.

The London makers, stated by Stonehenge, in the work quoted above, of the present year, 1856, to be reputed the first, are, alphabetically placed, Lancaster, Lang, Moore, Purday. The second is somewhat cheaper than the others; but Stonehenge rates his work at *cash prices;* and it is well known that all makers give a discount for that indispensable article. Purday has, perhaps, the widest reputation. I have my own favorite, as every sportsman naturally has; but as the preference is, perhaps, more in taste than in stern judgment—

"Between two blades, which has the better temper,"

it is not desirable to insist on it. From any of the four, there is no doubt that an undeniable piece may be procured.

Many of the old names, famous in the gun trade, are extinct, or exist as names only; the present owners of them having no relationship to the departed worthies, nor has the mantle descended on the pretenders.

To those who cannot afford the London prices, then I recommend the best provincial makers of England, unless they prefer, as I should, to build a gun in America, under my own eye, at the best provincial price.

Of the provincial gunmakers, the best, probably, and at all events the most generally known, is

Mr. Westley Richards; for it is idle, although he has a London establishment, with Mr. Bishop at its head, to speak of him as a London gunsmith, since his guns are notoriously made and finished at Birmingham, and sold at Birmingham prices. Mr. Richards' guns are well liked, and, as it is evident from the general favor in which he is held, give satisfaction; I have seen many handsome, well-finished, and strong-shooting guns from his shop, though the *tout ensemble* of their fitting and finish does not, as in fact it cannot he expected to, come up to the highest priced London guns.

My greatest objection to his guns is, that I think I have observed them to be soft. I do not mean soft-metalled, for that I regard as a merit, not a defect; but incapable of enduring hard usage, and liable to yield and give out disproportionately soon, as considered in reference to their price relatively to London guns. So far am I, however, from desiring to disparage his work, that, for persons who cannot afford to pay £50 or upward for a Purday, a Lancaster, or a Moore, or who consider that price enormous and absurd, as I know that some men do, I have nothing better to recommend, than that they should send their order, for exactly such a piece as they require, accompanied by the precise measure of a stock which suits them, to Mr. Bishop of Bond Street, when they will probably procure what will satisfy them, as well as the others would satisfy me, at a tar lower price. What the exact price of Westley Richards' best guns is at this moment, I do not accurately know; but I presume that it is from £30 to £35, from 150 to 175 dollars, with case and appurtenances, not including freight or duties; which would bring his best work here to the price of two hundred dollars, more or less. Mr. Lang's best double gun is stated by Stonehenge to be sold, in case complete, for £38, or 190 dollars, cash on the spot; and he further asserts, that "certainly it will be admitted that, for all the essentials desired by the crack shot, Mr. Lang's gun may lay claim to as high a standard as those of any of his rivals."

Besides Mr. Richards, there are other Birmingham makers, who turn out reputable work to order, and who are not to be confounded with the perpetrators of the detestable rubbish which finds its way into the United States, and is sold at almost every price from one dollar to one hundred.

Every principal shire-town in England, or nearly so, has some maker of high, at least, local celebrity; and some of these, as Parsons of Salisbury, Cartmel of Doncaster, Patrick of Liverpool, and others, whose names I do not remember, have become known and of good repute throughout England. Others have doubtless succeeded to these, since I have been a dweller in America, but little of their work has been, or is likely to be, imported; and no person is likely to come in contact with their work, unless he casually visit the spot of their operations, and he tempted of his own choice to purchase. It is needless, therefore, to consider these.

Below a hundred dollars I would counsel no man to buy an imported gun. There is a sort of gun, manufactured even by the best London makers, called a gamekeeper's gun, at £15 sterling, or 75 dollars, entirely plain, without engraving or any external finish. The locks are sound, well-working, and perfectly finished, though destitute of course of the last exquisite sharpness, smoothness and ring, which at once speak for the first-rate gun. The barrels are stub-twist, and may be relied on for solidity, safety, and excellent performance. I shot with one of these guns, in 1849, during a tour on the Great Lakes, and, though it had not certainly much beauty to brag of it executed beautifully and at long ranges, and was pronounced by "Dincks," a very competent judge, the best low-priced gun, and the cheapest gun, he ever saw. At my advice, a small number of these guns was sent out hither, for sale, at the lowest possible price; that is to say without any importer's profit, commissions or the like; and those of them which found purchasers, gave the greatest satisfaction. Their unpretending appearance, however, the incompetency of buyers to distinguish their real superiority to the lacquered trash of the Birmingham hard-waremen, and above all, the interested opposition of the vendors of such trumpery—who caused them to be written down by hireling scribblers, principally in the country-presses, though some of their lucubrations found their way into the Spirit of The Times—prevented the success of the experiment; and such guns never now, and probably never will, again, find their way into this market, even if ordered expressly.

Nevertheless, no gentleman visiting London, and desiring to procure a cheap, servicable, safe, though plain gun, can possibly do better than call on any one of the makers I have mentioned—Lancaster, Lang, Moore or Purday, and ask for a gamekeeper's gun. If he be a sportsman, and do not get a working tool up to his mark, he will be hard to please; but he must not expect any ornament, or any thing approaching to the high finish, or close and accurate fitting of pieces of four times its value.

For all guns of one hundred dollars, or under, I would earnestly advise all purchasers to have their own guns made to order in the American Atlantic cities, by American gun-makers of standing reputation. It will be understood, that the locks and barrels are all English made and English bored, though neither filed nor finished; and that they can be, and are, got up in New York, by several perfectly good and trustworthy workmen, in any style, from fifty to two hundred dollars; and I presume, and indeed understand, that the other principal seaboard cities of the Union are not far behind New York in this particular.

I have seen guns manufactured by Henry Tomes & Co. and by Henry T. Cooper, while he was in business, for 150 dollars, which, in all respects, I would myself have preferred to any one of Westley Richards' at any price; and I can cheerfully and truthfully say the same for guns of all descriptions, made by either of those excellent mechanics, John and Patrick Mullin of New York, while I have seen and handled guns at 75 and 50 dollars, by the former of the two makers last named, which I would have preferred to any hardware-shop Birmingham gun, by a nameless maker, with all its paraphernalia, at any possible price.

His fifty-dollar guns, of 30 inch barrel and 14 gauge, are, in point of real utility, excellent, serviceable, cheap, and perfectly safe arms. The purchaser can see them in the rough, before they are filed or finished, and see of what metal and stuff they are made; or, if he be at a distance, can commission his friend or agent to do so for him. The gun will not possess the finish, the lock will not work with the same unimprovable oiliness, sound-ness and clearness, as the lock of a three-hundred-dollar imported gun, nor will its barrels, probably, throw the shot with the same equality and regularity of distribution or force. Its details will not be as accurate, nor its joints and fittings as unimpeachable. But, if held straight, it will kill its game, sure and dead, at thirty-eight or forty yards; and what is much better, it *certainly* will not kill its owner— which, be it said, with all deference to Messieurs the importers thereof, cannot be predicated of any gun that ever was imported at any such price.

Every dollar over 50 and up to 150, will produce a dollar's worth of actual improvement, and intrinsic value in the article; but when we get beyond the hundred and fifty, the farther advance is for external show.

I know nothing beyond that, but if it seem good, to try Richards' at £85 sterling, with the duties added—though I would rather have the Mullin—or to go at once to head-quarters and get a London fifty-guinea, on whose shooting you may wager your life, with the certainty of winning, and of the gun shooting as well fifty years hence, as on the day of purchase. As Peter Probasco said to J. Cypress, jr., in the fisher's hut at Fire Islands, "Them's my sentiments, and you knows 'em!"

I said in the opening of this subject, that the double-barrelled fowling-piece is the only weapon and ultimatum of art for the sportsman. No greater number of barrels than two can be combined, so as to produce a manageable and effective piece; nor if there could, would the crack shot, once in twenty times, use a third barrel at three different birds, much less fire thrice at one. Than a crack shot, no other possibly could do so—if it he considered, how quickly a bevy of quail, all taking wing simultaneously, get out of the range of shot, and how rarely, when they do spring all together, even two barrels bring down their two birds clean killed.

All revolvers for sporting shot guns are out of the question; for more time is lost in revolving and revolving the chamber, than could be recovered by the quickest shot in time to kill even a second, much less a third or fourth bird; besides which, the weapons are unpardonably clumsy hideous, and unsportsmanlike, and fail entirely of execution as compared with ordinary chambered guns. Stonehenge gives a cut and description of a new breech-loading double gun, invented by a Frenchman, and improved by Mr. Lang, in which the barrels are raised from their connection with the false breech, by the turning of a crank, and expose the lower end of their calibre for the reception of a cartridge containing, in itself, the percussion cap, the powder, and the charge of shot, with a small brass pin, impinging on the percussion powder, attached to it, which, when the loaded barrels are again brought into their proper position and connection, stands up in a notch between them and the false breech made to receive it, and meeting the blow of the striker, discharges the gun.

Stonehenge speaks of this gun in terms of strong praise, and states his opinion, that "if as good in practice as it appears to him theoretically perfect, its invention will be almost as great an era in gun making as that of the detonator itself."

This language and praise are to me alike inexplicable. This gun has no nipple, no possibility of being loaded or fired except with the identical cartridge prepared for it, which is, and can be, only prepared at the shop which supplies the gun. It is true, he says, that the cartridge cases remain in the gun, and on withdrawal can be recapped and recharged many times; but, apart from the inconvenience of lugging about on your person a hundred or two, if you expect a good day's sport, of these cartridges —since the idea of a sportsman sitting down in the middle of a snipe-bog or a cock-brake, to recharge his cartridges out of a powder-and-shot magazine, which he must also carry about with him, is preposterous—what on earth is the shooter to do, if he takes it into his head to visit the Himalayas, or the Rocky Mountains, Canada or the Cape, or any other distant shooting ground (by no means impossible to, or unattempted by the British sportsman), where cartridges for Lang's breech-loading double-barrels certainly are not to be found growing on thorn bushes? Is he to carry with him, in heaven's name, a hundred barrels of cartridges on camel-back, or mule-back, or his own back, with the consciousness that these indispensables, once used up, his double-barrel is of less use even than a broomstick?

The want of simplicity is enough to ruin any invention; and this, it needs no prophet to foretell, must be inoperative, except as a pretty plaything to be used at home.

The gain, moreover, I should fancy from his drawing, is next to nothing; and I should judge that a quick smart loader would recharge both his barrels by the muzzle with a good flask and Sykes's patent-lever pouch, and cap them in the ordinary way, while his comrade is turning the crank, withdrawing the old cartridges, replacing the new—which by the way can only be done correctly under the eye, and hardly by touch—and bringing hack the barrels to their place.

The advantage in point of time can be scarcely, then, worthy of notice; and no gain of time is in truth requisite, in the case of shot guns. They can be loaded, fired, reloaded and refired, in the ordinary way, quite as rapidly as for ordinary purposes can ever be needed; and this every one knows, who has ever been present at an English battue, or has been obliged to sit down, as I have, a dozen times at least in my life, in the middle of a snipe-meadow, or of scattered bevies of quail, to let my barrels cool, before I have dared to reload them.

For rifle-shooting, especially in warfare, or in hunting on horseback, where the loss of time, the labor and inconvenience of forcing a patched ball down a tight, and, perhaps foul, grooved barrel, is great, the case is quite different. The gain is incredible, and the improvement, in fact, tantamount to the creation of a new weapon.

But, as applied to shot guns, I know but one case, in which breech-loading is desirable; namely, in very long, ponderous and unmanageable duck guns, where it is difficult to reach the muzzle and insert, much more drive home, the loading rod; and most of all, in the stancheon or punt gun, which is fired like a cannon from a carriage. Here the breech-loading system would work admirably, but it must be on. Perry's patent-arm plan, of which I shall have occasion to speak more anon, where the chamber can be loaded with loose powder and shot as easily as with the cartridge, and the nipples capped by hand, almost as readily as by the self-priming apparatus connected with it.

With regard to the weight, length, and calibre of double-barrelled fowling-pieces, there has always been and continues to be much diversity of opinion.

The sticklers for the old system adhere pertinaciously to the long barrel and small bore, the length to be increased as the calibre is enlarged. The upholders of the extreme modern school insist on gauges, such as were never heard of in the olden, times, and barrels proportionately short; maintaining that they will carry heavier charges with equal execution, and vastly increased handiness, especially in covert.

The old rule of proportion was 46 or 48 diameters of the bore to the length of the barrel; and on this Col. Hawker insists, consistent to the last, in his latest edition; advising that a gun of fourteen gauge should never be less than thirty-four or thirty-six inches in length, and that thirty-two inches is the proportion for a twenty-two gauge. I do not doubt that, for the mere carrying of shot, the extreme length will keep the charge together longer, and, consequently, that a three-foot barrel *will* throw its shot more regularly and evenly at sixty yards, than one of two foot eight; and that a twenty-two gauge gun of thirty-two inches length, will do so in a yet greater degree.

Therefore, if carrying shot to a great distance, say 60 yards, evenly, without reference to the quantity thrown, or any other consideration, be the test, a gun of twenty-two gauge and thirty-two inches would be the best in the world; but a gun, of twenty-two gauge and thirty-two inches, would not be of above 5 lbs. weight, and should not, at the utmost, be loaded with above 1

½ drachms of powder and ¾ ounce of shot—which shot ought never to be above No. 6 or 7. In other words, it would be a mere child's plaything and pop-gun. On the other hand, the gun of fourteen gauge, at the same proportion of gauge to length, should be, not as he recommends, three feet, but three feet 7 ²/₇ inches, and would probably weigh about twelve pounds. The colonel's advice, therefore, to use a thirty-four or thirty-six inch barrel with a gauge of fourteen, is, in itself, a compromise, founded on the sacrifice of force to ease of handing; since it would have been clearly preposterous to tell men to go out cock shooting with guns six feet long, weighing twelve or fourteen pounds.

But a much farther compromise is necessary, and it is now pretty generally conceded that the best and most useful gun, applicable to all kinds of shooting, and serviceable in all, is one of fourteen gauge thirty-one inch barrel, and 7 ½ to eight lbs. weight. Such a gun will carry a charge of ounce of 1 ½ shot to about 3 ½ drachms of powder, which is in the ratio of measure for measure, or seven to one by weight, and do its work well, regularly, evenly and effectively at forty yards—dispersing its shot, at that distance, over a circle of thirty inches diameter, so evenly that, supposing No. 8 shot to be used, no woodcock, quail, or single snipe shall be within that circle unpierced by one or more pellets—or, if larger shot be used, no ruffed grouse, prairie-fowl, or wild duck.

I do not intend, by any means, to indicate forty yards as the extreme distance at which such a gun will do its work fatally, but only as the distance at which it ought invariably to do it, killing every bird clean, if it be held so straight as to bring the bird aimed at within the circle. Beyond this it will often, I may say constantly, kill some shots at fifty, some fewer at sixty, and now and then one at seventy yards; moreover, such a gun will carry, when required, an ounce and three-quarters or two ounces of No. 1 or 2 shot, with 3 ½ drachms of powder, with great force and effect; it being remembered, that when we estimate by filling a measure of one capacity with pellets of different sizes, the measure of No. 10 shot being almost solid, will weigh at least one-third more than the same measure of No. 1, where the interstices are as numerous as the pellets. So that two ounces or rather the full of what is called a two ounce measure, in a shooting-pouch, of No. 1, shall not really weigh more than one and a half ounce of No. 10, by the same measure.

This then constitutes, according to my opinion, the gun above described, the most available for all purposes, and the most useful general shooting gun for all sportsmen who can afford but one gun for all work, that can be made.

It is sufficiently short and handy to be easily recoverable, and to shoot with murderous effect in the closest and most tangled brake. It is sufficiently close-carrying and hard-hitting to do its work, as well as any gun is ever needed to do its work, on the wildest game in the open. It will stop a wild duck going down wind with No. 2 shot at 45 to 50 yards, or with an Eley's cartridge at 70; and with ten slugs in a wire cartridge, a stag at the same distance will have but a poor chance before it, for it will throw the ten slugs into a twenty-four inch diameter.

I have never myself shot in any covert with a shorter gun, nor did I ever feel that I was giving any odds to those who did. I have never shot in the open with a longer or heavier gun, and I have always felt, that in shooting a hard long day through, I was taking large odds from those who did.

It must be remembered, which, for the most part it is not, that the great majority of birds killed are recovered dead, within twenty yards of the muzzle; that not one in fifty, in a day's shooting, is gathered over forty, and that none but a very crack shot, and he but rarely, shoots at a bird which is forty yards off when he draws the trigger, and which, if going away from him, or down wind, will be when killed at least ten yards farther.

It is safe to assert, that not one bird in a hundred killed is shot at when above forty yards from the trigger, and that birds so shot at, not one in ten is brought to bag.

By this, one may judge how much avail there is in talking about the necessity of having guns, which shall shoot evenly and strongly at sixty yards. No gun, I had almost said, ever did so; and would be of little avail if it did.

It cannot be denied that very short guns, so short as 26, 28, and even I believe 24 inch barrels, with gauges so large as 10 and 9, having the weight of the 14 gauge and 31 inch guns, have been found to shoot far better than had previously been supposed possible, carrying heavy charges, and not appearing so much deficient in range or penetration as to be manifestly inferior to the larger guns. For covert, their powerful load, and the comparatively large space which their shot covers, rendered them exceedingly fatal, and, for a time, they were all the rage with London makers, and some were even exported hither; but on the moors, and even in wild partridge shooting, in England, they did not tell, and for this country or British Colonial shooting, they never had any wide or general market. If one were rich enough to have a gun for every season of the year, one of these short wide-barrel London guns, by a first-class maker, of about lbs. weight, would be a very agreeable change for July cock-shooting, reserving the more ser- viceable 14 gauge for spring and fall snipe-shooting, and for autumn shooting in general. To persons who can afford one only, such a piece would be nearly useless, as it would be two to one against him, the year through, compared with his companion carrying a gun such as I recommend.

In any event, it is a more piece of luxury and cox-combry, scarce worthy of a sportsman, to affect a particular gun for every season; and, what is more, it is not unlikely to detract seriously from his shooting; even if it be built of exactly the same weight, bend and length of stock, and trigger-pull; since no two or more guns ever come up, much less shoot, exactly alike; nor does the same man ever execute equally with two guns.

Like the proverbial man of one book, the man of one gun is to be bewared. He is likely to prove an ugly customer.

In one ease, I should recommend the adoption of a different gun to the above, or the use of two of different sizes. That is, where the shooter has little or no upland shooting; by which term I mean snipe, woodcock, quail, grouse, prairie-fowl and hare, using it in opposition not to lowland, but to bay shooting, and depends for his sport on the shores, lagoons, creeks, and beaches, or even inland rivers and lakes; when I would advise, in lieu of the gun I have so often described, one of ten lbs. with two barrels of thirty-six inches, and 8 or 9 gauge. Such a gun is the most effective that can be had for single fowl or for small flocks, and for shore-birds, such as curlews, marlins, willet, plovers and the like. Where a sportsman is so lucky as to have a combination of the two kinds of sport, in nearly equal proportions, and follows both with nearly equal ardor, I know no plan but that he should have a gun of each description; for the heavy piece it would be too wearisome to carry over hill and over dale, and the lighter will not tell its tale with effect on sea ducks; while, if a fine and costly article, it will be seriously damaged by the sea mist and salt air; and the finer the finish and engraving, the greater the damage.

Such a gun ought to be, by choice, as plain as it can

be made. Every line of engraving is a positive drawback, only serving to bold rust. The maximum price, which I should hold it desirable to pay for a fowl gun of this description, is one hundred dollars, and for that, or even for eighty, any one of the New York makers I have named, will provide one of undoubted excellence.

Than this, I think no double gun should be made larger. For boat-shooting in the bays or beaches I recommend, what I always use, two single guns of fourteen to sixteen pounds weight, four foot barrels, and 5 gauge. They should be made without ramrod or pipes, which only renders them top-heavy, and provided with a solid loading rod having a round knob on the upper end, and a complete set of cleaning apparatus to screw in at the other.

These guns will carry four ounces of any sized shot from BB down to 4, and an equal *measure* of powder, and will kill with loose charges at 80 yards; with green cartridges at 100, sure.

They are English made, and imported; and can be had, the best, for 35 to 40 dollars. If they be top or muzzle-heavy, which they sometimes are, and which is a bad fault, and a great hindrance to quick shooting, the fault may easily be remedied, by taking off the heel-plate, scooping a hole in the butt, and running in a pound or two of lead. The restoration of balance, by means of this counterpoise, will far more than compensate the increase of the total weight; the rather that guns of this size are only to be used in boat-shooting, not carried in pursuit of game.

A very little practice will enable a hardy man and quick shot to use two single guns, laying down the one after firing, and snatching up the other; if not quite so rapidly as one double-barrel, quite rapidly enough to demolish a flock, by getting in both loads. I have, at this moment, one of the exact character described, so handy, that I can raise and manage it with ease with my left hand on the trigger-guard. For sea-fowling guns, the nipples should be of the inverted fashion, having the orifice like a funnel, large above and tapering to a point below; as the flame of the cap is thus more forcibly injected, which is needful, as the coarse-grained powder, which is preferable for sea shooting, will not enter the cones.

As to the makers, qualities, prices, or descriptions of guns needful to the sportsman, I have no word more to say; but as to the mode of choosing, a few hints may be found serviceable.

We will suppose a person, having made up his mind to what price he will go, and what description of piece he needs, to have found, by the assistance of competent judges, several guns the work of responsible makers, and in the hands of dealers on whose faith he can rely; and from among these to have selected some two or three, which he has ascertained, by testing them according to the instructions on pp. 11, 12, to suit him, as to weight, curvature of stock and trigger-pull—the last can be altered, if too hard, by the touch of a file. He should now proceed to try them by firing them in the open air, with a full charge of powder and shot, as prescribed before, at a distance of forty yards. The mark should be twenty-four sheets of thick tarred brown paper, large enough to contain an interior circle of thirty inches diameter.

Into this circle the gun ought to put its whole charge point-blank; I mean without more elevation than that given by the rib. The shot ought to be dispersed evenly, not strewed here in clusters of a dozen or more close together, and there with spaces of several inches intervening. A gun doing the first may be depended upon for killing, if held straight. With one planting its charge, as the second, it is hit or miss by luck. If a small part only of the charge is lodged in the mark at that range, and those wide apart and much dispersed, the gun scatters too widely, and consequently shoots weakly; discard it, therefore, on the instant.

If, on the contrary—but that will very rarely happen, at forty yards—the charge should be much, though evenly concentrated, in the centre of the mark, especially if it have put a great proportion of all its pellets through all the 24 sheets of paper, the gun is a wonder.

It is possible it may shoot *too* closely, that is, may tear its object to pieces in the hands of a dead-shot, or miss it clean with a novice. This is easily ascertained by trying it at a shorter range, say fifteen or twenty yards; and if at the former distance it concentrate its charge in the size of a tea-cup, it certainly does carry too close, and should also be laid aside.

But this I must add, that of all the guns I have ever seen, handled, or shot with, which amount to a pretty considerable number, I have never seen one which shot too closely. Nor do I believe that a gun ever did carry too closely, provided that it did not lose force by supererogatory friction, for a good shot. For it is the simplest of all things, to a person who is continually making allowances on almost every shot that he fires, if he finds that his gun hits too hard and tears its game, when too near at hand, either to give the animal time in the open, and let it get away to a just distance, which is always the better plan, or in thick covert to shoot a little wide, so as to avoid raking it with the body of a charge.

Generally, if one hear a person say that he prefers a scattering gun, he may be tolerably satisfied that it is because the speaker cannot shoot with a close-carrying piece, or, in other words, cannot cover his object.

Lastly, in regard of trials, it is not one or two shots that will thoroughly test a piece. Ten or twelve fires of each barrel, should the result prove satisfactory, and with little variation of effect, the same number of pellets, more or less, being put into the mark and through the last sheet each time, will be a sure proof of the quality of the gun, at the range of forty yards. A few shots may then be tried as corroboratory at twenty, thirty, fifty, sixty, and, as a matter of curiosity, with increased charges of powder and various elevations, at fancy distances, 70, 80, and upward, till you fail to touch the paper at all.

If, however, the gun perform thoroughly well, and to admiration, at forty yards, it will do so at all distances, and may be held capable of all that can be asked of wood and iron.

It must be remembered, lastly, that by increasing the quantity of powder to an equal charge of shot, you increase the force and velocity, but detract from the closeness of the shooting; and *vice versa*. A light charge of powder and a heavy one of shot will tell wonderfully for closeness, but not all for strength.

With wire cartridges, however, the results of charging are precisely the reverse of this. The heavier the charge of powder, the closer the cartridge places its shot, as well as the farther. The reason is obvious.

The utility of the cartridge arises from its power of keeping its shot together after being propelled from the muzzle, which it leaves as a single ball. According to the stiffness of the cases, this quality endures longer, and the cartridges are graduated and distinguished as blue, red, and green—the latter being fit only for sea-shooting, and often going several hundred yards before they burst, though they ought to open at 70, and deliver their shot, at its best, at 100. Therefore the heavier the charge of powder, the farther the cartridge is sent unbroken, and the closer will the shot he planted at any given distance.

I should, perhaps, add to this, in order to obviate the possibility of mistake, that these trials are directed for a general fowling-piece of 31 inches and 14 gauge. For ducking guns of all descriptions, a longer distance will be required correctly to test their properties.

For the double-barrelled duck guns which I have recommended for river or marsh shooting, of ten lbs. weight, three-foot barrels and 8 or 9 gauge, fifty to fifty-five yards should be the distance with loose shot, and the piece ought to execute at that range with the same effect as the lighter gun at forty.

The great fowling gun, again, of 16 lbs., four foot barrel and 5 gauge, ought to do its work with three or four ounces of shot, at sixty-five yards, as powerfully and with as much penetration as the others at forty and fifty-five.

Beyond this, I have nothing to say in regard to the choosing a gun.

If he will follow the instructions laid down above, the merest novice who wishes to buy, may be sure of getting what he asks for, and is willing to pay for.

The quality of what he gets, must, after all, rest with the amount that he is willing to pay.

I shall now proceed briefly to teach how to use the gun when it shall be chosen. How to carry; how to clean; how to load; how to learn to shoot it.

I cannot make a man a crack shot, but I can show him how to be a safe one. "*Legere et scriber,*" says J. Cypress, Jr., *"est poedagogi sed optimé collineare est dei."* Reading and writing come of schoolmasters, but a crack shot is the work of God.

THE GUN, AND HOW TO USE IT.

After becoming possessed of a good gun, in accordance with the means, object and idea of the individual, the one thing essential is to know how to use it. And this knowledge, once acquired, lasts for ever, yet does not last unchanged, or, like most sublunary things, change only to deteriorate; for what is at first acquired with difficulty and much painstaking, gradually becomes a habit, ripens into a second nature, and, constantly improved by practice, by experience, by freshly-discovered resources and trials of the power of the weapon, shall be at last, almost, as it were, an innate instinct, acting without deliberation or forethought as if on the profoundest calculation, and accomplishing results, in the twinkling of an eye, to arrive at which scientifically would require the solution of intricate problems.

The master of his gun once, moreover, is master of the art for ever, and of all guns; and let what improvements or changes soever take place in the science, none will occur, in which he will not immediately participate, and find his ancient superiority still available.

For all improvements simplify, facilitate, add, in a word, to the power of the weapon, or to the celerity of the performance, or to the convenience of the performer.

If the change render it more difficult to shoot well, it is a retrograde step, not an improvement. For example, the percussion system is now, in spite of all old-fashioned prejudice and opposition, an admitted improvement on the old flint-and-steel system; and one, not the least, of its advantages is, that it has so much simplified the art of shooting flying, that there are now ten good shots, where there was one, forty years ago.

Consequently, the person who had learned with much toil and labor to shoot excellently with the old flint lock, took up the new percussion piece, and found himself at once, with no farther trouble, twice as good a shot as he was before. It was to him as if his old gun had suddenly doubled its celerity and accuracy of aim. It is certain that no good shot, with flint and steel, ever found himself a bad one with percussion, even on the first trial. Equally certain it is, that, take twenty crack shots with the percussion, and give them the best and most perfectly finished Joe Manton flint-and-steel lock, and the first week they will not kill three fair shots out of ten; in any given time, not one will shoot as well as he did with his copper caps, and probably one half of them will never become respectable shots at all.

In the like manner is it, of all other improvements; it is comparatively easy to advance from skill in an unimproved art, with the improvement of the appliances, to excellence. It is almost impossible, excellence being attained with worthy implements, to retain that excellence practising an inferior method, which must be relearned with inferior means.

Now, in using the gun, there are three principal points to be considered; so that the art may be properly divided into three heads: How to use the gun safely—that is, with the least possible danger to yourself and others; how to use it effectively—that is, with the greatest power of bringing down, under all circumstances, the object at which it is directed; how to use it serviceably—that is, so that it shall be always ready for service, so that it shall suffer the least from being constantly used, and endure the longest wear and tear without deterioration.

The maxims for using a gun safely, are few in number, and simple; but they can never be infringed without serious risk, either to the shooter himself, his companions, or innocent, unconcerned bystanders. No one has a right to incur these risks himself, from mere carelessness, much less to inflict them on others. In my view of the facts, there are extremely few cases of accidents with fire-arms, as they are called, involving loss of life, which do not argue the last culpability; and I wish that, by the law, they were rendered culpable misdemeanors, and punished with fine and imprisonment, instead of being regarded with sympathy and commiseration.

The first is, never, under any circumstances, whether you know it to be loaded, or believe it to be unloaded, point your gun, or allow it to be pointed, in the act of handling or carrying it, toward any person.

This is the only sure rule of safety, and it is an easy one; for, like all the rest, after a time it becomes an instinct to carry a gun, so that the carrier, and those around him, shall all he alike safe from the consequence of an accidental discharge. Such discharges, on the contrary, though care may lessen their frequency, can never be entirely prevented. A thumb will occasionally slip from a striker in the act of cocking the piece; a brier will catch a trigger or hammer; a foot will miss its stephold, and a fall explode the cap; lastly, the casual failure of a portion of the lock may let off the gun, without the least *maladresse,* inexpertness, or negligence on the part of the shooter. Unquestionably, no man ever shot constantly for many years, who has not had his gun discharged in his hands inadvertently, without his intentionally pulling the trigger, on some occasion; although with a careful, observant, and expert person, such occasions will be rare indeed. If such things happen frequently to a person, however safely he may carry his gun, he must be an incurably inexpert bungler, one of those unfortunates whose fingers are all thumbs; and with such persons there is but one course to take—not to shoot with them at all.

There have been several patent inventions of *stops* of various kinds for preventing the discharge of a gun, even on pulling the trigger, unless the piece be actually at the shoulder, and the holder intend to fire.

I utterly disapprove of all these; first, because they tend to encourage carelessness directly, by making the person trust to the infallible quality of his gun, which *cannot* go off, instead of to his own caution; secondly, because, however good in theory, I never saw one which was certain in trial; in proof of which I can say that I have never been so often missed, or so nearly shot, as by some brilliant genius letting his gun go off, in the very act of demonstrating the impossibility of its going off; thirdly, because all the stops I have ever seen, do occasionally prevent the discharge of the gun when the holder wishes to discharge it. Therefore, I uphold care and constant observation, as the only sure gravitating stop.

First, then, in carrying the gun, it is necessary so to carry it, that, if discharged, its contents shall fly harmless, as regards yourself or others.

It will be found necessary, for relief to the muscles, in a long day's shooting, to carry the gun in many various positions; but in all it may be carried so as to render its casual discharge nearly harmless. If carried on the right forearm, with the butt backward and the trigger guard on the arm, the muzzle should point directly to the ground. If on the right shoulder, with the gripe in the hand and the locks on the shoulder, the muzzle should point directly upward. If on the shoulder, with the butt backward and the barrels grasped in the hand, the muzzle should point directly to the ground. If on the trail, the muzzle should be pointed directly forward; but the gun should never be so carried, unless when the shooter can *see* that there is no one in front of him. If in the hollow of the left arm, with the gripe lying in the hand, and the barrels diagonally across the person, the shooter must see that no person is, or can be, in range of it; so also, when, in walking up to a point, or to game marked down, he bears his gun with the muzzle diagonally advanced, his hand on the trigger guard and his thumb on the striker; or, when he levels the gun, in the act of taking aim, he is bound to see that no one is in the line of fire.

There is a very safe way of carrying a gun in thick covert, where you expect snap shots, which I have seen little practised—it is to gripe the stock with your right so that the forefinger can command the trigger, and the thumb the striker, and, with the left on the barrels immediately before the trigger guard, to bear the piece perpendicularly, muzzle upward, with the elevated rib toward the body, almost in the attitude of a soldier presenting arms. If a bird rise, a simple and easy movement simultaneously drops the sight to its level and brings the stock to the shoulder; while in forcing his way through coppice, it assists rather than hinders the shooter, by parting the branches before his face.

I recommend its practice as worthy of attention.

Than these, I know no other way in which it is allowable to carry a gun under any circumstances.

Next, as to the condition of the locks, in carrying a gun. When a piece is loaded and capped, the strikers must never, under any possible circumstances, be let down, much less carried down, on the caps. This is the more to be observed, because it is by far the most common, and commonly conceived to be the safest, way of carrying a gun. I do not think I ever saw a countryman carry his gun otherwise, until indoctrinated with much labor into doing so.

It is infinitely the most dangerous way in which a gun can possibly be carried, for these reasons: First, any blow on the back of the striker, while it is down, will explode the cap and discharge the gun, as may easily happen from a fall on a stone or on hard ground, without either raising the hammer or touching the trigger. Secondly, a branch or brier catching the hook of the striker, drawing it back any where short of the half-cock catch, and then releasing it—as it will do twice out of three times—will infallibly fire the gun.

At half-cock, in ninety-nine cases out of a hundred, the same brier or branch will bring the striker to full-cock, and then no harm is done. In the hundredth instance the niece would be fired.

From personal experience I may say that I have, probably, in the course of my shooting, had my locks full-cocked from half-cock, from fifty to one hundred times—fired from half-cock never.

At full-cock, a gun can be discharged *only* by a branch or brier catching the trigger; then it must *invariably* be discharged. No catch of the striker can do any mischief.

Consequently, the comparative safety stands thus:

There are two accidents, by which the locks with the strikers on the nipples may be discharged, and by either of these they will be discharged nine times out of ten.

There is one accident, by which the lock on the full-cock may be, and by that it will be, *invariably* discharged.

There is only one accident by which the lock at half-cock can be discharged, and by that it will not, ninety times out of a hundred.

I never, to conclude, object to shooting with persons who shoot with their guns habitually carried at full-cock. Most quick shots always do so; and some argue, with some show of reason, though I do not agree, that it is safest so to do. I have shot for years with men who do so, and never saw an accident occur; besides which, they are of necessity careful. With no man, who carries his strikers on his caps, would I walk in company ten minutes, much less hunt a day with him.

To load a gun, which has been recently fired, leave the striker of the barrel just discharged, down upon the cap which it has exploded; let down the other to half-cock, or, if at half-cock already, let it stand there; drop the butt, so that the piece shall stand perpendicularly before you, with the trigger guard and ramrod toward your face, at about a foot distant from the body.

Hold the barrel lightly, at about two inches below the muzzle, between the three first fingers and thumb of the left hand. With the right draw out the powder flask from the pocket in which you carry it; cover the orifice of the charger with y0ur forefinger; invert the flask; turn off the charger spring with the ball of your thumb, giving the flask a slight shake. Let the spring fly back with a sharp click, which will cut off the communication, and, if the flask be a good one, will obviate the possibility of an explosion.

I will here observe that Dixon's patent flask, with the steel spring on the outside of the top, is the only one which ought to be used by any person who regards safety, convenience, and rapidity of loading.

In the little cut above one of these implements is shown, of the best construction, together with a double patent lever shot-pouch of Sykes's patent, also manufactured by Dixon of Sheffield, and sold by all considerable gunsmiths. I esteem it preferable for convenience and quickness to any belt or contrivance I have ever tried, both for carrying shot and loading. The best material for the powder flask I hold to be tin, made in two halves, and soldered along the edges. It not unfrequently happens, where explosions take place in the horn, either from defect in the mechanism, or from carelessness in the loader's pouring the powder into the barrel without cutting off the communication, that in flasks so constructed the two halves are simply blown asunder, instead of being shattered to atoms, and that the owner escapes with a scorched, instead of a maimed, right hand.

But to return to the loading. You then toss in the powder as quickly as is consistent with accuracy, return your flask, insert a cut wad in the barrel, draw your ramrod, drive down the wad sharply and ram it *home* on the powder; remembering not to grasp the rod, much less cover the tip of it with the palm of your hand, in ramming down, but to hold it only between the tips of your fingers and thumb. In case of an explosion, this difference in the mode of holding it will just make the difference of lacerated finger tips or a hand blown to shreds.

For the same reason, never hold your nose over the muzzles, as if you want to look down the barrels; you cannot see the charge in the chambers, any more than you can find truth at the bottom of a draw well.

Your powder home, drop the ramrod into the undischarged barrel, by which yon will ascertain whether the load has started on the firing of the first, as it will do sometimes, and create some risk of bursting a barrel, and if it have, will drive it hack into its place. Pour your shot into the barrel you are loading, insert another cut wad on the top of it, ram it down sharply, and return the ramrod to its pipes. If, by any accident, a shot have run down into the barrel which contains the ramrod, do not attempt to draw it by force, which will only jam it harder, but invert the piece, give it a shake, and out will come both shot and ramrod.

You are now loaded—recover your piece, bring the lock to half-cock, remove the broken cap from the nipple, and see if the powder be up to the mouth of the orifice. If it be not up, there is much danger of the piece missing entirely, or making long fire; rap the lower side of the breech smartly with the hand, holding the nipples downward, which will usually bring the powder up. If it fail, try the cones with the pricking needle, and, if needful, pour in a grain or two of powder, put. on the copper cap, and press it down tightly with the ball of the thumb, to insure its fitting so closely that it will not readily fall off.

Nothing is so vexatious as a miss fire, and by these precautions, and the use of good materials, it is rendered all but impossible.

Cut wadding for a double gun is indispensable; it is cleaner, more expeditious, safer. Tow and loose paper are both dangerous; the former from its liability to remain ignited in the barrels, and fire the second load, the latter from its tendency to slip, at the shock of the first fire, and leave a vacuum between the powder and shot, which will often produce a burst.

Wads can be readily cut at home from pasteboard, cards, old bandboxes, old hats, or the like, with a cutter, which always accompanies a good gun, numbered according to the calibre, a mallet, and a piece of sheet lead, on which to rest the substance to be cut. They are, however, to be bought of all sizes, in boxes of 250 each, at all gunsmiths' shops, so cheap as to render it a waste of time and trouble to cut them, unless in an emergency, when the stock is expended, and there is no store at hand whence to replace it.

There was formerly sold a patent metallic English wad, which I approved, both on account of the small bulk it occupied, and that it kept the gun clean; I have, however, seen none lately, and they seem to have gone out of fashion. A species of medicated or oiled wad is now sold for the same purpose; and it is recommended to mix a few with the common stock, so that one will be occasionally used, as it is claimed to clean the barrels. These I neither praise nor the reverse. I do not know what medicament is that applied, and some are highly injurious to metal.

The best gunpowder for upland shooting, by many degrees, in my opinion, is Curtis and Harvey's diamond grain, No. 2; next to that, Pigou and Wilkes', and of late years, an admirable Scotch powder—I believe the Roslin mills. But I consider Curtis and Harvey's the cleanest, quickest, strongest, best, that I have ever tried. Dupont's American powder is undoubtedly strong— perhaps stronger, if strength alone were the test, than any other—but it is so irremediably filthy, that I abominate the sight or mention of it. It were not too much to say, that ten shots fired with Dupont's powder foul a gun more than five and twenty with any of the reputable English or Scotch powders.

I consider the best powder that ever was invented for large guns, especially for sea shooting, where the salt air decomposes the ordinary qualities, to be Hawker's ducking powder, manufactured by the same makers I have named, with preference, above.

Any of the anticorrosive English copper caps are good; I think Walker's the least so, and Starkey's central fire water-proof the best. I have kept these a week in a tumbler of water, and known them to go off without a single miss or long fire. Eley, celebrated for his famous cartridges, has invented a cap lined with India rubber, which is said to be superlative, and to answer for punt guns, over which the spray is continually falling so as to render extra expedients necessary to secure sure firing; these, however, I have never seen. All the good London makers now manufacture their own caps, which to furnish to their customers, and I have never used better than some from the house of Moore & Gray, Edgeware Road.

With regard to the sizes of shot, there is much difference of opinion. I consider No. 8 sufficiently heavy, unless in case of birds being unusually wild, when I would use No. 7, or what I greatly prefer, Eley's cartridges of No. 8, for all upland game, all the year through.

Even at fowl, I am convinced that most men err both in loading too heavily and in firing too large shot. No. 4 is, in my judgment, as large shot as any fowling-piece can ordinarily carry. No. 2 is large enough for any thing except geese, out of any gun, but for them one may use BB, or Eley's green cartridges with SSG.

The farther rules for safety are these: never get into a wagon without taking off your copper caps, even if it he only for a drive of ten minutes; and it is well also to wipe or brush the nipples, after removing the caps; for the percussion powder will occasionally adhere about the orifice, and will explode under a blow as readily as the cap itself.

On going into a house, never take off the copper caps. Men often do so, thinking thereby to render them safe in ease of their being thrown down by dogs or played with by children. In that case, the only safe plan is to place them where none of either the probable offenders can get at them.

The danger in reality, is increased tenfold by removing the caps; for to do so is to represent the loaded gun as unloaded and innocent. Nothing but a very small hoy indeed takes up a capped gun, without perceiving it to be loaded; and it is rarely, if ever, with such pieces, that accidents happen.

With loaded guns left uncapped, scarcely a week passes, but we see that some unhanged idiot has had, as it is glibly termed, the misfortune to blow out the brains of his sweetheart, wife, or child, by capping a piece which he supposed to be unloaded, and snapping it at the head of his victim.

The writer can only say that, should he ever sit on a jury where one of these unfortunate gentlemen shall be tried for such an accident, his misfortune will probably be increased by having to serve out a sentence for manslaughter, or murder in the second degree, in the State prison.

One would not suppose it necessary to write for the information of sane folk, that it is not altogether safe to put the muzzle of a gun into his mouth, and then for one to pull the trigger with his toe.

I have, however, within a month, read of two deaths occurring so nearly in this manner, that I am led to doubt the inutility of the caution.

One genius, having got the cleaning rod of his rifle

jammed, so that he could not withdraw it, cocked the piece, took the rod in his teeth, pulled might and main, and finding that it still did not come, pulled the trigger with his toe.

I am sorry to say that it is stated, although I do not altogether believe it, that the cleaning rod and ball both went out at the back of his neck, without doing him much harm. I say I am sorry, for if the story be true, such a fool ought not to live.

In the other case, the sufferer wished to ascertain if his piece were loaded or not, by trying whether the air would draw through it. To this end he clapped the muzzle into his mouth, and began to suck; then, remembering that so long as the striker lay down on the nipple, that alone would prevent the ingress of the air, he proceeded to half-cock the lock with his toe. Of course, his toe slipped, and very naturally his brains were blown to the four winds.

It must not be supposed, that these "modern instances" are either jokes or "weak inventions" of the author. The former anecdote appeared in the columns of the National Intelligencer, the latter in the New York Daily Times; both relations bearing every mark of authenticity, the names of the sufferers, the time and place of their exploits, though not the verdict of the coroner, which one might conjecture would run in the old style of "sarved 'em right, too."

Who shall say, after this, that it is unnecessary to state the danger of pulling triggers with the muzzle in the mouth?

I shall now, for the sake of continuity, alter the order in which I have heretofore considered the modes of using the gun, under the three heads into which I first divided the subject.

The learning to shoot, and the various details and degrees of shooting, are in themselves an art, and I therefore prefer to treat them separately, postponing them to what is for the most part mechanical, and, however useful, and indeed necessary to be known, easily explicable to and attainable by any person, not actually deficient in intelligence.

It is hardly necessary to say, that the residuum of the gunpowder exploded, and of the igniting substance of the copper caps, has the effect of producing the worst sort of oxidization of the metal of the barrels, in a greater or less degree, according to the temperature and humidity of the atmosphere.

The finest barrels are rusted the most easily, and suffer the more detriment by rusting. Of course the fouler the gun, the greater the evil that arises from its being left foul. In hot weather barrels suffer infinitely more than in cold, and in wet than in dry. When dampness and heat are combined, the mischief is yet augmented; and, probably, the worst conditions that can be supposed are when to dampness and heat a salt atmosphere is superadded.

No man, who owns a fine gun, or any gun which he values, ought ever to put it aside after use, without cleaning, even if he have fired but a single shot.

Again, every man who loves his gun should make it a point to clean it with his own hands. It is all very well in Europe, where the sportsman has a gamekeeper at his elbow who knows how to clean a gun, better than he does himself, and who takes as much pride in having it clean as he, to trust it to his servant.

I have shot, more or less, twenty-five seasons in America, and having body-servants all the time, never had one to whom I would intrust the cleaning of a valuable piece. I have always cleaned my own gun before sleeping, or if I have been too much beaten with work to do so, have invariably, after seeing it as well done as a man could accomplish at night, given it a thorough and fresh going over, before using it in the morning.

The mode and process is as follows:

Bring your locks to half-cock, take the ramrod out of the pipes, and the barrels out of the stock, screw the brass jag into the lower end of a solid cleaning rod—not one of the trumpery, jointed ebony or mahogany sticks which come in the gun-case—but a tough, seasoned hickory staff, of nearly half an inch diameter, about four inches longer than the barrels, with a saw-cut hand-piece. Wrap the jag as thickly with the finest and cleanest tow, as the bore of the barrels to be cleaned will admit. Moisten this tow, and insert it into the muzzle; plunge the breeches of both barrels into a bucket of cold water, some four or six inches deep. Some persons advise *hot* water; not so I. Hot water cakes and hardens the dirt in the barrels; cold dissolves and loosens it. Work the rod up and down, like the sucker of a pump, first in one barrel, then in the other, constantly changing both tow and water, until the former comes out of the barrels unsullied; the latter can be pumped through them pure and limpid.

Should the barrels be leaded, which all writers say occasionally occurs after very hard and very rapid shooting, when they become so much heated as to melt the shot in its transit, so that a part adheres to them—though I confess that a leaded barrel is a thing I have yet to see—a wire brush, or a little fine sand sprinkled on the tow, may be used. If the brush, it should be of brass wire, as softer, and less liable to scratch the polish of the barrels than iron; if sand, the less the better. I have never used either in my life; and I have, at times, shot very hard—to the extent, I doubt not, of several thousand shots in several single seasons, and my guns have always been in as good condition as those of my friends and neighbors.

I have adhered to a practice, however, which I strongly recommend to others, of having the breeches of my gun taken out at the expiration of every shooting season, by an experienced gunsmith, so that the whole interior may he inspected, and the least flaw, morsel of extraneous matter, or rust spot, detected and removed, if judged necessary, by dry reaming.

The barrels thus cold washed, wipe them dry externally, and pour into the muzzle of each, from the spout of a tea-kettle, nearly boiling hot water, until they run over at the brim. Reverse them and let them drain, standing erect in a corner, in the sunshine, on the hob of the kitchen grate, for five minutes, or by the register of a hot-air furnace. Wipe the cleaning-rod dry, replenish the jag with clean dry tow, as much as you can force into the muzzles, work it up and down as quickly and sharply as you can, constantly changing the tow, until not only no touch of moisture is sensible on the swab, but the barrels are perceptibly heated through by the friction.

It is not an unlaborious piece of work, I assure my readers; and if they be, like the royal Dane, in a degree "fat, and scant of breath," they will puff and blow, and their muscles will complain before the task is accomplished. Nevertheless, the work will be well repaid by the performance.

The tow may now be moistened, at the most, by two drops of clarified oil, of which anon, and may be run down each barrel. The cavities around the nipples, and all the exterior grooves of the barrels about the ramrod-pipes, elevated ribs, &c., should now be rubbed clean with a bit of flannel, or the finger of a kid glove stretched over a slip of pine wood, and then brushed lightly with a proper brush—a soft tooth-brush is as good as any—moistened, as before, with clarified oil, and rubbed with a piece of chamois leather or buckskin until dry; the striker, and above all the cavity of it, which impinges on the nipple, should be cleaned out, and oiled and dried in the same manner. But, unless the gun has been exposed for a long time to small penetrating rain or snow, has been immersed in water, or been thoroughly saturated with salt air, or unless some obstacle or hitch is perceptible in their working, I do not recommend the removal of the locks.

Every time they are removed and replaced, something is lost of the exquisite finish and fitting, where the woodwork and the metal come together; which is one of the principal points of superiority in London-made guns to all others; it seeming impossible in them that the air itself, much less a mote of dust or a drop of dampness, should penetrate the accurate suture.

The lock-plates externally should he rubbed and oiled, as should the trigger-guard, the heel-plate, and, in fact, all the iron work of the stock. The wood, which in the finest English guns is now put up merely in oil, with no French varnish to be scratched at the first encounter with stock or stone, and thenceforward always to show bruised and ragged, needs only plenty of elbow grease and a little furniture oil to keep it in perfect condition. The ramrod must be oiled, reinserted in its pipes, and the gun is clean, ready to be shot again to-morrow, or to be laid by in its case until once more wanted in the field.

If the latter, lay a treble-folded linen rag, dipped in the clarified oil and pressed dry, between the striker and the nipples; lay a single fold of the same over each muzzle, and force it down with a wad inside it, about two inches into the barrel.

Clarified oil is made by putting a handful of rusty nails, old iron, or shot, into a bottle of the best salad oil. In less than a month all the impurities of the oil will sink and collect about the metals, and the residue, when drawn off carefully, instead of itself promoting, will prevent oxidization.

"From the peculiar construction of detonating locks," I quote from a clever little English work by "Craven," under a title similar to my own, "they should not be snapped either with or without the copper caps, except in the act of shooting. When the gun is loaded, the flash of the detonating powder never enters the inside of the barrel; but if snapped upon the caps, when the gun is unloaded, it drives the detonating gas into the barrels, which creates rust;[8] and if done without the caps, the works are liable to be injured, by reason of the cocks meeting no resistance in their fall, as in flint locks.

"The detonating pegs, cones, or nipples will last a season's hard shooting—" I have known them to last half a dozen—"but should by no means be used after the holes are worn large by repeated firing; as it will weaken the force of the gun, and damage the locks."

Should it be found necessary to remove the locks—and this will be *necessary* whenever the gun shall have been immersed in water, exposed to heavy rain, snow, mist or salt air, and whenever any roughness or rigidity shall be discovered in the working of the locks, and *advisable* at least so often as at the beginning and end of every season—the mode of doing so is as follows:

Take out the lock screw, which passes through from the left to the right side immediately in front of the cock; and with a gentle shake, or a very slight tap on the inner side of the strikers, the locks will be dislodged from their places. On no account, in case of their adhesion, insert any thing between the wood and the metal of the locks; to do so will invariably bruise the softer

8   This gas is far more injurious to the metals than that evolved from the combustion of gunpowder, or than that arising from the two powders in combination.—H. W. H.

substance, injure the close fitting of the parts, and make way for the admission of rain or water.

I will here observe that bar-locks are by far the better. Back-action locks, though they wore at one time the rage, do not ordinarily work so smoothly as the others, in consequence of the form of the scear-spring, and, unless the stock be made thicker and more clumsy in the gripe, which is in itself both an eyesore and a defect, materially weaken that part of the gun.

If the lock, when taken off, be bright, clear and dry, nothing will be required but to wipe it off with a bit of dry wash-leather; woollen stuff is not so good, as bits of the lint or thread are apt to remain behind; to brush away any dust or old oil which may remain about the joints and screws of the springs from the last cleaning, with a dry-feather, and then with the same instrument to apply a very small quantity of oil, clarified as above, to those parts which work one into the other.

If, however, rust be any where established, or if much dirt and foulness be coagulated in places where it cannot easily be got at, it will be necessary to dissect the locks.

To do so, the following rules, published on the first introduction of the percussion system by a leading London gunmaker, are the best and safest to follow:

"I have found it a good plan, on taking the parts asunder, to drop the screws, keeping them carefully unmixed, into a dinner-plate, containing clarified oil to the depth of the eighth of an inch, and to wipe them dry with a piece of wash-leather before replacing them. The same thing may be done, advantageously, with the nipples when taken out of the breeches, and in this case it will be well to draw through the tubes a needle well charged with floss silk, which will collect and remove any oil which may have entered, and which, if suffered to remain, when the gun should be loaded, intervening between the powder and the cap, would, almost certainly, cause a miss, or at least a long fire.

"Let down the cock.

"Cramp the main spring sufficiently to remove it," with the small lock-vice which accompanies every complete gun-case but be careful not to *over*-cramp, as one may so break or injure the spring.

"Take off the bridle.

"Press scear against scear-spring with the forefinger and thumb of the left or right hand, according as the lock may be a left or a right one; and having, with the forefinger of the other hand, pushed back the cock as far as it will go, let the scear -spring go hack gently, when the pivot of the scear is easily lifted out of the hole, and the scear taken out.

"Turn out the scear-spring screw, and take out the spring.

"Unscrew and take out the cock." To do this, by no means wrench it off by forcing a screw-driver between the cock and the plate, but loosen it by gently tapping the inside of the cock with a bit of soft wood.

"Take out the tumbler."

This done, wipe all the parts thoroughly dry, remove the dry rust, if any, by means of a little oil and a burnisher, lightly oil the whole machinery, again wipe it dry with a piece of wash-leather, and it is ready for reconstruction.

"To put them together again, put in tumbler, and screw on cock, so as to be down.

"Put cock rather backward, and screw on scear-spring.

"Push cock back as far as it will go; put pivot of scear into its proper hole, and then taking hold of scear with the thumb, and of the top of the cock with the forefinger of the right hand, if a right-hand lock, and *vice versa* if a left, compress the spring, and move the lock forward and down.

"Push forward the swivel, so that it may not interfere with the screw, and drawing the cock a little forward, slip the two holes in the bridle upon the heads of the scear and tumbler pivot, and screw on the bridle.

"Having let down the cock, and pushed forward the swivel as far as it will go, cramp the main-spring, hook the end of it on the swivel, move it up to its place on the lock plate, and unscrew the cramp."

When a fine gun is to be laid aside for any considerable length of time, during the absence of the owner, or under such circumstances that it cannot be readily examined and overhauled, the following plan will be found admirable for its preservation.

Stop the orifices of the nipples with small pegs of pine wood, plunge the barrels, breech downward, into hot water, pour into the muzzles melted lard, tallow, or suet, carefully tried out and clear from salt, until the barrels are completely full; oil them copiously, without, with pure clarified neat's-foot oil, or loon-skin oil, which is better; and if laid away for half a dozen years, they will be found, when cleaned, in perfect condition. To clean them, plunge the barrels, as before, into hot water, and stand them near the lire until the grease within, being completely liquefied, can be turned out; the barrels should be then washed, dried, and cleaned as usual after a day's shooting, the pine pegs removed from the nipples, and they will be ready for any service.

Loon-skin oil, mentioned above, is thus made. Cut away with a sharp knife all the fat, nearly half an inch in thickness, which, comes away, adhering to the inside of the skin, when the bird is flayed; try it out in an earthen pot or crucible, purify by inserting old nails or shot for ten days, draw off the oil, and bottle.

It is the sovereignest thing in the world to prevent rust, especially the rust arising from sea-air; I learned the use of it from observing that the gunners at Barnegat, Egg Harbor, &c., constantly, when out on the bays, keep a piece of loon-skin in the pocket of their pea-jackets, and therewith wipe, from time to time, with the fleshy or fatty side, the metallic parts of their fowling-pieces. Perceiving the effect of this, I improved on the plan, by trying out and bottling the oil, and from long trial can pronounce it the best detergent and preventive of rust.

A few words on the rifle, that most American of all fire-arms, as adapted to sporting purposes, and to field use as opposed to target practice, and I pass on to more interesting, if not more indispensable portions of my subject.

The ordinary old-fashioned rifle of the American backwoodsman, which did its work of extermination on the red Indian, and the fatal volleys of which told with effect so deadly on the disciplined battalions of England during the wars of the Revolution and of 1812, has had its day; it is superseded; crowded out of its place by newer and more puissant arms; its mission is ended, whether in the field of the chase or of real warfare.

It was a ponderous, unwieldy, long, ill-balanced barrel, of weight so great, as, while it was rendered thereby irksome to carry, and difficult even for a strong man to fire but from a rest, to prevent all recoil, and to make it as steady almost as a fixture in any hands capable of balancing or aiming it.

The ball was ludicrously small, varying from 80 to 120 to the pound, and the charge of powder in proportion. The object of the hunter was extreme precision at exceedingly short ranges, the densely wooded wilderness, which was alike the hunting ground and the battle field, presenting insuperable obstacles to seeing an object, much more drawing a fine sight on it, at a distance exceeding a hundred yards.

To this must be added, that in the old days of scouting, Indian fighting, and forest hunting in the Atlantic States,, both lead and powder were matters to the woodman worth almost their weight in gold—that it was desirable to get as many bullets, as could by any means be compassed, out of a pound of lead, and that so valuable a thing as a charge was never to be wasted, unless with the certainty of bringing down an enemy or sending home a meal.

In the state of the country then prevailing, a shot was oftener obtained within fifty yards than beyond that distance; and it may be assumed that within one hundred, a ball of one hundred to the pound may be lodged in a stationary mark, by a hand and eye used to such shooting, with such precision as to insure death to the object aimed at.

At this time the art of gunmaking of all kinds was rude in the extreme, and the commonest of all prevailing errors was the almost universal belief that extreme length of barrel, whether in the rifle or fowling-piece, produced corresponding length of flight to the missile.

Rifle barrels were not unfrequently made of five feet and upward in length, and the hall was made to take two or more spiral perfect revolutions within the barrel previous to its expulsion. The art was in its infancy; and as no pieces were made which could outshoot these old-fashioned clumsy implements, while, from certain necessities of his position and habits, certain peculiarities of his character and temperament, the American backwoodsman became perfect in the use of the weapon, the weapon itself came to be regarded as perfect, and itself and the marksman who wielded it, were regarded with mingled apprehension and admiration.

Still it was never adopted by any other nation, and never has been used, in the true sense, as a sporting weapon—I mean as one used to kill game for a sport and pastime, and not for the value of the game. Its extreme inadaptability to rapid firing, especially at things in quick motion, its comparatively limited range, the want of weight in its hall, which, unless it hits its object directly in a vital spot, is of little more effect on large game than a pellet of shot, all combined to render it inefficient and unpopular.

It was soon found, moreover, that it was the weight and not the length of the barrel that did the work— that a half rotation, or, as some insist, a third, within the barrel, gives all the rotatory motion to the ball which is desirable; and lastly, that weight in the ball itself is necessary for distant firing correctly, independent of the fact that an ounce bullet, inflicting a wound not of necessity mortal, will disable a man or animal, where one of 120 to the pound will be carried off, harmlessly for the time, in the very vitals.

With this came the first change. The short ounce-ball yager rifle was adopted generally on the prairies against large quadrupeds, and was found to outrange the small piece infinitely, and, with equally good shooting, to plant its balls as accurately.

For a long time the double-barrelled English London-made sporting rifles were the *ne plus ultra* of the weapon, placing both their ponderous balls with extraordinary powers of penetration in the same spot at three hundred yards, and doing their work fatally at twice that distance.

During the period of European improvements in this arm, science made no advance in America, save in what may be called the frivolities and fripperies of the art. Target-shooting from rests, with telescope sights, patent-loading muzzles, and other niceties, very neat, and doubtless telling also in the practice-ground, but wholly useless and ineffective in the field, came into vogue with all the rifle-clubs and companies of nearly all the original thirteen States, owing partly to the disappearance of those species of game against which it was employed.

In the European armies the soldier's rifle, though effective at long ranges, was ill-finished, clumsy, and not by any means a weapon with which to allow men, much less to teach them, to become first-rate shots. The first move in the right direction was the heavy British two-grooved military rifle with the belted ball. Its range was found to be what was then thought immense, its precision great, and it was an available, manageable, telling, and killing weapon.

As a sporting piece, it still to a certain degree holds its own, though it has one bad fault—a fatal one for troops in active warfare—that it clogs in rapid firing, and soon becomes so foul as to render it impossible to load.

This in turn was superseded by the Minie rifle, used by the French chasseurs de Vincennes, the principle of which is duplex. First, it contains a hollow projection, sharp-pointed, running from the base of the breech perpendicularly into the chamber, which bursts the cartridge when it is driven into it, and through which the igniting power of the cap is carried directly into the centre of the charge. Secondly, the ball is so contrived as to expand, after the impulse is conveyed to it, fill the grooves of the barrel, and cut its way out, instead of merely holding its way out by means of the cuts made in it, as it was forced down in loading.

This weapon has made a complete revolution in the art of war. The Minie rifle executes with such precision at such ranges as to render all other fire-arms useless. A good shot can, and does not unfrequently, bring down his object at 1000, and even at 1500 yards. Artillery have been silenced with it before they could come into grape-range; and such is its appalling force and penetration, that at the bloody battle of Inkerman the Minie bullets, falling into the serried columns of the Russian foot, were found, in many instances, after the fight was ended, to have pierced three and four men in succession, inflicting ghastly and fatal wounds on all.

To this otherwise formidable weapon, a breech-loading principle has been adapted in Europe; but it is as yet slow, incomplete, and in one, which seems hitherto to be admitted as the best weapon of the kind, the Enfield rifle, liable to clog after firing, so as to render it difficult or impossible to load.

We now come to the various American patent arms, recently invented; and one of these I consider as, beyond all doubt, the best rifle ever invented, and destined to supersede all others, both for the chase and for actual warfare—I mean Peny's breech-loading rifle.

I have already had occasion to speak of the revolving and breech-loading principle, as applied to fowling-pieces, and have given my conviction that no advantage is to be gained by the adoption of either. On coming to consider the same principle, as applied to the rifle, we must distinguish between that weapon as required for military and for sporting purposes; the qualifications of the two being widely different.

For the former purpose, it is often necessary to tire a maximum number of shots, at a vast range, in a continuous stream, with great successive rapidity, almost in a minimum space of time.

For the latter, to fire two or three shots almost instantaneously, either at one animal constantly in motion, and increasing its distance from the firer, or at two, or possibly at three animals starting before him, simultaneously, and going from him at great velocity, is the *ne plus ultra*. Of revolvers, there are several kinds recently introduced, two of which are noticeable. Colt's and Porter's patent revolving arms—the former, on account, of its celebrity and excellence, *as a pistol,* for use in brief, rapid encounters; the latter, on account of its utter worthlessness for any purpose. As applied to a military *rifle,* Colt's revolving chamber fails, for several reasons. First, it cannot be made of sufficient calibre to carry any ball of telling weight, at long range, without being monstrously unsymmetrical and unwieldy. Secondly, after four or six shots have been discharged, the cylinder must be removed and reloaded by a slow and complex operation, during which the bearer is virtually unarmed, and liable to be ridden over by horse or charged with the bayonet, while unable to offer any resistance. Thirdly, it is difficult to be cleaned. Fourthly, it cannot be loaded, at all, but by means of its own peculiar apparatus—which lost, it is all but useless. Lastly, if injured, or out of order, it cannot be repaired by any ordinary armorer or gunsmith.

As a military weapon, therefore, it may be pronounced useless—this objection not being understood as applying to cavalry or boarding *pistols,* to be used only during close, rapid combats of a few seconds or minutes' duration, without continuous firing. For these are of admitted excellence.

For sporting purposes, though the rapidity and number of its discharges are all-sufficient, the difficulty of loading, the want of sufficient calibre, and the consequent failure at long ranges, are conclusive against it.

Moreover, it is clumsy in the hand, and singularly unsightly—nor are these slight or trivial objections; for of two guns, the one symmetrical and the other the reverse, the former must needs, *coeteris paribus,* shoot the better; as being the more handy and manageable in taking aim. Porter's rifle has a perpendicularly revolving cylinder, loading on the outer edge; and if any flaw should occur in the metal, causing an internal communication between the chambers, so that a discharge should ensue, four or five of the balls would take effect on the person of the firer, and the whole fabric would be burst and blown to atoms.

Add to this, it has all the faults ascribable to Colt's arm, with this in addition to them: that aim is taken not along the barrel, or over the axis of the ball, but along a sort of outrigger, divergent at the base and convergent toward the muzzle of the piece. By an arrangement of screws, it can be so adapted, that these two convergent lines, the one made by the sight of the shooter and the other by the flight of the ball, shall meet at any given distance; beyond which they will necessarily intersect. But, when once regulated for one distance, if fired at an object much nearer, the lines will *not* meet by some inches or feet; at one much farther, the lines will cross, with the same effect of missing the object, however true the aim. It is therefore, at best, a weapon which can only be used effectively at *one, known and given, distance;* and is utterly useless at any other range, until the difference shall have been calculated, and the machinery rearranged—an operation requiring time, and, of course, utterly inconsistent with field service.

Of breech-loading pieces, we will say that they are the great desideratum of military gunnery; that the superiority of them to muzzle-loading arms is greater than that of percussion to flint-and-steel locks; perhaps as great as that of musketry to archery.

For sporting, however, the gain is not so great. No breech-loading rifle has probably ever been made, with which the best and most rapid marksman could fire two shots, loading for the second, at one animal running at speed away from him, or across him—unless it were, once in a thousand times, on a perfectly open and level plain, at a very large object—much less could bring down two animals in quick succession, leaping up and taking flight at the same moment.

In point of rapidity of firing, therefore, for sporting purposes, no breech-loading rifle can ever equal, much less surpass, a finely made, accurately-sighted, double-barrelled hunting rifle, such as are turned out by Purday, Lang, Moore and Gray, and other London makers.

The obstacles to the success of all former breech-loading arms have been—First, the difficulty of so arranging the juncture of the chamber with the barrel, as to prevent the escape of the gaseous ignited fluid, at the moment of discharge. If this subtle fluid escape, it will speedily eat away the metallic faces at their point of junction, so as to render the arm useless; independent of the fact, that if, as must necessarily be the case, the escape vent be contiguous to any portion of the shooter's person, this fluid will seriously scorch him, and may set his raiment on fire. Secondly, the liability of the movable portion of the arm, and the crank which turns it, to become clogged by foulness, after repeated and rapid firing, so as to be bound, stiff, and, at last, wholly immovable. Thirdly, the complicity of their workmanship, the difficulty of cleaning them, their liability to get out of order, and their incapability of ordinary repair. Fourthly, inadaptability to any but their own peculiar ammunition; and lastly—their want of symmetry, and consequent unfitness for fine, rapid, accurate and workmanlike shooting.

To two of these faults, and two of the most serious of these, Sharpe's rifle, which has of late acquired so much Kansas notoriety, is with justice held liable. The gaseous fluid *does* escape dangerously, where the two metallic faces slide one against the other; so much so, that I have seen a person seriously scorched, in firing a few shots rapidly; nor can I doubt that, after a few hundred shots, the efficiency of the weapon would be seriously affected by the burning away or melting of the metal; as occurs in the vents of cannon and the touch-holes of flint-and-steel guns, after much rapid firing. The other fault is its extreme clumsiness and want of symmetry.

Perry's arm. which I have mentioned above, and of which a sketch is inserted on the following page, is liable to no one of these charges.

I speak positively, on conviction founded on long use, frequent experiment, and most accurate examination.

I have a rifle of this plan, carrying a ball of 80 to the lb. if round, of about double that weight, if acorn-shaped— which I have fired several hundred times, with my bare hand exactly under the point of junction, and never have been sensible of the least escape of gas; nor are either of the metallic faces in the slightest degree burnt, corroded, or altered in appearance, by the sharp firing to which they have been subjected.

From forty to fifty shots have been fired in succession, with cartridges made from Dupont's filthy gunpowder, and, though the operation of opening and reclosing the breech was, in a slight degree, checked, it, was not seriously impeded. With cartridges filled with good sporting powder, I have fired thirty shots a day three days in succession, without cleaning, for the purpose of testing its operation, and have found no difficulty with the arm.

The military pieces, both carbines and pistols, have the loading-breeches arranged to play somewhat more easily than those of finer fabric; and I prefer the former, as equally free from the escape of the gas, and as more convenient in service.

The weapons are—as will be seen at once from the following sketch, displaying, first, the rifle closed and ready for firing; second, the rifle with the trigger and trigger-guard turned forward, and the orifice of the chamber thrown upward, to receive the charge; and third, the loading-breech, taken out for the purpose of cleaning—singularly symmetrical, handy, and even elegant of form.

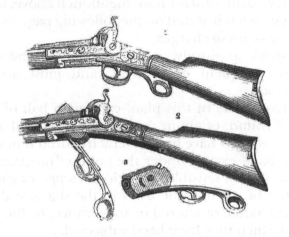

Ten shots can easily be fired, to hit the mark, by a practised hand, within the minute; and I have never taken in my hand any gun, which it is easier to bring to the shoulder and eye, on which it is more ready to take a swift and sure aim, or which shoots more truly or at a better range.

It is extremely simple, the commonest smith being able to repair every part. No gun can be cleaned with greater facility, since, on the removal of the breech by the withdrawal of two pivots and a guide-screw, the light is admitted to the interior of the barrel, at the base, so that the smallest speck of dust or oxidization can be at once detected and removed.

The base of the loading chamber, which receives the charge, is furnished with a hollow thorn, or *tige,* as it is termed in the Minie rifle, which tears the cartridge, and, being inserted by a screw, is itself removable, so as to render the chamber also pervious to light, air, and water, for purposes: of cleanliness. No ordinary gun can be cleaned so rapidly and thoroughly; nor can it be ascertained of any other, so surely, whether it is clean or not, before laying it aside.

To this may be added, that it is the safest of all arms; since, while loading, the trigger is removed from the lock on which it operates, and the cone with the copper-cap subtracted from the hammer, not returning into position so as to be subject to discharge, until the chamber is again looked into its place as conjoined with the barrel.

The ordinary load is a cartridge, containing the powder and ball, or slug, which is merely thrust into the chamber, when it is torn as described above; and so soon as the guard is drawn back to its proper place, the arm is ready for firing, inasmuch as, if desired, it is a self-primer.

The stock contains a long hollow tube or reed of brass, enclosing a spiral spring, which, when filled with thirty copper caps, is inserted at the butt, and at every return of the breech to its place after the cartridge is received, the old cap falling off as it is deflected, fits a fresh one on the nipple.

A peculiarity however, and a most important one, of this arm is, that, should the supply of proper cartridges run out, it can be loaded quite as readily, though not quite so fast, with a common horn and patched bullet, as with its appropriate charge; or, that if by any chance the breech should become fixed, it can be charged like any other piece from the muzzle with a ramrod; and that, either when thus or otherwise loaded, it can be capped by the hand, precisely after the manner of any other variety of the firelock.

With the cartridge, hand-capped, it can be fired deliberately five or six times in the minute; and I should think, though I have never tried it, three or four times, if not more, with loose ammunition.

If these, however, were the only recommendations of this arm, it would have been needless to waste words upon it, as applicable to sporting purposes. But it has another unrivalled superiority to any fire-arm I have ever seen—its range and power of penetration.

The small-calibre gun, of which I have spoken, does its work tellingly and killingly at ranges which used to be considered impossible, three and four hundred yards' distance. But the short cavalry carbines of 22 or 21-inch barrel carry a round ball of ½ oz. and an acorn-shaped one of twice the weight, which does fearful execution at 500 paces. I have seen a round ball, from one of these short pieces, pierce two three-inch wet oak planks, at a foot distance asunder, and then bury itself, eight inches deep, in the body of a tulip tree.

The military rifle of the same pattern with a ball of about ¾ oz. round, ½ oz. conical, has been proved capable of striking the size of a horse at the enormous distance of 1400 yards, and with a force as fatal as its range and accuracy are tremendous.

Tried before a military board in Canada, against the Minie rifle, it beat that queen of weapons, as it has been styled, out of sight, in all the three great desiderata—accuracy, range, and force of execution.

All these points being taken into consideration, I am inclined to prefer Perry's breech-loading rifle, even as a sporting weapon, to any gun ever yet invented; adopting, for that purpose, a very simple modification of its ordinary form. For use in close covert, and still more on horseback, in which condition, whoever has fried it knows that it is almost an impossibility to load a rifle, its superiority is inconceivably pre-eminent; and, even in common use, the saving of the actual labor of forcing the patched ball down a foul barrel, is a matter of no inconsiderable moment.

A good rider might load, fire, reload and fire again,

a, carbine of this construction, while sitting in his sad-
dle, with his horse at full speed, almost as readily as he
could do so on foot.

For buffalo-hunting, in the great plains, no weapon
could by any means compete with this; and were I about
to stake my life on the continuous and unvarying performance of any fire-arm I have yet tried, this is that on
which I should determine the risk.

The cause of its superior carriage is simple and easily explained, and is clue to its peculiar construction; producing by a different mode the same effect as is obtained
by the expansive bullet which forms the peculiarity of
the Minie rifle. In the ordinary rifled-barrel the ball is
driven down through an arrangement of sharp-edged
spiral grooves, which cut it into ridges and furrows in
its descent. On its projection, it passes out, retained in
its position within those grooves by the ridges previously cut in it; which mode of exit communicates to it the
rotary motion, whence its efficacy.

In the Minie rifle, the hollow conical hall is made to
expand by a wedgelike appendage, forced into it by the
explosion of the powder, and so fills the grooves, which
had not previously acted on it, and cuts its way out, gain-
ing its motion by its exit, not by a form impressed on it
in its descent. In Perry's arm, the chamber, and the ball
inserted into it, are both larger than the grooved barrel,
through which the latter is to be propelled; and the pro-
jectile, which enters the barrel, for the first time on the
discharge of the piece, a perfect sphere, is found, after
its emission, to be cut into an irregular cylinder, deeply
grooved and ribbed. The effect of this in the attainment
of accuracy is self-evident.

Why the excess of friction does not, as theoretically
it should, *diminish* the velocity and force of the projec-
tile, I cannot explain. It would seem that so far from
doing so, it *increases* both.

At all events, the matter is not one of theory, but of practised and established proof.

These guns can be made to order, at the factory in Newark, N. J., of any dimensions, calibre, form, weight, and finish requisite. If, happily, the manufacture had been set on foot anywhere else, in the United States, the arms would, undoubtedly, have long ago attained the repute they deserve, and would have been in general use.

But, according to the wont of the inefficient, unenterprising, pennywise and poundfoolish system of business of the twopenny community among which it is located, after being brought to perfection and proved satisfactorily, at some considerable expense, the small farther advance needed to set it in operation before the public, is not forthcoming; and, in consequence, the best weapon in the world remains comparatively unknown, while half a dozen mere pretenders are reaping golden premiums.

This arm can be, and is, made double-barrelled quite as effectively as single, and can be finished and ornamented up to any desired limit.

I should choose, for my own use, a double barrel to carry a conical ball of precisely one ounce weight, the round bullet being proportionably lighter, of from 28 to 30-inch barrel—the shorter length, if to be used principally, or much on horseback—with a weight of not to exceed ten pounds. It should have a plain fowling-piece stock for quick shooting, and rather an open V shaped backsight to facilitate rapidity of taking aim, though it might be furnished, also, with a telescope back-sight, and thread-and-ball end-sight, for target practice and rest firing.

For off-hand shooting and real work in the field, such gimcrackeries are useless and ridiculous.

I should prefer the gun to be finished in plain blue

steel, without any ornament or engraving, as easier to keep clean, less likely to absorb rust, and on the whole more sportsmanlike. Such a weapon can, I presume, be furnished of the best quality for about one hundred dollars, and I will insure it to shoot to the builder's satisfaction, and to kill deer, horse or man, if held fairly on its mark, at any distance from 500 to 1000 yards.

The mode of selecting a rifle to suit the shooter, is identical with that of choosing a shot gun. The way to ascertain its operation, is for the buyer to have it tried in his own presence, at arm's length and at rest, at long and short ranges, with the wind, against the wind, and across the wind—which last, if it be blowing any thing like a respectable breeze, is the hardest test of all—by some one in whose shooting, if he be not confident of his own, he may have perfect reliance. If it execute quickly, surely and forcibly, he may be sure he has got what he requires. But, by all means, let him insist on trying it, or seeing it tried, in the open. No testing in a gallery of fifteen or thirty paces is worth sixpence, as a real proof, either of the weapon or of the shooter; and none but a tyro would dream of purchasing on such a childish assay. Distance and penetration are the only true tests. At twenty feet a schoolboy's steel cross-bow, with a deal bolt, will snuff a candle; at a hundred yards it will hardly hit a house.

If, notwithstanding all that I have written, the hunter lean to the old single rifle, let him select one of not less than a ½ ounce round ball, seven or eight pounds' weight, and 33 to 36-inch barrels, by any American maker, and he can scarce go wrong.

If he want a supereminent double, let him pay Purday, Moore or Lang, of London, fifty guineas for his last and best turn-out, and he will not he disappointed; but in my mind, if he prefer a double, he will do well if he cause each barrel to be separately sighted at the breech and on the end, instead of in the ordinary method, which sights both intermediately along the dividing elevation.

What is lost of elegance in appearance, in this mode, will be more than overbalanced, whatever the gunmakers may say to the contrary, in precision of fire.

And with these brief remarks on the rifle, and the mode of choosing it, I shall pass, with no farther pause, to the consideration of the *modus operandi*—the how to *use* the gun of whatever kind in the field; how to learn to shoot deliberately, accurately and correctly as to principles; how to kill on the wing, or at full speed, with loose shot, and how at rest, or in rapid motion with the single ball.

This, after all, is the whole that I can attempt by precept. Some men take to shooting almost by instinct, as a thoroughbred setter does to pointing and backing, *de race*, as the French have it, by the accident of birth; others cannot by any toil of practice or amount of indoctrination be tutored into acquiring it. The eye, the finger, the nerve, the temper, have all something, more or less, to do with it; and, no more than a poet, do I believe that a crack shot can he made, save by the special ordinance of nature.

Still if one cannot be made a poet, he can at least be taught the difference between blank verse and rhyme, between Milton's Lyeidas and Christy's "Old Uncle Ned;" and, if he can never be brought to cut down his twenty consecutive shots, clean and quick in close covert, with the *sang froid* of an artist, he can, at least, be taught to fire his gun off without killing himself, his neighbor, or his dog; and, unless he be the clumsiest and slowest of the human kind, to kill a fair proportion of his shots decently and creditably, if not brilliantly or like an artist. It may be a consolation to beginners to know that a strong inclination toward field-sports and shooting rarely occurs, where practice, if persevered in, will not ultimately insure proficiency. In a lifetime, I remember but two instances of men, passionately fond of shooting, who never could compass even the humblest mediocrity, but continued to the end blazing at every thing, slap-dash, hit or miss, and seemingly as well content to make a noise, as to kill game like a Lord Kennedy or a Captain Scott.

In conclusion, no one need despair. The introduction of percussion locks has so simplified the art or science, call it which you may, of shooting on the wing, that it is much rarer now to find a dismally bad performer than a crack shot.

The latter was in my boyish days, *rara avis in terns;* nowadays, every second man is a fair shot, and every sixth, of those I mean who hold to the gun at all, an artist. In the mean time,

> *æquam memento rebus in arduis*[9]
> *Servare mentem,*

and be "deliberate promptitude" your motto and the mark for your attainment.

9   Remember in difficulty to preserve an equal mind.

HOW TO LEARN TO SHOOT,

The next tiling, after becoming the owner of a gun, or before it, as may be, is to learn the rudiments of the art of shooting, and this is only to be done by constant and careful practice.

The great point of difficulty, and the method of avoiding it, are well described in the following sentences, which I quote from the "Oakleigh Shooting Code," a work of decided merit, though not free from, what I must esteem, heresies.

"We think," says the author, and herein I fully agree with him, "that the generality of shooters use a gun properly, as regards throwing the end of it upon the object aimed at and drawing the trigger, and that any inaccuracy of aim must be attributed to the eye not being in the proper place when the aim is taken.

"The habit of missing seldom arises from inability

to throw the end of the gun straight upon the bird; but from the eye not being directly behind the breech, which it necessarily must be for good shooting.

"If there were a sight at each end of the barrel," as there is in the rifle, "it would be requisite to keep shifting the gun. until both sights were in a line between the eye and the mark; that, however, with a gun not well mounted to the eye and shoulder, would be too complex an operation; for, before it could be accomplished, a swift bird would be out of reach; it follows, then, that the shooter's attention should be directed only to the sight at the top of the barrel, and the breech end should come up mechanically to the proper level.

"If the sportsman will take aim alternately at objects on his right, on his left, on the ground, and in the air, without moving his body or taking his gun from his shoulder, he will at once see the difficulty of keeping the eye directly behind the breech. To be a proficient in shooting, he must in some way be able to do that mechanically; for, when aiming at a moving object, his attention can only be paid to placing the end of the gun on that object. When bringing up a gun to the shoulder in a gunmaker's shop, it is easy to bend down the head to the exact spot for looking along the sight-plate; but it is a very different thing when shooting at birds on the wing. The best way to prove whether a stock suits, or, in other words, whether the user of it can bring it up, as it were, mechanically, and without an effort, to the proper place, is to fire hastily, on a dark night, at a lighted candle placed against a wall, at about forty paces distant."

This, it may be observed, is very well for one who is already "a shot," to try a gun; but it gives no clue to the attainment of the skill which enables the gunner to cover his object quickly and correctly. What follows is excellent.

"When a person is nervous, or afraid of recoil, he

naturally raises his head, and consequently shoots above the mark; on firing he unconsciously throws his head back, and then, seeing the bird above the end of the gun, he fancies he shot under it, when the reverse is the fact.

"We may also observe, that if the shooter do not keep his head down to the stock, he will probably draw it aside, so that his aim will be as if taken from the left hammer, which would of course throw the charge as much to the left of the mark, as raising the head would above it.

"The main point, then, in taking aim is *to keep the head down to the stock and the eye low behind the breech*. The sportsman, who can from habit or practice, invariably bring his eye down to the same place and keep it steadily there, so that he always begins the race from the same starting point, will distance all competitors."

This is indisputably true, and all old sportsmen, who shoot sufficiently well to reason on, and account for the causes of their shooting ill, on some, one or other, day, whether from being physically or mentally out of order, long out of practice, or other accidents, are aware of this habit of throwing up the head, when unsteady, at the moment of firing. The same malpractice will be frequently produced, even when a person is steady, by the trigger, which is expected to yield to the accustomed pressure, not giving way without a jerking pull; and still more so by the cap, after giving the ineffectual click of a miss-fire not followed by a report, suddenly exploding a second too late. The head is nearly certain to go up, and the shot to be wasted above the mark.

The writer, doubtless, does not intend to be understood as asserting that, after keeping his eye low down behind the breech, the practised shooter takes aim at a flying bird, or running animal, as he would do with a rifle at a mark, along the barrel. The beginner must do so in a degree, but so soon as the facility of so doing is acquired, the practice must be laid aside; or the learner will never rise to any thing above mediocrity, but must always continue a *poking* shot.

This is the cause which renders it so extremely difficult for a person, who has become by long practice a first rate rifle shot, and has grown by use perfectly *one* with that weapon, ever to become a crack shot on the wing.

He dwells too long on his aim, and follows or *pokes*—as it is technically called—*after* his bird, and rarely attains the art of cutting it down, sharp and sure, at a snap shot, as it flashes across an opening in a brier brake, or twists among thickset saplings.

The art to be acquired is this: to bring up the gun with its sight on the object, or so much above, below, or before it, as you intend to tire, of which more anon, having the eye, the breech, the point of the gun and the mark in the same plane of elevation or depression.

One other thing I believe to be equally indispensable, which I have never seen mentioned in any written instructions on the subject of shooting; that the top of the barrels should lie, when the piece is at the shoulder and the aim taken, flat and square across the eye, so that a level rested upon them should be in the exact plane of the horizon.

Unless this be the case, the lines of sight along the patent elevation and of the projected shot will not be identical, much less the lines of fire of the two barrels, and consequently the aim will be faulty.

The following precepts will be found, I think, to embody the best method of acquiring the mastery of this; and here I would beg to caution my young readers, that these indoctrinations are not merely intended for the use of those who do not shoot at all; but for all those—whether they shoot well at the mark, off-hand or at rest, whether they are dead sure of a robin on an apple bough, or a high-holder on the summit of a dry, dead tree, or not—who do not shoot *well* on the wing.

I believe it to be a common error with young shooters in America, where every boy, who lives in the country, has more or less use of the gun early in his teens, to continue too long content to shoot sitting, to learn to shoot *too well* sitting, and to acquire a habit of taking such an aim, oven when using shot, as would insure killing the object with ball.

Such a habit, once acquired, has to be unlearned, before great proficiency can be hoped for on the wing, or at, running objects; and I would undertake, with far more confidence of turning him out a crack shot, a young man, who had never fired a gun in his life, than one who was sure death to a chipping bird on a rail, or a ground squirrel on a stone wall, at forty yards.

This is not the case in Europe, where the children of the wealthy, of landowners especially, are taught to ride and shoot, from their youth upward, as regularly as to read and write; the latter especially, if not solely, with a view to shooting on the wing—and where the children of the poor, unless, unhappily for them, their parents chance to be either poachers or gamekeepers, do not shoot at all.

But in America, it is generally and undoubtedly the case. It is the fact, which renders the rural and even urban population so easily convertible into soldiers; and which, when they are converted into soldiers, renders their fire so deadly.

There are in every community hundreds on hundreds of men and boys, who never had a rifle in their hands, yet who on first taking one up will shoot with considerable accuracy, and in a week's practice will be marksmen. They have been all their lives learning, with the fowling-piece, to be bad shots with that weapon, and capital shots with a weapon of which, perhaps, they have never heard.

This is precisely what they have got to unlearn, *ab initio*, before they can become good shots at game; but their acquired skill will yet do yeoman service, when they need it, with the rifle, which is more than can be said on the other side of the question; since it is hard, indeed, for the crack flying-shooter to become a great rifleman. In fact, excellence in the two branches of the art is so rare as to be thought, by many, incompatible. Such is not, however, the case. There are some persons so constituted, that all fire-arms seem equally familiar to them, and that what is the fruit to others of patience and practice, is to them an instinct, as it were, rather than an acquirement.

To learn to shoot from the beginning, then, with most persons, is a matter of time and patience; and the first steps, as is the case with almost every new pursuit, are slow, tedious and unamusing.

"Before attempting to use the loaded gun, the shooter, whether young or old, should always make himself thoroughly master of it. Many of the accidents, which so constantly occur, arise solely from a neglect of this precaution; but if the sportsman be early drilled into the notion that he has a dangerous yet useful weapon in his hand, he will seldom forget the importance of the precept. One or two points should be most sedulously impressed, the most important one being *never to point the gun, at any time, by design or otherwise, at any thing, but the mark intended to be shot at.* It is astonishing how often this is neglected. Guns are often pointed at females with a desire to frighten them, or at dogs, cows, or other objects in mere wantonness; or again, whilst carrying the gun, its muzzle is held so as to point to every part of the visible horizon. All this is unsportsmanlike, unsafe, and worse than useless. With this proviso kept steadily in view, even at full cock, the gun is perfectly safe except from bursting." The above quotation, as well as several which follow, is from Stonehenge's "Manual of British Rural Sports," and is well worthy of attention, as are the remarks ensuing on the first lesson of shooting.

Previous, however, to using the plan hereafter indicated, I would recommend that the learner should be placed in position, that is to say, with the left foot advanced, the knee slightly bent, about eighteen inches in front of the right, on which the weight of his body should rest; holding the gun at the level of his hip, with the butt below his right elbow, his left hand grasping the front of the trigger-guard, perpendicularly to the barrel, the gun being at half-cock. The thumb of his right hand should be on the striker, and the finger nail of the fore-finger touching the inside of the trigger-guard, before the trigger.

In front of him there should be a whitewashed wall, with a black mark, the size of half a dollar, at about the level of his eye. On this mark he should steadily rivet his sight, and raise the gun to his shoulder, cocking it with his thumb, while in the act of bringing it up, and then lower his cheek to the stock.

It will not as yet be necessary to attempt to take any aim at the object, or to rectify the first direction. The lesson to be acquired is, first, to attain the knack of cocking the gun quickly, yet deliberately, while it is in motion from the hip to the shoulder; and secondly, to gain the habit of instinctively throwing the point *toward* the object to be aimed at.

The gun should not be snapped, or the trigger drawn; and when, by a few hours' practice in these motions, the pupil can perform them readily, handily and surely, it is wonderful how much is already gained.

Nothing is so much to be guarded against as dwelling on the sight, poking about to get the aim, or keeping the gun long to the shoulder. This facility acquired, the next step is to learn to bring with equal quickness, ease and deliberation, the lock back from the full-cock to half-cock, while in the act of lowering it from the shoulder, without making any pause or separate motion. This is done by placing the ball of the thumb on the striker, as if in the act of cocking the piece, and holding it gently in check while the trigger is drawn with the forefinger, yielding to it, nevertheless, and letting it descend slowly, until it almost touches the nipple. Then by drawing it back until it ticks, the sound showing that the cock is safely secured.

When considerable facility has been acquired in these motions, the faces of the strikers may be lined with a thick piece of cork or felt, so as to preserve the cones from the effects of the blow, and the pupil may be directed to pull his trigger, the moment the gun is at his shoulder and his cheek down to the stock, still without attempting to take or correct his aim, more than he has already done by fixing his eye on the mark, without removing it thence, until after the trigger is pulled. The instant it is pulled, the muzzle must be lowered and the butt withdrawn from the shoulder.

This practice should be persisted in, under the supervision of a careful, kind, and steady instructor, half an hour at a time for many days; care being had, never to hurry or agitate the learner, either by impatience, or by rebuking any clumsiness or oversight. Encouragement is needed, not rebuke; and practice can alone make perfect.

It is, also, advisable not to persevere, at any one time, so long as to weary the pupil; who will soon begin to feel proud, as he acquires handiness, In perceiving his aptitude with the piece and his quick control of the mechanism; and will take more and more interest in the lessons, as he finds, even at the quick practice I have described, that he catches occasionally sights of the mark over his barrel.

All this should be done *invariably* with both eyes open.

The next lessons are merely for the acquisition of steadiness. They are first to snap the locks, cocking and uncocking the piece, as before, with caps only on the gun. In this case, a good wad of well greased rag should be rammed into the breech of both barrels, and it will be better, also, to pour a drop of oil into the orifice of the nipples, as the explosion of the percussion powder is most detrimental to the gun, which should be cleaned at once, when the lesson is ended.

This lesson should be practised, as before, while pitching up the gun at a mark, and may be varied by occasionally, at *uncertain intervals,* loading the gun with extremely light charges of powder, the pupil not knowing when the powder is inserted, and when he shoots with the caps only. This will give him confidence and steadiness, and will effectually prevent him from flinching, unconsciously, in anticipation of the flash and report.

Observe, that nothing is so much to be avoided as the startling him, at first, by a broad flash and loud report, to which he must gradually and imperceptibly be habituated; or, afterwards, by an overloaded and kicking gun.

When this has been all steadily gone through, for some time, and both quickness and fearlessness have been acquired, I would proceed to the lesson which Stonehenge recommends as the first; but even this I would modify.

"Provide gun-caps, &c.," says he, "in a good-sized room at night, then get a lighted tallow candle, and place it at about two yards' distance on an ordinary table, liaise the gun to the shoulder," from this time with the left eye closed, and, still without seeking to take deliberate aim,—Stonehenge says, "with deliberate aim—pull the trigger. If the aim be good, and the bore of the gun about 16, at that distance the candle will be extinguished, or, at least, its flame will be visibly affected." If the first, proceed again and again as before; but if not, and if the flame be but little agitated, the learner will now begin to rectify his aim, by sighting the lighted wick as quickly as possible, until he finds himself able to blow out the flame, with moderate rapidity, twice or thrice out of five times.

The next step, when this has been mastered, is to fix a black mark of the size of an ordinary playing card, on a white wall or fence, at about twenty paces distance; or a white mark on a black wall, and then to practise at it, as before, firing powder only, bringing the gun up quickly, cocking; it while raising, and bringing it down the moment it is discharged; still taking care not to pause or dwell upon the aim, but to fire on *the first catching sight*, even if the sight appear to be an inch or two wide of the mark, at the time of drawing the trigger.

The knack of bringing the sight up, and the eye down, correctly to the true level, will gradually be improved with practice; and precision will be obtained imperceptibly and by degrees, far more rapidly than one would expect. But the habit of dwelling on the aim, and poking about with the muzzle in the hope of at length fixing the sight point-blank, if once acquired, is so difficult to be shaken off that I may almost say it is impossible. After a while, still loading with an exceeding light charge of powder, it will be advisable occasionally, and when the shooter docs not expect it, to put in about half an oz. of small shot, and let him, as before, fire at the mark on first sight.

If he be aware that the gun is loaded, he will be nervous with endeavor to aim more steadily; and without doing so a whit, will do so far more slowly. Not knowing when to expect shot, and when mere blank cartridge, he will blaze away just as unconcernedly as ever, and speedily finding that he comes, as he very shortly will, to plant his shot in and all round his mark, firing as soon as the heel-plate is at his shoulder, he will quickly acquire perfect confidence in himself, and that unconscious equanimity, which is the cause, as it is the invariable consequence or accompaniment of being a good shot.

After this habit is well acquired, and the sitting or stationary mark can be hit almost to a certainty, it is wonderful how nearly the pupil has arrived to being a good flying shot, even before he has attempted to shoot on the wing.

Let him now commence at small, short-winged birds, as they rise slowly from the grass, or flit across open spaces from tree to tree, still keeping his eyes riveted on the object while bringing up his piece, and firing instantly.

If the former lessons have been perfectly acquired, and he be nearly sure of' striking his stationary mark at snap shots, he is certain ultimately of becoming a quick and sure shot on the wing, and he will not fail to bring down his object, now and then, even from the first.

Practice and coolness will do all the rest; and it is necessary now to guard against one malpractice only— never to take down the gun from the shoulder, when it once has been levelled, without firing, from the idea that it is not correctly aimed, and from the fear of missing, is a positive and invariable rule.

To do so, is to become undecided, unsteady, and to falter more and more, until he have lost all nerve and ability to judge how the aim is taken, or what he is about at all.

To shoot at all risks, with deliberate rashness or recklessness, if I may so express myself, is the only true maxim. If the shot tell—well and good. All is done that is desired, and the chance of doing so is doubled by the careless confidence with which it is done.

If the aim be falsely taken, the distance, speed or motion of the object miscalculated, if cool, the shooter will easily come to judge where the error lay, and to see at once why he missed; whether he over or under-shot, whether he fired before or behind, to right or to left of his object; and this point once gained, wonderfully easily will he correct the errors and improve.

After this, almost everything is acquired that is needed. Constant practice, and careful attention and observation, must make every one, who has got thus far, one day or other a good shot.

He must know from his teacher, and learn from his own observation, that in order to hit objects rapidly crossing him, going from him, or coming toward him, he must shoot in advance of them in order to hit—above them, if they be ascending, below them, if they be falling.

The allowance to be made will vary in proportion to the distance of the object from the shooter, and the velocity at which it is travelling, when he fires. For it must be remembered that the shot, which is propelled from his barrel the fraction of a second after he pulls the trigger, has to travel a considerable distance, from twenty to fifty yards or upward, before it can reach the object, which, unless it be progressing before it in a direct line, will have changed its position, and will be some inches more or less in advance of the place at which it seemed to be stationary, when the sight was taken.

What this change may be, is uncertain; for calculating it, no rule can be given. According to the velocity of the object, the force and direction of the wind, and twenty other chance circumstances, it will vary, so that hardly in two instances will the variation coincide. Yet habit, practice, and deliberate observation will so far conquer all difficulties, that a crack shot, with a bird, or birds crossing him at any distance from fifteen to fifty paces, with or against a positive gale, will instinctively and without a pause calculate the allowance to be made, pitch up his piece and cut down the objects, one after the other, as if they were hanging motionless in a dead calm.

The best practice for this purpose, not merely for the novice, but for the old hand who by any accidental circumstances has got out of use, and one which cannot fail to produce its effect, is to shoot at large-sized turnips pitched into the air with the utmost force and vigor of a powerful arm, in all possible directions, diagonally, across, and toward, or away from, the shooter, by a clever and practised assistant.

With a tyro, the lesson should commence by tossing the turnip directly before him, slowly upward; and as he improves and attains certainty in hitting it, increasing its velocity and altering its direction.

The learner, after a few trials, should avoid shooting at the turnip when at its maximum elevation, for while in that position, it hangs for a moment in the air virtually motionless, and then presents a stationary shot. He should, therefore, as soon as he is tolerably sure of it, when at its height, begin firing as it rises or descends, by which means he will easily learn what allowance is to be made for speed and distance. When he is master of this, let it be first tossed, then hurled, as I have said above, diagonally across him, away from, or toward him; and by the same degrees, imperceptibly he will come to such skill, that he will never, or scarcely ever, miss it. So soon as he can accomplish this (and I have seen scores of boys who have done so, and could do so in a great measure myself, before I had ever thought in my most sanguine dreams of firing at game), he can—my word upon it—kill any bird that flies under any circumstances, except it be in very dense covert, which requires practice arranged in the same manner, among bushes and shrubbery of greater or less intricacy.

By causing the assistant instead of throwing the turnip into the air, to bowl it along the surface of the ground, in all different angles and directions, up hill, down hill, over the level, across knobby, hillocky ground, which will cause it to bounce and bound into the air, between large trees or among brushwood, the pupil will learn to hit it *thus* as easily as when in the air, and will then be as certain on *running* as on flying game.

Beyond this, in the art of shooting, there is nothing to be learned beyond coolness, steadiness, the immovable nerve, the self-possession which nothing can disturb, the inventive and instinctive resource, which can always devise a mode of action to meet any emergency; which comes, and can come, only from long use, and that habituation which becomes, in time, a second nature.

It is certain, however, that any youth who has good eyes, quick faculties, who is apt with his hands, not having, as the ordinary saying is, all his fingers thumbs; who observes, thinks, and can control his nerves in a reasonable degree, can—if he will consent to be patient, to practise precisely according to the rules which I have prescribed, not trying to jump to conclusions before he has taken in the rudiments—and will become more than an ordinarily good shot.

That, if he be neither irrecoverably nervous and rash, nor irretrievably slow and timid, if he have ordinarily quick eyesight, quick wits, and quick hands, he must be, if he obey orders, beyond the possibility of failure.

If he be unusually stout of nerve, cool of temper, rapid of sight, sure of observation, and apt of hand, he will probably become as successful as a marksman and a shot, as he would at any thing else to which he should turn his superior faculties.

If, however, he be purblind, a blinker, clumsy and helpless with his hands, dull-witted, weak-nerved, timid and a dolt: I should strongly urge it on him and his friends, that he should let the gun alone, for he is never like to do much with it, unless it be to shoot his friend, his sweetheart, or himself—none of which are the legitimate, though I am sorry to say they are but too frequently the casual, ends of amateur gunnery.

For learning to shoot with the rifle, a mode of practice must he adopted almost diametrically opposite to that prescribed above.

The charge of a shot gun, expanding in width in proportion as it increases its distance from the muzzle of the piece when it is charged, will cover, at forty paces from a strong, well-shooting gun, a circle of a yard in diameter, with its pellets so regularly distributed, that any bird found within that circle must receive two or three missiles, and sent so strongly that any one of these must break a pinion bone. At sixty paces the circumference of the shot will be greatly enlarged and the force nearly as greatly diminished; still a good gun ought to kill a bird to a certainty in the *centre* of the circle, and generally any where within it.

It is evident, therefore, that with a shot gun at medium distances, the aim need not be taken with exact precision on the object. It must be a considerable divergence of the line of aim from the line of flight of an animal going directly from the shooter, probably an inch or so at the muzzle, which should produce a clear miss at forty yards. In some cases, when the animal shot at is close at hand, it is necessary to shoot wide of it, in order to prevent its being shattered to pieces by the shot; which, for a few yards, goes together in a compact mass.

I remember once striking a woodcock going directly before me so squarely with the whole body of the charge, at some ten or twelve yards from the muzzle, that all we ever found of it was the extremities of the two wings below the pinion joints.

The result was, of course, unintentional, but the shot, for a shot gun, was a bad one—for a rifle it would have been perfection, as the ball would have struck the bird centrally at whatever reasonable distance.

The farther distant the object is from the shot gun, the more is close-aiming needed, since at long distances it is only in the centre of the circle of their distribution, that the pellets of shot fly close enough to hit, or strong enough to pierce and bring down the game.

With a rifle the operation is wholly different. The missile is a single one, of inconsiderable size, and has no divergence whatever to right or left of its flight, if the barrel be itself true, and truly sighted. It is of course liable to fall lower than a direct horizontal line from the muzzle, since all projectiles descend in a parabola, and that liability we guard against by elevated sights. What is *called* a point-blank shot, for there really exists no such thing, is merely a shot which we fire from the ordinary elevation of our piece, without extra allowance made, at the centre of the mark.

It is clear, therefore, that in aiming with a rifle, absolute precision of aim is positively requisite. There is no space for chance or good fortune even in a minimum degree. The ball must be sped exactly to the identical spot which it must hit, and the divergence of a hair's breadth at the muzzle will grow into inches or even feet as the range increases.

Therefore the aim must be taken with the utmost deliberation and certainty, and must be maintained perfect, which can only be done by great steadiness of nerve, perfect coolness of temper, and sufficient muscular power, until not merely the trigger is drawn, but the ball is dismissed from the barrel.

I am satisfied that in rifle-shooting, the more misses by far occur in consequence of the shooter disturbing a correct aim, and diverting his barrel never so little from the true line, by the act of pulling the trigger, or by flinching from the flash or report, than of his taking a false direction in the first instance.

If, therefore, nerve be valuable to any shooter, to the rifleman it is indispensable. The slightest tremor, even the motion communicated by the act of breathing laboriously to the muscles of the arm and shoulder, is sufficient to disturb the truest aim and spoil the finest shot.

It is impossible, therefore, for one half at least, if not more of mankind, to become even fair rifle shots, with any possible amount of practice, but to all men, who have good eyes, iron nerves, sufficient physical strength and phlegmatic tempers, it is a certainty, beyond calculation, that they can become first-rate rifle shots with sufficient practice.

It is far easier to become a tolerable shot even on the wing with a shot gun, than a passable marksman with the rifle. But of those who shoot at all with the rifle, there are a hundred splendid marksmen, where of those who affect to use the shot gun there is one really crack shot.

In learning to shoot with the rifle, therefore, the first requisite is to see the end sight through the orifice of the back sight exactly on the mark—the second, to keep it there steadily for a length of time, a second or two at least—the third, to pull the trigger exactly when the sights are most centrically and steadily on the mark, and never to pull it otherwise—the fourth, to pull the trigger and endure the little shock of the discharge, without the smallest jerk, start, or trepidation.

To teach how this is to be done is impracticable, beyond saying that it is to be done. Practice and coolness can alone effect the ability to do it, even with those constituted by temper, physical and moral, to obtain the power. One thing may be premised, that it is well, if not actually necessary, to hold the breath from the moment the sight is taken until the ball is fairly discharged.

One eye must, of course, be closed in rifle shooting; but, as I have said before concerning the shot gun, the other eye should be riveted on the mark before the rifle is brought to the shoulder, and while it is rising, by which means it will find the sights in opposition the most easily, and often almost without an effort. Though it is necessary to *get* a sure aim before firing, it is not necessary to dwell on it before doing so. Every second between the having taken true sight and the giving fire is a second lost, or worse than lost; for the longer the rifle is held to the face the greater the tension of the muscles and the nerves, and the likelier are both to shake and give way. The first true sight is always, with all fire-arms, the *best* sight, and a quick shot has as much, or more, the advantage over a slow shot, with the rifle as with any other weapon.

It is perfectly easy to be at the same time a quick and a deliberate shot with a rifle, just as it is with any other weapon, and the union is of course invaluable.

In learning to shoot with the rifle, therefore, celerity of taking aim and the habit of giving fire instantaneously when the aim is taken, are the points to be practised most diligently—the latter more especially, since on the simultaneous action of eye and finger everything depends.

I particularly advise and caution beginners against the habit of firing the rifle from a rest, and I advise them as early as possible to practise at objects in motion. A person may have acquired perfect precision and certainty

in shooting with rests and telescope sights at the smallest objects, and at long ranges, and yet may be totally
incapable of taking a steady aim, where he can obtain
no extraneous support, even at a large mark.

In field shooting at game, it is not once in fifty times
that it is practicable to shoot with a rest, other than such
as may be obtained from his own person by the shooter.
And as target-shooting is only the practice by which he
proposes to fit himself for the end, not the end itself, it
is as such that the shooter is to regard it.

In the Middle States, where there is but little game
to be shot with the rifle, the rifle-clubs are, in my opinion, taking a wrong direction, as both the style and
character of their weapons, and the manner of their
shooting, are utterly unsuited either for the chase or
the field. Their best and most landed marksmen would,
from what I have seen, read, and heard of their performance, make very poor work in field or forest-shooting
with "the deer before the hounds."

Again, it is highly advisable to practise at long ranges, at least two and three hundred yards, for on the prairies, where now only game exists of the species to be
followed with the rifle, in sufficient numbers to render
the sport of great moment, a majority of the shots fired
will lie within those distances.

In speaking of the necessity of taking a direct and
exact aim at one small point, when shooting with single
ball, I do not, of course, mean to say that the small point
to be aimed at is always identical with the small spot to
be hit, and that no allowance is to be made for velocity
of motion or distance of the object.

Far from it. Allowance must be made when an
animal is crossing at speed, even greater with the rifle
than with shot gun, unless the shooter have the knack—
which, if he have it, is perhaps the best—of keeping his
hand and muzzle continually moving, so as to have his

aim continually covered, even after the trigger is drawn and the shot fired. Where the motion of the animal shot at is steady, such is the better plan, but where it bounds, or rises and falls in sweeps and curves, an absolute allowance in advance will perhaps on the whole succeed better.

If a ball be aimed directly behind the bend of the shoulder in a deer—which is the proper place where to strike the heart—taking the animal to be crossing the shooter at 75 or 100 yards, the deer will have moved so far, while the shot is discharging and the bullet travers-ing the space, that the latter will take effect far back in the ribs, and therefore fail to inflict a deadly wound. In such a shot, therefore, the aim should be taken at the forward point of the shoulder, or the edge of the chest in advance of it, and that aim will probably plant the missile in the exact spot desired.

At a longer range, yet a greater allowance must be made in advance; but to do this the shooter must calcu-late exactly how much he means to give, and then aim directly on a spot at the level he wishes to cover, precise-ly so far in advance of his mark.

The better way, I think, of doing this is, first to cover the exact spot which it is desirable to strike, and then, carefully keeping the sights in line, to sweep the muzzle forward six inches, a foot, or more, as it may be judged necessary. At a deer crossing at speed at two hundred yards' distance, an allowance of one yard in advance of the point of the chest, and above or below it accordingly as the animal is ascending, descending, or running on the level, will not be an inch too much.

On level ground it is well to shoot a little low of the object, as it is better to take the deer on alighting from his bounds, especially if he be in bushy covert or underwood.

All allowances of distance, as also for the force of a

cross wind, however, are matters of judgment and calculation, as are the ranges at which the shooter is actually
firing; and practice is the only true way to obtain correctness of judgment, and of eye-calculation.

It must always be remembered, however, that every
one who has acquired the skill to shoot off-hand, necessarily possesses that which enables him to shoot with
a rest; and that he who can surely strike an object in
motion can strike one at rest with tenfold certainty.

To conclude, I advise no person who desires to
become a proficient with both weapons, by any means
to touch the rifle until he has made himself a perfect
master of shooting on the wing; and then never to practise with single ball at a mark for any length of time,
without diversifying his practice by shooting at turnips,
bowled or tossed, as described before.

If he do, he will lose one skill, as he acquires the
other, even though he may be an old craftsman and a
capital shot.

The habit of waiting and following for an exact aim,
with the sights in line, will stick to him, and incline him
to dwell and follow his birds on the wing, in a manner
which, as it has been shown, is destructive to quickness,
style and handsomeness of killing.

No one, however good a shot, has ever returned,
after a campaign with the rifle against deer, or what
you will, to the snipe-meadow, without finding that he
requires some days' practice before he can cut down the
long bill so soon as he tops the rushes, with the precision and instinctive swiftness he had before he visited
the prairie or the forest.

For the person who desires, above all things, to be a
first-rate performer with the shot gun on the wing, who
is so, and who only cares about rifle-shooting as a super-
fluous accomplishment, for which he expects to find
little occasion and less exercise on its legitimate game

in the field, I advise that the rifle be let alone *in toto.* So nearly do I hold the two accomplishments incompatible in their perfection.

I do not mean that a first-rate flying shot may not shoot enough with the rifle not to be a complete bungler, not to miss a deer or a man standing at a hundred yards; but I do mean that if he be ambitious, and once get so far with his rifle, he will be apt to proceed, until he succeeds to the utmost, and then—good-bye! to his lightning-like dash and swiftness on the wing.

The same is, more or less, the case, *vice versa;* but as it is, I believe, quite impossible that a person, who has become by years of patient practice a perfect and unerring rifle shot, without any early knowledge of the shot gun—as is the case with hundreds on hundreds of foresters and woodmen in the West and East—can ever, by any amount of practice, at a late day in life, become a crack shot on the wing, so will the attempted practice of it interfere the less with his old acquired habits.

If there be two things on earth, which, to be done *well,* must be done *young,* they are to shoot on the wing, and to ride across-country. They cannot be learned old, more than it can "to speak the truth."

THE DOG.

After the gun or rifle, the great essential, as to the mere killing of game, is his dog to the sportsman; but when we regard him as the living, the intelligent, the more than half-reasoning companion, the docile, obedient, enduring, uncomplaining servant, the faithful, grateful, submissive, affectionate friend, and not unseldom the last mourner of the dead master, unmourned by all beside, "when men have shrunk from the ignoble task of watching him who led them;" we must think of him as something widely different from the tool of wood and iron which we fashion, how perfectly soever, merely to be the senseless and unconscious instrument of our skill.

The wonderful tractableness of the dog, his facil-fault, and—be it added—his master's disgrace, if he ever lose his teachings, or if he ever require severe or cruel punishment to maintain it.

Nine dogs are cowed, ruined and rendered irretrievably worthless, by cruel flogging for small causes,

or for no cause at all, where one is spoiled for want of
it; and, even in early breaking, the constant resort to
the whip must be regarded as a proof that the breaker
is incompetent to his business by milder and more legitimate means.

Still, the whip, I do not mean to deny it, must be
used in the commencement; the animal must be made
acquainted with its power, and taught to know that it
is the ultimate consequence of refractory conduct or
obstinacy.

The great point to be gained is to make a dog aware
that he has done wrongly, before he is punished; the
great point to be avoided, the punishing him, so far as
he knows, for no offence; that is, when he is ignorant of
any wrong-doing.

When punishment is to be inflicted, it should be
done with a sharp, tough, slender whip, capable of
inflicting stinging, painful strokes, but incapable of cutting, as a cowhide; or bruising, as the heavy thongs one
often sees used for the purpose. A stick should never be
laid to a dog, unless it be a slender birchen twig, or the
like, for it almost invariably bruises. The ears should on
no account ever be pulled so as to give pain, for to do
so is almost sure to produce deafness; though it is very
well to pinch them gently as a sign of rebuke, and perhaps to box them slightly with the fingers, while rating
and scolding the animal. When intelligent, and kindly
treated, it is remarkable how sensitive dogs are to repri-
mand, and how intensely they dislike to be held gently,
but forcibly, down, and rated and reproached for several minutes together by their master.

I have a Newfoundland dog in my possession, certainly a most singularly intelligent and attached animal, which, after having committed any escapade and
returned to follow at heel, if one turn round the head
to look at him and merely say—"Ain't you ashamed,

sir?"—will dodge from side to side, still keeping close to heel, in order to avoid the reproachful look, so as to render it impossible to catch his eye, and will follow, with his stern lowered between his legs, looking ludicrously disconsolate and unhappy, till he is forgiven and again admitted to favor.

In conclusion, I would say, that to *kick* a dog under any circumstances is an act of utter and unpardonable brutality—a bone may be broken in an instant, and a valuable animal destroyed, when no such result is thought of, much less intended by the human brute, who practises the savagism.

I once took all my dogs out of the hands of an otherwise undeniable dog-breaker, to whom I had determined to intrust three or four puppies, for no other reason, than that I saw him once punish a young pointer on the snipe meadows, where no rod or switch was at hand, by kicking him.

Once a kicker!—I said to myself, a kicker always! and as I had no desire to have one of my fine young dog's ribs broken, and then be told that he had unluckily died of fits or of the distemper, I removed him from the strong probabilities of that fate; as I advise all my readers to do, under the like circumstances.

Before I have done with this part of my subject, in order to avoid being misunderstood, I will add, that when correction is needed, it should be given, in kindness to the sufferer, in earnest, and once for all; so that he shall remember the infliction, and need no repetition. One sound flagellation, when really deserved, will do twenty times the good, morally, and not inflict half the suffering, physically, of twenty, or twenty times twenty, insufficient, teasing corrections, which keep the dog in constant agitation and irritation, without making him once really care about it, or remember it.

A dog, when he has once learned what a whipping

is, will be sufficiently warned by the mere sight of the instrument of flagellation, shown menacingly, with a word or two of objurgation. The menace must not, however, be repeated *in vain*, or it will be a short time only ere it lose its effect, from the offender perceiving that no execution follows.

In such cases, with old knowing dogs, who are as much aware as their master that they are doing wrong, if they neglect warning and take no heed of threats, two or three smart cuts, with a long rating, is as good in its effect as half an hour's flagellation. Where the offence is very grave, such as rushing in on a fallen bird, breaking point from jealousy of another dog, chasing violently heedless of the call, paying no attention to the call or whistle, refusing to come to heel or down charge; where the fault evidently arises from wilfulness, and not from accident or the casual wantonness of high spirits, as when a dog has been long confined without being shot over—then indeed chastisement must not hide his head.

The sportsman should, however, always have a careful heed to causes, and to the actuating motives of his dogs, before he punishes. I have seen good, careful, true-nosed dogs flogged for flushing birds; when it was evident to me, from their coming to the point instantly, and looking around with a deprecatory glance, that the fault was accidental, or, in fact, no fault at all, but the consequence of existing circumstances; perhaps the failure of scent owing to the state of the ground, or of the atmosphere. Again, I have seen a martinet punish dogs, what I call cruelly, for not *sitting down* to charge, on snipe ground, where the water was three inches deep and as cold as ice; when the poor brutes *were* standing to charge, perfectly passive, with ears and sterns lowered, and only failed to squat, on account of the state of the ground.

But it is needless to multiply instances. In the former case, all that is desirable is a gentle "Have a care, Sir! Have a ca-are, Don!" in the latter, when a shot should be again fired on good dry ground, to insist on the charge being made in the most perfect style, with the paws extended and the nose down between them.

By the way! if a dog be at all unsteady, the only sure plan is to make him charge, *whenever a bird rises,* whether shot at or not. In fact, it is better always to make him do so, steady or not; and, if a retriever, never to allow him to gather a dead bird until he have pointed it.

Thus much as to general rules, for dogs in general. When we come to the several varieties, I shall speak somewhat more largely; but as this work is intended chiefly for young sportsmen and beginners, I shall not enter into dog breaking, of which they are not supposed to be capable, even if in positions and circumstances where they might attempt it. Neither my subject nor my limits will permit.

In like manner, diseases, remedies, except the very commonest and most simple, do not come within my subject or sphere; in such cases, the best thing to take is *advice.* Young beginners, who seek to cure by dosing and drugging, are pretty sure to kill. Those who wish to learn what is necessary of such things for accomplished sportsmen, will find what they want in "Dinks and Mayhew on the dog;" the former excellent authority on breaking, the latter on medicine; in my own "Field Sports;" and in "Blame's Canine Pathology," and "Youatt on the Dog."

Dogs should be warmly but airily housed; heartily, but not heatingly, fed—old Indian meal, mixed with oatmeal, suppawn, is the best general food, with a small quantity of salt, which is a preventive against worms—occasionally some vegetables may be added, and once or twice a week, sheep's-head broth, the water in which meat is boiled for the house, or greasy slops of any kind;

milk and buttermilk, whenever they can be spared, are excellent additions—they should have abundance of water, abundance of exercise, be kept scrupulously clean and dry, and their condition and efficiency will well repay the care.

The dogs most used by sportsmen in this country are, or ought to be—"The Setter; the Pointer; the Cocker; the Water-dog; the Newfoundland; the Deerhound; the Foxhound; and the Beagle." To each of these I shall devote a few remarks, as to their characters, qualifications, points and uses; to the services and localities for which they are the best fitted; how to get them good; how to keep them so; and how to use them to the best advantage.

I shall not go into minutiae of breeding or natural history—such disquisitions will be found elsewhere, in the works I have named above, and in many English books, which cannot be too highly recommended; I would particularly specify Colonel Hutchinson, on Dog breaking; Scrope, on Deer stalking; Colquhoun, on the Moor and the Loch; and Hawker, on Seafowl shooting; who are the best authorities on their several respective specialities,

I may here add, that the field for wild-sports, and the market for sporting dogs, like the course of Empire, "westward take their way." The failure of game in the Eastern and Middle States renders it yearly more and more difficult to break dogs on the Atlantic seaboard, or to obtain well broke dogs thereon.

English broke dogs do not succeed any where in America, owing to the difference of the ground, the game, and the mode of limiting it. English bred dogs, however, of all kinds, with the single exception of the Russian setter, are the best for all purposes, indeed, the only dogs worth having.

THE SETTER.

First in the list of sporting dogs, without a moment's hesitation, I place the Setter.

For—although the pointer possesses many excellencies, among others greater docility, or rather, perhaps, greater retention of what he has learned, with less inclination to run riot and require partial rebreaking, after he has long lain idle, than the setter—which qualities certainly render him preferable for very young shooters, or for residents of cities who shoot but a few days in the year—I must agree with that agreeable sporting English writer, "Craven," that "the first place among shooting dogs must be awarded to the setter.

"In style and dash of ranging, in courage and capacity of covering ground; in beauty of form and grace of attitude; in variety of color and elegance of clothing; no animal of his species will at all bear comparison with him."

I will add that, in endurance of extreme fatigue; in supporting cold and wet; in facing thorny brakes

and tangled covert; in travelling with uninjured feet
over stony mountain ledges, across plains bristling with
spiked sword-grass, or over burnt coppices ragged with
jags and stubbs; and generally in working, day in and
day out, for weeks, or through a season together, the
setter distances the bravest pointers I have ever seen.

His temper too is usually milder, he is a more affectionate and friendly dog—this praise is not, however,
due to the Irish variety, which is apt to be savage—and
is, in my opinion, also a wiser and more intelligent and
sagacious animal; although he is so much more frolic-
some, larking and high-spirited, that it is, undeniably,
more difficult to keep him in command, and more necessary to rule him with a strict hand and observant eye,
than the pointer.

For the made and complete sportsman, therefore,
I without a moment's doubt advise the adoption of the
setter, especially for America, where, or at least in the
greater part of which, almost all the shooting is either
covert-shooting or marsh-shooting; for both of which
branches of sport I consider one setter as equal, for the
quantity of service to be got out of him, to two pointers, and for the satisfactory style of doing the work, and
the cheerful endurance of the toil without suffering, yet
more superior.

On this subject, I shall quote the brief opinion of
"a gentleman, a large breeder of sporting dogs," from
a work of "Craven's," which I feel myself the more justi-
fied in doing that he often, and once in this very work,
borrows from me, not only not rendering credit where
it is due, but inventing a "Mrs. Harris" in the shape of
an *American* correspondent, to bear the weight of my
offendings.

"I have tried all sorts," says he, "and at last fixed on
a well-bred setter as the most useful. I say well-bred, for
not many of the dogs with feathered sterns, which one

sees nowadays, are worthy of the name of setter. Pointer fanciers object to setters on account of their requiring more water, but there are generally sufficient springs and peat-holes on the moors for them, and even in the early part of September a horsepond or ditch is to be met with often enough. For covert or snipe-shooting the setter is far superior; facing the thorns in the covert, and the wet in the bogs, without coming to heel shivering like a pig with the ague. I have always found, too, that setters, when well broke, are finer tempered, and not so easily cowed as pointers. Should they get an unlucky undeserved kick, Don, the setter, wags his tail, and forgets it much sooner than Carlo, the pointer. My shooting, lying near the moors, takes in every description of country, and I always find, that after a good, rough day, the setter will out-tire the pointer, though, perhaps, not start quite so flash in the morning.

"I always teach *one*, at least, of my dogs to bring his game, which saves a world of trouble, both in covert and out of it, but never allow him to stir for the birds until after loading."

The writer is an Englishman, which accounts for the allusion to the moors and the early part of September, which are not applicable to this country, but I preferred to let it stand and comment on it at leisure.

Our summer shooting, in the hottest part of the year, from July through August, is only for woodcock, and lies *invariably* in wet ground, and almost invariably in covert; in no case, therefore, at this season is the setter likely to suffer from thirst, and so to prove inferior to the pointer, which really has the advantage over him in supporting extreme *dry* heat. Where the shooting is in thick coverts, the setter has the best of it.

Again, in the autumn shooting, which does not commence until the end of October, there is much more of cold than of heat to be endured, and, the springs and rivers being ordinarily full, there is never any difficulty of procuring enough water for the thirstiest of dogs.

On the grouse-mountains in Pennsylvania, and among scrub oaks and burnt woodlands, I have found the well-feathered legs and full toe-tufts of setters to give them great advantage over the barefooted pointers, which I have frequently seen the necessity of hunting in buckskin boots.

In the southern country where quail-shooting, or partridge-shooting, as it is there termed, is followed in sultry weather, the lands are so irriguous and so well watered as a general thing, that the setter need not suffer, while the great preponderance of snipe and marsh-shooting gives him the preference.

The only portion of the United States, in which I should consider the pointer preferable, is the dry prairies of the West, where it is frequently indispensable to carry out water for the dogs in grouse-shooting, which takes place in the intolerably hot weather, on those treeless plains, of August and the earlier part of September.

A prodigious quantity of nonsense has been written under the pretext of ascertaining or deriving the original breed and stock of the setter—some writers insisting that he is a treble or quadruple mongrel, part setter, part pointer, and some add, part Newfoundland and part foxhound.

One sporting writer—wonders will never cease!—and he a man of some repute both as a sportsman and an authority, has actually given a receipt in one of his works, for manufacturing a setter. He desires the aspirant for the possession of a perfect dog of this breed, of which he records his own opinion, that it is the best in the world, to cross a foxhound with a pointer, and to recross the progeny with the low small Newfoundland of St. Johns. The offspring of this last cross is to be the given setter.

And this, as if there were not half a dozen pure and distinct families of setters reproducing themselves to the smallest distinctive mark of shape, coat and color, generation after generation, in England alone, without taking into consideration the Russian and Irish varieties.

He had precisely as well, in order to raise a London dray-horse, have desired the breeder to cross a jenny ass with an elephant to give size, and then to recross the progeny with a bear in order to gain courage and a hairy coat.

The truth, and it is now generally admitted—certainly admitted by all physiologists and natural historians—is, that except the spaniel, the setter is the oldest and purest of all the sporting breeds. In fact it is, itself, neither more nor less than a spaniel of the largest size, cultivated by the selection of the best types for parents, by superior food, good housing, and judicious crossing, not with different varieties of the dog, but with various families of its own distinct variety, until it has been brought nearly to perfection.

The habit of setting or pointing its game, which is now an instinctive and natural qualification of its race, was originally an acquired trick, taught by diligent breaking. Centuries of tuition have rendered that acquired trick an hereditary gift, so much so, that no good judge of animals would now think a young setter worthy of being put into the breaker's hands, if he did not point naturally and without instruction.

This conversion of foreign and acquired tricks into hereditary and congenital powers, transmitted from sire to son, is extraordinary; but this is by no means its most extraordinary phase. Every sportsman, who has kept and reared families of pointer puppies—in which variety, as I have said before, this retention of acquired habits is even more common than in the setter—must often have observed the whelps, under four months of age, when no instruction has ever been given them, nor have they acquired any apprehension of men, not only pointing the chickens and pigeons, in the stable yard or in the street, but backing one another in their points.

Now backing is entirely, and from the beginning, a bit of tuition. There is no movement resembling it in the natural action of a dog, nor, if there were, could it, be of any service to him in a state of nature, but rather the reverse.

It is assumed, no one can say with how much plausibility or truth, that the assumption and retention of a stationary attitude, on coming upon a hot scent, is merely an adaptation to our uses, by the breaker, of a natural peculiarity of the dog intended by nature for his own behoof.

On scenting his game and crawling up as he still does, almost on his belly, and elbows, to the immediate proximity of it, the animal naturally, it is said, paused, in some instances couched—as does the cat or leopard—in order to collect its energies and contract its muscles for the fatal spring. This pause, it is added, man has seized; taught the animal to prolong it; and so adapted it to his own purpose. It surely can be no native instinct implanted by the Creator in the dog from the beginning; since no animal possesses an instinct, which to possess would be useless, much more injurious to itself.

How a dog standing stock still, as if in a half cataleptic state, with eyes glaring, lips slavering, tail rigid, back bristling, and limbs quivering with excitement, motionless and attempting to effect nothing for ten minutes, or half an hour, until the bevy of birds takes to its wings and away, should help him in a state of nature to get his supper, is inconceivable; but that because one dog on scenting game assumes this strange position, his friend who is hunting in company with him, instead—as one naturally would suppose him likely to do—of rushing to share the fun and partake of the spoils, should do the like, is far more wonderful; as, where it does not naturally exist, it is infinitely more difficult to teach.

Naturalists have classified dogs under three principal, general divisions; *veloces,* the swift; *feroces,* the savage; and *sagaces,* the intelligent; of which the greyhound, the bull-dog, and the spaniel are respectively the types. To the latter species belong all the dogs which hunt by nose, having as their anatomical character, according to Blaine, "the head very moderately elongated; parietal hones not approaching each other above the temples, but diverging and swelling out, so as to enlarge the forehead, and the cerebral cavity. This group includes some of the most useful and intelligent dogs."

The anatomical distinction first named is probably the cause, as well as the sign, of the superiority of this variety of dogs, as it gives room for the capacity of brain, which, whether in man or the inferior animal, invariably indicates and produces superiority of intellect.

In all the spaniels proper, the eye is full, liquid, and speaking: the nose well developed, with large and open nostrils; the coat silky, soft, and in some cases much waved, and almost curly. The colors of the various families of this variety are almost innumerable, varying from pure black, white and yellow, tan, liver and orange, to ring-streaked, spotted and speckled, with all these tints two by two, and sometimes three by three; as black and white, with tan spots about the eyes and muzzle, and tan feet. The ears are generally long and pendulous, and are the most curly part of the body. The legs, belly, and stern are deeply flewed or feathered with a long fringe of soft, silky hair, and the feet are protected with tufts about the ancles and between the toes, which afford much defence to these delicate portions of the body.

Of this family, the setter of pure English blood is the largest variety, perhaps improved by culture—I say, perhaps, for I do not find any real reason for believing that it has been enlarged in the process of time, and there is certainly less distinction between it and some of the large varieties of what are called true spaniels, and which are in appearance pony-built setters, than between some of those varieties themselves, as the clumber breed and the King Charles.

The only permanent structural distinction if it can be called so, is the size of the ear, which is smaller, and looks as if it had been rounded by art. This peculiarity is, however, shared by the Newfoundland dog, who is admitted to be spaniel.

The coat also is somewhat coarser, though still in the best families excessively soft, silky, and beautiful, and waves rather than curls as in the proper smaller spaniels. Especially about the ears is this texture of the coat observable. Setters, however, differ in this respect, and I have seen dogs, and once owned one—and he was, perhaps, the very best I ever did own, a liver and white dog called Chance—which was as curly about the ears and poll as an ordinary water-spaniel.

I do not know the pedigree of this animal, and it is possible, though barely so, that he might have a cross of water-spaniel in his blood. It is not, however, probable, for the water spaniel is an exceedingly rare dog in the United States, so much so that in a residence of five and twenty years, I have not seen half a dozen of the race. His character and conduct showed nothing of the spaniel, which is the most riotous and hard to break of all sporting dogs, for he was singularly docile, cool-headed, and, though the best retriever I ever saw, was almost, if not quite, the stanchest setter, both at the point, and the down charge.

The chief cause of the question which has arisen concerning the origin of this beautiful and sagacious animal, it appears to me, is simply the new name, which with the improvement of field-sports, the subdivisions which have been introduced, and the nicer distinctions which have been of consequence required, has come into use, it would seem, within the last century.

I find it variously stated, that the spaniel was first taught to set in the reign of Edward II., and that he is mentioned in a MS. treatise by the grand huntsman of that monarch, so long ago as 1307—and, again, that Dudley, Duke of Northumberland in 1335, first systematically broke in setting dogs.

One objection, and a very material one, to the latter version, being the fact that Robert Dudley was not Earl, much less Duke, of Northumberland in 1335, but Henry Percy.

A curious document, which is probably the earliest legal instrument of this nature on record, is in existence, having been preserved by Mr. Daniel in his Rural Sports, proving that in the seventeenth century setter breaking was an understood and regularly managed branch of business.

Singularly enough, this document is a contract between a Worcestershire farmer and a namesake, and doubtless a collateral ancestor, of my own—since a branch of my family were early settled in that county— which would seem to show that I come honestly by my love of field- sports, as a matter of inheritance from past generations.

"Ribbesford, Oct. 7, 1685.

"I, John Harris of Willdon, in the parish of Hastlebury, in the county of Worcester, yeoman, for and in consideration of ten shillings of lawful English money this day received of Henry Herbert of Ribbesford in the said county, Esq., and of thirty shillings more of like money by him promised to be hereafter payed me, do hereby covenant and promise to the said Henry Herbert, his ex'ors and adm'ors, that I will from the day of the date hereof, until the first day of March next, well and sufficiently maintain and keep a Spanile bitch, named Quand, this day delivered into my custody by the said Henry Herbert, and will before the first day of March next, fully and effectually traine up and teach the said Bitch to set Partridges, Pheasants and other game as well and exactly as the best sitting doggers usually set the same. And the said Bitch so trained and taught shall and will deliver to the said Henry Herbert, or whom he shall appoint to receive her, at his house in Ribbesford aforesaid, on the first day of March next. And if at any time the said Bitch shall for want of use and practice or o'rwise forget to sett game as aforesaid, I will at my cost and charges, maintain her for a month or longer as needs may require, to traine up and teach her to sett game as aforesaid, and shall and will fully and effectually teach her to sett game as well and exactly as is above mentioned.

"Witness my hand and seal the day and year first above written.

"JOHN HARRIS his X mark.
"Sealed and delivered in presence of
"H. PAYNE his X mark."

The fowling-piece not being at that time invented, nor indeed brought to any perfection a century later, the object of breaking the spaniel to set was the netting of birds, which is now regarded as rank poaching. The training was, however, identical; and stanchness was, if possible, more necessary, inasmuch as drawing the net over the covey requires longer time than merely to walk up to the game, then than now. The price, as the value of money then stood, is very large. At all events, the passage proves the antiquity of this mode of training, and further shows, at that day, that the identity of the setting spaniel with the other breeds of the same dog, was not questioned.

It is worthy of remark, that the term setter is very recent; the animal, when all its present habits and characteristics were fully developed, retaining the name of *spaniel*. Gay calls him the "creeping spaniel," and Thomson, that accurate observer and close describer of nature, thus writes of him, in terms that leave no question as to what manner of dog he alludes to:—

> "How, in his mid-career, the *spaniel* struck
> Stiff by the tainted gale, with open nose
> Outstretched," &c.

It is stated by Mr. Blaine, that the setter is still called in Ireland the English spaniel. If it be so, it would go far to disprove the generally received idea that the Irish setter is an original family, if not, as some suppose, *the* original stock. I doubt, however, both the fact, and the deduction.

In my "Field Sports" (vol. i. p. 325), I surmised that "the Irish dog is undoubtedly the original type of the setter in Great Britain."

I have, since writing this, seen reason entirely to alter my opinion; which was induced by the large admixture of Irish blood which has been introduced into many of the choicest English families, those especially which run to orange and white with black noses and muzzles; one family, in particular, with which I had most acquaintance. The races are, however, I think, now, where not intentionally interbred, entirely distinct.

The English dog is distinguished by his inferior bone and stoutness; superior grace and delicacy; the greater length, silkiness, and curl of his coat; his blandness, affection, good-nature and docility; in all which points he much more closely adheres to what we now call the spaniel, than does his Irish cousin.

I am inclined to think that black, black and white, pale lemon-colored and white, and perhaps—though I speak this doubtfully—liver and white, are the true and distinctive colors of the English setting spaniel. I somewhat doubt the liver-colored, because I observe, first, that it is distinctively the water-spaniel color; and secondly, that where that color prevails, one is apt also to find a greater tendency to curl—another water-spaniel sign—in the hair.

I also believe, that wherever orange or deep red is found in the English breeds, especially coupled with the black nose and palate, there is an Irish strain.

Sure I am that, as a rule, though of course there are exceptions, the red or red and white dogs are the wildest and the most difficult to break.

In choosing an English setter, the first thing to examine is the head; it should be broad and expansive between the eyes and across the brow, with a high bony process extending upward from the base of the skull to the ridge of the occiput. The nose should be rather long than broad, the nostrils well opened, soft and moist— the latter condition being a proof of good health and a *sine quâ non* to the possession of great scenting powers. The eye should be large, soft, and bland, and the whole expression of the face amiable and gentle.

In this last point of physiognomy I put much faith— I never saw a good dog with a *bad face;* nor a thoroughly bad one, with an intelligent, open expression of countenance.

There is as much difference in dogs' faces as there is in that of men; and I should as much expect to find the qualities of a Walter Scott, a Napoleon, or a Washington, in a being with the face of Hogarth's bad apprentice or of a Jew prize fighter, as I should think to find a dog, with a cross, spiteful expression, a curt nose, thick jaws, and a narrow brow with a deep cleft between the eyes, a first-rate animal for intellect, memory and affection.

For the rest, a pendulous jowl and hanging lip are a defect in a setter, as they are the reverse in a pointer. Medium-sized dogs are the best, both for endurance of work and for convenience of transportation; besides which, I consider great size and heavy bone, especially if coupled with harsh coat, a symptom of coarse blood.

A setter should be high and thin in the withers, snaky in the neck, roomy in the chest, long in the arms and quarters, short in the lower legs, round and cat-like in the feet, well fringed or feathered on belly and legs, and well furnished with pad and toe-tufts. The bone of his tail should be slender; however well, and it cannot be too well, feathered; his coat cannot be too soft and silky, nor can he, in all respects, be too beautiful.

His beauty is a sign of the purity of his race; and in some sort—which I fear is rarely or never the case with us men—an indication of superior intellectual qualifications; but then it must be remembered that, although every clog is, at one period of the existence, a puppy, one never has heard of a canine fop, or, except in the old fable, of one who used a looking-glass.

The points of the Irish setter are a more bony, angular and wiry frame, a longer head, a less silky and straighter coat, than those of the English breed. His color ought to be a deep orange-red, or orange-red and white; a common mark is a strip of white between the eyes, a white ring round the neck, white stockings, and a white tag to the tail; all the rest deep red.

Unless the nose, palate, and lips are black, they are not in Ireland esteemed pure; and I consider the point a test of blood and a proof of hardiness in all breeds; I doubt a liver-colored, and detest a flesh-colored, muzzle.

The characteristics of the thorough Irish setter are, often savage ferocity of temper, always extreme courage, high spirit and indomitable pluck. They are naturally wild, and given to riot to the verge of indocility, require much breaking, I had almost said continual breaking, a jealous eye, a resolute will, and a tight hand over them. With these, they are of undeniable excellence.

They are not, however, by any means the right kind for young sportsmen, or for any sportsmen but those who are constantly in the field whenever game is in season; for such, their hardihood and pluck renders them invaluable.

They cross well with the English setter, if it can be called a cross, when it is but an intermarriage of cousins, and the progeny lose something of the temper and gain something of hardness.

The only remaining pure variety of setter to be noticed is the Russian, which is rarely or never met with in this country.

It is an admirable creature, docile, good and gentle, to a charm. Enduring, beyond any other race, of cold and wet, and dauntless beyond any other in covert, but more susceptible of heat and thirst than the others of his race.

He is, I think, rather taller than the English or Irish dog, muscular and bony; his head is shorter and rounder than that of his family, and, like the rest of his body, is so completely covered with long, woolly, matted locks, tangled and curly like those of the water-poodle, only ten times more so, that he can hardly see out of his eyes.

His color is black, black and white, or pale lemon and white. I never saw one of any other color. I never have seen a pure one, though I once owned a half breed—a most superior animal—in America, nor are they common or easily attainable in England.

I learned to shoot over one in England, which I was permitted to take out alone, because it was well known that "Henry could not spoil Charon;" and almost everything that I know of shooting that old Russian taught me. He would not drop to shot, if a bird were killed, but dashed right in to fetch; yet I never saw him flush a bird of a scattered covey in my life; for if the fresh birds lay between him and those killed, he would set them all one by one. In the same way, if a hare were wounded, which he knew by the eye by some indescribable sign which no man could descry, he always chased and never failed to retrieve him. If he were missed or went away without a shot, he would charge steadily enough; but if two or three shots were missed in succession, particularly in the first of the morning, home he went in disgust, in spite of all threats or coaxing.

Russian setters have what is called more point, they couch lower, and steal in more silently on their game than any other dog, consequently they are the best in the world over which to shoot game, when it is wild. Could they be procured, I think of all sporting dogs they are the most adapted for ordinary American shooting, and the best of all for beginners. They have less style, and do not range so high as the English or Irish dogs, but that is no disadvantage for America, where there is so much covert shooting.

Setters should range wide and swiftly, with the head well up; dogs which puzzle on the ground except on bad scenting days, or in emergency on the cold trail of a wounded animal, have generally bad noses; they should,

if hunting two together, cross each other regularly on
their beat, if singly, quarter the ground evenly in front
of the shooter; they should, at each turn, invariably cast
forward so as not to come on old ground, and never
cross backward, behind the shooter. This is a very bad
fault, causing much delay and loss of time, and it is hard
to cure when once acquired.

The habit of quartering ground well is little understood, or taught, even by professed breakers in America,
though it is of first importance. Most dog breakers are
content, when a dog stands stanchly on his game, backs
his comrade, drops to charge at the word, and retrieves
cleverly, to let him run about the ground as he will at his
own pleasure.

There is no greater error. A dog, which does so, will
beat much of his ground twice or thrice over, and leave
much altogether untried, so that not only will much
time be lost, but much game will be passed over.

The man who shoots over dogs or a dog broken to
quarter and beat his ground truly, will get twice as many
shots on the same ground, and in the same time, with
another hunting animals which meander at their own
sweet will.

If I *must* shoot over a dog unsteady at his points and
unsteady at his charge, but a good ranger and quarter-
er of his ground, or over one as stanch as a rock, who
ran about after his own pleasure, and were shooting a
match, I would take the former, confident that I could
make up by the quantity of game found for the other
defects.

These are the points which the young shooter
ought to regard in choosing his dog, though, if he be
wise, he will take some experienced friend to counsel.

Let him remember, that it costs no more to *keep*
a good dog than a bad one; that a dog properly kept,

having been well bought at a proper age, lasts probably, apart from accidents, five or six years, or more;—unless he be so unhappy as to live in Newark, New Jersey, where the inhabitants throw strychnine, the deadliest of all poisons, broadcast, in the streets, without the interference, if not by the direct encouragement, of the city government—that it is, therefore, the cheapest plan in the long run, to buy a good dog; and lastly, that there is no such thing as buying a good dog at a low price.

A well-bred, well-looking, well-broke setter, or pointer dog, has just as real a market value, apart from any fancy price, which may go to any amount, as any merchandise in the world, and is exactly as sure—almost surer than any —to realize it; since there is always a greater demand than there is supply; and since gentlemen, as opposed to dealers, are rarely, if ever, tempted by price to part with animals which suit them. Many sportsmen would regard an offer as an affront, akin to that of proposing to purchase his family plate or his family pictures.

The best rule for teaching a dog to quarter his ground, and, when taught, to keep him at it, will be found in "Dinks on the Dog," as on breaking generally.

The above precepts for choosing a dog by his action are equally referable to the setter and the pointer, although the latter is something slower, steadier, and closer in his ranging. Otherwise, there is no difference in their style of finding or pointing game. For it is a singular thing that in America, for some reason which I cannot comprehend or conceive, and for which I never heard so much as a plausible conjecture, the pointer and setter lose the distinctive action whence they derive their distinctive names.

In England the pointer *invariably* stands his game, and almost invariably *points* it, by raising sometimes a fore leg, sometimes a hind leg.

There the setter, if not invariably, at least nine times
out of ten *sets* his game, falling prostrate as if shot, and
lying so close as often to show only the tip of his erected flag above the stubble or turnips. I have often had a
brace of setters go down so suddenly, when shooting in
high turnips or potatoe ridges, the eye being casually off
them at the moment, that it required some trouble to
find them. When very close on their game good setters
never fail to do this, and it is unusual for them to point
except at hedgerows, or on running game.

In America, wherever I have shot, East or West, in
Canada or in the States, I have but *twice* in five and twenty years seen a setter *set*, and then it was accidental; so far
as this, that the dog usually stood. It is worthy of remark
also, that, on my first arrival in this country, I shot over a
dog which was bred in my own family and which I broke
myself in England. I do not think I ever saw him point
in his old country; I know I never saw him set in his new.
After I lost him, I for many years imported dogs of the
same family, which traced back to Lord Clare's red Irish
breed and Colonel Thornton's celebrated black dog
"Death," and always with the same result—not one of
them ever *set*.

I should like vastly to arrive at something, concerning this strange point in natural history, but it defies
conjecture.

I omitted above to say that in my own opinion, for
choice, perhaps I should rather say for fancy, the best
colors for English setters are pure black; pure white—
the latter very rare—red and white, or lemon and white,
with black noses; black and white, or black and tan.
Roan, or fleabitten dogs, whether red and white speckle, called strawberry, or black and white speckle, called
blue, are unobjectionable.

But I have something of a prejudice against liver
or liver and white setters; as I regard the colors as

belonging, of right, to the water-spaniel, or to the pointer, and therefore indicating the suspicion of a cross. In the same way I always suspect red and white, or black and white, in a pointer, for the converse reason. I may here add that I regard the cross of the setter and pointer, commonly known as the dopper, as an abominable mongrel.

There is a breed of black and white and tan setters in the United States, known as the "Webster setters," the original stock having been imported by that great statesman, from, I believe, Lord Derby's kennel. It has not generally turned out well, the blood generally showing softness and timidity in the field. To this I have heard of but one exception. I deem the color altogether doubtful and suspicious. Still it remains to be said that the old saying of horses stands good of dogs—that good ones are always of good colors, and that there is no absolute rule in these, more than in men,

"To trace the mind's complexion in the face."

Before concluding my notice of this dog, I will add that I see lately a much lauded and advertised strain of blood quoted as the "Harewood Setters." Of the merits or alleged origin of these dogs I know nothing. But if they are attributed to the noble Yorkshire family of that title, I fancy there is either some error, or that the strain is very recent. I have known the late and the present Earls of Harewood from my childhood; I lived within six miles of their seat of the same name, and hunted regularly for many seasons with the late Earl's foxhounds; I can, therefore, assert without the possibility of error, that up to my leaving England they had no distinctive strain of setter blood, but often used our Irish strain, of which I have spoken. They may, within the last twenty years, have gotten up a distinct family, but the time is short wherein for a breed to win a celebrated name— and as Lord Eldon said— "I doubt."

THE POINTER.

This dog, which it may be admitted, whatever its intrinsic or comparative merits, is the most suitable, for many reasons, to the use of the young sportsman, is not, at least in its present form, an original or natural animal.

This is the more worthy of remark, because many modern writers, those more particularly who are opposed to the setter, have endeavored to discredit the latter by overlauding its rival, as if the pointer were the type, and the setter an offshoot produced from it, by some process of crossing.

So far, however, is this from being true, that the pointer is itself a manufactured subvariety, although now so well established, that it appears capable of reproduction, like for like, even to the peculiar characteristics of individual families, almost *ad infinitum;* whereas, as we have seen above, the setter, so far as can be ascertained by any investigation, is the natural, aboriginal, spaniel stock improved by care and culture, but not by inter-breeding.

The type of this dog is unquestionably, in the British Isles, and the countries which have been thence supplied, the Spanish pointer; but how that variety of the genus arose, by what crossing it was produced, or when it was first known, is now beyond ascertaining.

It was first introduced into England when the art of shooting on the wing began to be general, replacing the old sport of netting birds, for which the mute spaniel, taught to set, since that time improved into the modern setter, had been used. Its erect position while in the act of pointing, and its lower and more careful style of ranging, as well as its superior steadiness, were the qualities which, on its first introduction, caused the preference to be given to it for open shooting; and such are, with justice, the superior excellencies still attributed to it, by those who prefer it to its rival, the setter.

In form, structure and general appearance, the pointer would appear to be an intermediate link between the spaniel, the smooth-haired hound, and perhaps the ferocious dog of the bull type—the structure of the head, the cerebral development, and the olfactory apparatus clearly connecting him with the former species, his coat, his general shape, and his fine stern pointing to the gaze-hounds, and his heavy jowl, pendulous lips, broad chest, and crooked fore legs, assimilating him to the pugnacious varieties.

The old Spanish pointer is now almost extinct in England and America, and deservedly so; for, although his admirable powers of scent, not surpassed by those of any animal, and his great tractability, are undeniable points in his favor, he is an ungainly, misshapen creature, a slow-traveller, an awkward mover; and, though large-limbed, strongly-boned, and to an unpractised eye powerfully made, is for the most part so ill put together and slackly coupled, that he is incapable of long and severe work, except at a foot's pace.

The improved English pointer, which is the dog generally in use under the name of pointer, is a cross of the original Spanish dog with the fox-hound, or the grey-hound, or both—the union of the two affording probably the best existing form. There are now numerous subvarieties, in the shape of distinct families, raised and maintained by different amateurs in the British Islands and elsewhere, recognized apart by particular characteristics of form, color, and style; which characteristic peculiarities they transmit with the blood, all springing from some cross of the Spanish dog with some of the other strains indicated above, yet sufficiently remote from the original stock to allow of inter-breeding, without any danger of deterioration from *in-breeding*, as it is termed, or incestuous breeding, so as to obviate all necessity of farther intermixture of foreign blood, as of the various hounds mentioned above.

Of these English varieties, some are nearly as coarse, heavy-shouldered, and slow as the old Spanish pointers; some are almost as slender, thin-flanked, and whip-sterned as the greyhound; and some with deeply feathered sterns and sharp noses, showing a strong cross of the fox-hound.

The first of these varieties is faulty, for the same reason as the old Spanish dog; they do not get over the ground with sufficient rapidity to allow of a reasonable bag being made in reasonable time; they are apt to knock up, owing to their weight and faulty structure, and they are painfully ugly to behold.

The second fails from the natural consequences of over delicacy; his coat is too fine, he cannot endure cold or wet, he cannot face the lightest covert, he cannot do half a day's work in proper form. If hunted alone, he will find little or no game, if in company with other dogs, he will do the backing to their pointing, but no more. He is a sufficiently worthless dog any where, but in America particularly worthless, because particularly unfit for those very specialities of work which he should be particularly fitted to perform—covert-shooting and snipe-shooting. For the former of these purposes the pointer is, I may say, *never* used in the British Isles; for the latter, when old and steady, he is generally preferred.

The third variety is liable to two objections; he is apt to stoop too much, and puzzle for his scent on the ground, hound-fashion, instead of drawing handsomely with his head high; and he is inclined to run in and chase, especially on hares and rabbits, from which vice it is frequently very difficult to break him.

The best form of the pointer is the medium between the first two varieties; and a dog of this kind, of the proper shape and style, well bred, well broken, and well hunted, will be found to do his work for courage, stoutness, scent, and endurance of heat and thirst, as well as, if not better than, any other variety of dog that is used in the field.

For docility, tractability, and tenacity of memory, never forgetting what has been once thoroughly taught him, he is undoubtedly superior to all dogs; and, on this account, he is to be recommended for all beginners, for all occasional shooters, who have small opportunity for keeping their dogs in constant practice, and for all persons, in general, who are averse to extra trouble, and who, for the sake of having everything to go on smoothly and in even tenor, are willing to sacrifice something of dash, spirit, style and show.

The weak points of this dog, I have touched upon before; they are—want of endurance of cold and wet; which may be set off against their greater endurance of heat and thirst; inferior dash, impetus and ability—not courage—to face severe, thorny covert; which may be set off against superior docility, tractability and steadiness; and, lastly, somewhat inferior speed and stoutness, and decidedly inferior beauty, sociability, and affection to the individual who hunts them.

For the young shooter, however, this latter inferiority is, perhaps, in some sort an advantage.

The pointer is more apt to hunt willingly for anybody who carries a gun, whether he know him, or not; and hunts more after his own fashion, with less interference from, or reference to, the shooter; nor is he so apt to take offence at the failure of his Companion to kill the game which he has found for him, a habit which setters, especially such as have been much shot over by sure killers, often acquire and carry to a ludicrous extent.

The true form of the very best kind of English pointer is so well laid down by "Stonehenge" in his "British Rural Sports," that I cannot do better than to quote the passage entire.

"The points by which these dogs are generally chosen, are—First, the form of the head, which should be wide, yet flat and square, with a broad nose, pendulous lip and a *square tip;* the pointed tip indicating too great a cross of the foxhound or greyhound. Secondly, a good set of legs and feet, the former strait and bony, and well set on at the shoulder, and the latter round and the pads hard and horny. Thirdly, a strong loin and good general development, with sloping shoulders. Fourthly, a fine stern, small in the bone and sharp at the point, like the sting of a wasp, and not curved upward. This form of stern, with a vigorous lashing of it from side to side, marks the true-bred pointer as much as any sign can do; and its absence distinguishes the foxhound cross, which gives a very hairy stern, with a strong curve upward and carried over the back; or the too great amount of greyhound blood, marked by a small stern also, but by one whose diminution commences from the very root; while the genuine pointer's is nearly of the same size, till within a few inches of the point, when it suddenly tapers off. Great injury has often been done by breeding in-and-in for many generations of pointers. A sportsman begins life by obtaining a brace which do their work to perfection, and he is the admiration and envy of all his sporting friends as long as they last, which may be, perhaps, five or six years. From these he breeds others, which also maintain his fame; and he expects to be able to continue the same plan with the same blood for fifty, or in some cases, sixty years. He is so wedded to it that he fears any admixture, and for two or three litters he does not require it; but at last he finds that though his puppies are easily broken to back and stand, they are small, delicate, and easily knocked up, and are mere playthings in the field."

Than these remarks, as to the points and formation of the pointer, I can add nothing. As I have before observed of the setter, of this dog also the medium size is preferable. It is more easily conveyed from place to place, whether in wagon, boat, or railroad ear, and, if strongly built and well put together, will stand more work than a heavy, oversized animal.

As to setters, again, and horses, so of pointers, it may be said that good animals are always of good colors; still there is a choice, and for reasons apart from real fancy or love of beauty.

Colors more or loss indicate races, and the prevalence of some colors, therefore, indicate more or less admixtures of blood to be avoided, or sought after, as it may be.

The pure original pointer colors, as drawn from the original Spanish stock, are plain unmixed liver color, and deep tawny, darker across the shoulders than elsewhere.

Both of these, therefore, going with the thorough pointer shape, are undeniable.

To liver and white, with a liver-colored nose, there is

no possible objection as to genuineness, while the light tint is favorable as far more easily seen in thick autumnal covert, than the self-color, which greatly assimilates to the dead leaf.

Lemon and white, orange and white, tawny and white, particularly if coupled with a black nose and lips, are, in my judgment, highly objectionable, as indicating a cross of setter, which I abominate in the pointer.

Pure white is rare, but unobjectionable; plain jet-black is also faultless; but where the black and white are joined, I suspect foxhound blood; and if to these be added the smallest dash of tan, whether in the shape of eye-spots, muzzles, or feet, I am sure of it.

Tan eye-spots are sometimes seen in plain black dogs; and there is a famous but rare English family so characterized; and if there be no white whatever, I should rejoice in the possession of a pointer so colored.

So also in liver, and liver and white dogs, are tan eye-spots found and regarded as beauties, rather than defects. Lord Derby's excellent kennel turns out admirable liver and white dogs, so characterized, and of a stamp well adapted to American shooting, as possessing perfectly pure blood, and quite sufficiently high and fine a strain, without over delicacy of coat, and with sufficient stoutness for rough work.

There is little more to note in reference to the pointer; but there obtains a common error or prejudice in relation to one of his occasional characteristics, which it may be as well to refute.

One of the marks, so common as to be almost an invariable characteristic, of the old Spanish pointer, is what is commonly known as a double nose; and, in my opinion, and that, I believe, of most real judges of the animal, an exceedingly ugly characteristic, amounting nearly to a deformity. This double nose consists in a deep cut or furrow between the nostrils, causing them to a casual observer, and on a slight inspection, to appear disunited.

In the French pointers, which are for the most part coarsely-bred, ill-made and worthless animals, this mark, owing to the superabundance in them of Spanish blood, is general; and it is surprising to me that Mr. Youatt should describe it as "materially interfering with their acuteness of smell."

This, however, is not the error which I propose here to correct, but the converse of this; which I have found, in all countries, particularly among uneducated or partially educated sportsmen, to be a prevalent idea—that, this double nose is an indication of, and as it were a guarantee for, the existence of an unusually good nose in the animal so marked. This external furrow can, I conceive—and I am borne out in my opinion by the judgment of Dr. Lewis of Philadelphia, celebrated alike for his medical and sportsmanly abilities—have no effect or influence one way or other on the scenting capabilities of the animal, being wholly unconnected with the internal olfactory apparatus.

How the idea should have originated, it is simple enough to see—the old Spanish pointer is, beyond dispute, an animal of superior powers of scent, and he is often double-nosed. Hence came the superstition that the superior scent is due to the ugly furrow between the nostrils, though it might have been as well ascribed to the slack loin, or thick club tail, which are equally characteristic of the breed.

So well established is this creed in my part of the country, that a neighbor of mine told me the other day, with great glee and exultation, that he had got a double-nosed setter, the only one of that kind he had ever seen, though he had seen many pointers such.

He was urgent to know whether I had ever seen a double-nosed setter, and was not a little astonished

when I replied that I never had, and sincerely hoped I
never should; for that, while in a pointer it is simply a
deformity, of no actual consequence, in a setter it is a
certain indication of a cross of Spanish pointer blood;
about the worst cross imaginable.

It may be added, that the Spanish pointer is not
unfrequently ill-tempered and surly.

Of the action of pointers in the field, whereby to
judge of them, I shall speak hereafter, under the head
of Field Management.

THE COCKING SPANIEL.

The best of all dogs, beyond a question, for woodcock shooting exclusively, particularly in the summer season, or even for autumn shooting in covert, is the spaniel. It is little known as yet in this country; and it is extremely difficult to procure them, either purely bred or thoroughly broken, and unless they be both, no animal is more worthless.

In England, they are used entirely for all covert shooting, where dogs are employed at all, which is not the case in battues; the game, in these, as I must consider them, unsportsmanlike butcheries, being driven up by beaters. The reason of this preference of the spaniel is twofold. First, he does the work better than the pointer or setter can do it; secondly, it is an injury to the latter species to inure them to this sort of work, which is not suited to their habits, instincts, or style of hunting.

Those dogs are naturally endowed with great range and speed of foot, and ought, if high bred and endowed with good noses, to stand their birds steadily at long distances.

These are the points and excellences of line setters or pointers; the proper stage for which is, in England, the moors, or the open partridge stubbles and turnip fields; here the prairies, for grouse, the open stubbles for quail, and the snipe marshes.

If they be duly qualified to hunt these grounds in style, and to find their game fast and well in such situations, they will, in covert, range entirely out of shot, will probably overrun and put up many birds, quite beyond the shooter's range, or, coming to a dead point, at a quarter of a mile's distance, with heaven knows how much brush and brier intervening, will be missing half of the time, or will have, instead of themselves hunting, to be painfully hunted up by their owner.

Over and above this, being used to hunt under the constant supervision of the sportsman's eye, where the least error is observed and the least fault rated, finding themselves under less restraint in covert, they are apt to become careless and to run riot. To this habit they are more particularly led by two causes, both of which must often occur in shooting in heavy coverts, especially in summer, when the leaf is full—first, that frequently coming on points unobserved by the shooter, who has lost and cannot find them, they are kept standing such a weary time, on the game, that they become impatient, flush it wilfully, and come away unchidden, because unremarked.

Second, that the shooter himself, instead of himself walking or beating up his game over the point, as he ought to do, too often, for the sake of securing a shot which, from the badness of ground or thickness of the brake, he would otherwise be apt to lose, hies the dog on, and encourages him to flush, at one moment, probably punishing him for doing the very same thing, some twenty minutes later.

Thus it is clear that pointers or setters, when in the

very best possible training and condition for open shooting, which is their natural work as well as their *forte*, are not suited for covert shooting.

It is also clear that covert-shooting is likely to be disadvantageous to their steadiness, and to render them, unless carefully and judiciously hunted, wild and riotous.

If, on the contrary, they are thoroughly broken and inured to covert shooting, they get into a slow, pottering style of work, lose their range, their speed of foot, and in a great measure their dashing style and carriage.

Once or twice in a lifetime, one may find a brace of dogs so perfect, so steady, and so well up to all kinds of work, that they will range the opens at full speed, heads up and sterns down, and again when brought into covert beat every inch of a ground at a trot, and never stir out of gunshot of the sportsman; but it is, as I have said, but once or twice in a lifetime.

These are the just reasons, why pointers and setters are in England, rarely, if ever, used in woodlands.

Here the case is altered, since with the exception of snipe-shooting on the marshes and grouse-shooting on the prairies, there is in America no distinctly open shooting. In the Northern States and provinces, especially, where autumn shooting is and must ever be the principal and choicest pursuit of the true sportsman, open shooting and covert shooting are so inseparably combined, from the habits of the birds pursued, that no line of distinction can be drawn.

The quail, which is the principal object of pursuit, must be found and roused on his feeding grounds, in the stubbles, orchards or meadows, and, when once scattered, followed up and killed in the densest and heaviest brakes and coverts.

To find them, the greatest speed and the widest range is necessary; to finish up the scattered bevies in good style, the closest and most accurate, inch by inch ground, or foot, hunting.

The perfection of the thing, if means permitted, would be of course to drive the open grounds with setters or pointers, and then, when the game should be driven into covert, to couple up these, and let loose spaniels wherewith to beat the brakes and thickets.

This, however, would require such a number of dogs and servants to be kept, so large an expense and so systematic a pursuit of the sport, with consequent expenditure of time and attention, as few or no American sportsmen are willing or able to bestow on what is, to most men, but an occasional and rare pastime.

For the most part, then, we must rest content with our setters or pointers, and must satisfy ourselves with overcoming to the best of our abilities the difficulties which we must encounter.

Nevertheless, I would strongly recommend it to such sportsmen as have the means, the leisure, and the opportunity, to procure a brace of good and well broke cocking spaniels, at least for summer cock-shooting. It is not only the true method, but it is far more exhilarating and exciting, it is less fatiguing, and, as it gives the sportsman far more opportunity of choosing his own position for shooting in the paths, runways and glades, instead of being forced to blunder into thickets in order to drive up his game, it is by far the most killing mode.

The spaniel naturally gives tongue on his scent the moment he strikes it, hunts it up with the rapidity of light, and springs his bird or starts his hare with a rush.

By education he is made to hunt mute, or at most to express his delight at finding the hot scent streaming up to his nostrils by a suppressed whimper, to track the game foot by foot, pausing to note the vicinity and whereabout of the shooter, and to give tongue only when it is flushed.

This steadiness and closeness of range and of dropping to charge the instant the shot is fired, and lying hard until ordered to "*hie on!*" is all that is required of the spaniel; but that *all* is not a little; for the spirit in the small bodies of these active and indefatigable little animals is of the most indomitable, and it requires steadiness, patience, firmness, equability of temper in the highest degree, and at times severity, to break them into discipline, and to keep them in it when broken. But this once accomplished, they are all but perfection.

"There can scarcely be a prettier object," says Mr. Youatt in his admirable work on the dog, "than this little creature, full of activity, and bustling in every direction, with his tail erect; and the moment he scents the bird expressing his delight by the quivering of every limb, and the low eager whimpering which the best breaking cannot always subdue. Presently the bird springs, and then he shrieks out his ecstasy, startling even the sportsman with his sharp, shrill, and strangely expressive bark.

"The most serious objection to the use of the cocker is the difficulty of teaching him to distinguish his game and confine himself within hounds; for he will too often flush everything that comes within his reach. It is often the practice to attach bells to his collar, that the sportsman may know where he is;"—this precaution is far more necessary with the pointer in covert—"but there is an inconvenience connected with this, that the noise of the bells will often disturb and spring the game before the dog comes fairly upon it.

"Patience and perseverance, with a due mixture of kindness and correction, will, however, accomplish a great deal in the tuition of the well-bred spaniel. He may at first hunt about after every bird that presents itself, or chase the interdicted game; if he be immediately called in and rated, or perhaps corrected, but not too severely, he will learn his proper lesson, and recognize the game to which alone his attention must be directed. The grand secret in breaking these dogs is mildness, mingled with perseverance, the lessons being enforced, and practically illustrated by the example of an old and steady dog."

"This beautiful and interesting dog—" adds Dr. Lewis, speaking of the *cocker,* in his American Edition of Youatt—"so called from his peculiar suitableness for woodcock shooting, is but little known among us, except as a boudoir companion for ladies. He is, nevertheless, extensively used in England by sportsmen for finding this bird, as also the pheasant; and no doubt, if introduced into our country, would prove equally, if not more serviceable, in putting up game concealed in the thickets and marshy hollows of our uncleared ground."

There is no doubt that such is the case. An excellent and accomplished English sportsman, Mr. Joseph Tarret, who shot for many years in New Jersey with great effect and success, used these dogs exclusively, and few, if any sportsmen of the day could beat his bag.

Dr. Lewis states in another passage that the larger variety of spaniel, known as the springer, is owned in the greatest purity in the Carrollton family, and is also in possession of Mr. Keyworth of Washington City.

Captain Peel of the Royals, late of H. M. R. Canadian rifles, better known to the sporting world as "Dinks" of Amherstburg, who has been recently serving in the Crimea, but may be shortly expected to return, has a fine strain of this blood, which I can earnestly recommend from my own knowledge and experience.

The three varieties of spaniel principally used in pursuit of game are the "cocker," the "springer," and the "Clumber spaniel," which is, on the whole, the best in all respects as a sporting animal.

The cocker, a likeness of which, adapted from a magnificent engraving by Ansdell, is prefixed to this paper, is the smallest of the three varieties.

He is seldom above twenty pounds in weight, has a short blunt nose, an excedingly full, soft, liquid eye, and bears a strong resemblance to the King Charles, and Blenheim breeds, with both of which he is, probably, more or less connected. His color is usually dark orange and white, or lemon and white; sometimes black, white, and tan, or plain black and white, and yet more rarely black and tan. This last color is ascribed by Mr. Youatt to an admixture of terrier blood; but I think incorrectly. I would attribute it wholly to the King Charles blood, with which the cocker shows much connection, and the most when he is of this color. The snub nose and large soft melting eye of the cocking spaniel is as remote as possible from the elongated, sharp muzzle, and keen quick visual organs of the terrier.

"These dogs," says Stonehenge, "have very delicate noses, and work well in covert for a short time, but are soon knocked up, and cannot compete in endurance with either the springer, or the old English spaniel."

They are the liveliest, the prettiest, and the most active of the whole family.

The springer is somewhat larger, "has a smaller eye," I quote from the Manual of Rural Sports, "and a more pointed nose, and with a more impetuous nature than the cooker, requiring more coercion than he, and far more than the Clumber spaniel. He is generally of about thirty pounds weight, with a party-colored coat of liver and white, yellow and white, or black and white."

All the varieties should be hung "with ears that sweep away the morning dew," should have coats long, soft, waving—not curled, except about the ears—and glistering as floss silk. Their tails should be short, stout, and, like their legs, deeply and densely feathered.

The Clumber spaniel is a stouter, shorter-legged, rougher-coated dog, with a broad nose. "In him," continues Stonehenge, "there is the full development of brain and of the cavities of the nose, which gives the power of smelling with the greatest nicety, and also that of discriminating scents; thus the true Clumber spaniel will distinguish readily the foot-scent of the pheasant from the cock, and will throw his tongue differently; and they may readily be kept to either, or allowed to hunt both, according to the fancy of their masters. In size these dogs are about thirty-five or forty pounds—generally of a liver color, with very large heads, long ears, and broad noses; bodies low, long and strong, covered with long hair, not very curly but with a strong wave, legs very straight and strong, with good feet. They also have great powers of endurance, but are not fast, and are on that account well suited to covert-shooting. Their note is deep and musical, and they are under very good command, when well broken. Numberless breeds, somewhat resembling the Clumber, are met with throughout England, and of all colors and almost all forms, commonly called old English spaniels. Most of them have nearly the same kind of developments, though few come up to him in all the qualities here enumerated; there is generally too fast a style of hunting, or too little courage, or a want of steadiness, or some deficiency or other."

In another part of the same volume, this able and discriminating writer says of this dog—"The Clumber spaniel is the best I have ever seen, being hardy and capable of braving wet with impunity. His nose is also wonderfully good, which its full development in point of size would lead one to expect. They are bred so much for hunting cock that they own the scent very readily, and seem to delight and revel in it, giving generally a very joyous note on touching upon their trail. The true Clumber may be easily kept to feather, and though they will readily hunt fur when nothing else is to be had, they do not prefer it, as most other dogs do."

The Clumber breed is that, which I have mentioned

above, as owned in great purity by Captain Peel, and is the dog which I would especially recommend to all sportsmen, young or old, for July cock-shooting.

I am well satisfied that over two or three of these unwearied and dauntless dogs, which, where water is plenty, would work willingly from dawn till sunset of a July day, a good shot could double his bag with one half the walking and labor he would be obliged to exert over setters or pointers.

It is true, that they require constant attention, firmness, steadiness and temper; but so do all dogs. These, I think, not more than most others, excepting always the steady pointer, certainly less than the headstrong and fierce Irish setter.

Moreover, the attention of the sportsman is at all events required to fewer points. To hunt close and mute, and to drop to shot is all that he has to ask, and, if asked becomingly, he will not be disappointed.

To conclude, no one, I believe, who has ever shot cock in a wet July brake of alders, or what is worse, in the ravine of a Maryland *branch*, over Clumber spaniels, will ever voluntarily return to the setter or the pointer, however pre-eminently superior at their own work, and over their own line of country.

THE WATER-SPANIEL.

This beautiful, sagacious, and useful species, like the
varieties last described, is not so general in this country, as he deserves to be, the rather that many districts
inland, to the westward and southward more especially,
are singularly adapted to his use.

A portion of his blood is not unfrequently to
be found in imperfectly bred setters, and although it
unquestionably detracts from the value of the animal
as a purebred species, it is the least objectionable of all
the crosses. It does not produce obstinacy and inferior
sagacity, as is, I think, usually the case with the pointer cross; nor headstrong wildness, evincing itself in an
uncontrollable desire to chase fur, which is the consequence of a foxhound admixture. It generally shows
itself in an increased degree of curliness in the hair, particularly about the poll and ears, the latter being also
larger, longer, and far more fleecily covered in the pure
setter. The qualities which this variety seems to give, are
great readiness and facility in retrieving, and superior

fondness for the water. Neither of which points are detrimental, but rather the reverse, to the setter. The very best setter I ever owned, whose pedigree I do not know, showed strong indications of a remote water-spaniel cross in his hair and color, though in form and habits he was a perfect setter. I never saw so good a retriever, nor a steadier or stancher dog, though I have seen hundreds fleeter. One thing is certain; water-spaniel blood does not produce riot, since the dog is eminently docile.

I approve of no cross-breeding in dogs of established races; yet if I had a family of fine setters, which in the course of years had become too nearly connected from want of intermixture of some other pure but distinct setter blood, and none such were attainable, I would not hesitate to use one cross of water-spaniel, and should not doubt of improving the stock in the second generation from the admixture.

"Of this breed," says Mr. Youatt, "there are two varieties, a larger and a smaller, both useful according to the degree of range or the work required; the smaller, however, being ordinarily preferable."—In this point I do not agree with Mr. Youatt. The larger dog is, to my taste, the purer bred, the lesser being often interbred with the land-spaniel, and for American shooting in particular, far superior. "Whatever be his general size, strength and compactness of form are requisite. His head is long, his face smooth, and his limbs, more developed than those of the springer, should be muscular, his carcass round, and his hair long and closely curled."

In the best and purest breeds, while the face itself is perfectly smooth, the poll, the ears, and the sides of the neck are clothed so densely with long, soft, silky, curled hair, that the countenance appears to be set in an Elizabethan ruff, and the ears are absolutely *ringletted*. The only *true* colors of this dog are liver or liver and white. Any others indicate mixtures of foreign blood.

"Good breaking," Mr. Youatt continues, "is more necessary here than even with the land-spaniel, and fortunately it is more easily accomplished; for the water-spaniel, although a stouter, is a more docile animal than the land one.

"Docility and affection are stamped on his countenance, and he rivals every other breed in his attachment to his master. His work is double; first, to find when ordered to do so, and to back behind the sportsman when the game will be more advantageously trodden up. In both he must he taught to be perfectly obedient to the voice," or *dog call,* "that he may he kept within range, and may not unnecessarily disturb the birds. A more important part of his duty, however, is to find and bring the game that has dropped. To teach him to find is easy enough, for a young water-spaniel will as readily take to the water, as a pointer puppy will stop; but to bring his game without tearing it, is a more difficult lesson, and the most difficult of all is to make him suspend the pursuit of the wounded game while the sportsman reloads."

He must, in a few words, be taught invariably to beat his ground, crossing and recrossing it in endless intersecting semicircles, never beyond twenty paces distant from his master, and to hunt *mute.* The latter being far easier than with the cocker, springer, or even the Clumber dog, since the water-spaniel does not give tongue so fiercely or so instinctively as his land congener.

Secondly, he must drop to shot, at the report of the gun, and lie steadily at charge, until he be ordered to go on, when he will recover wounded birds with inconceivable cleverness, following them foot by foot through tussocky bogs, thick flag tufts, and the most closely tangled marsh grasses, or diving after them in deep waters, till they shall give out in their own element, from mere weariness.

For wild fowl shooting in large inland lakes he is invaluable, merely as a retriever, particularly where there is much reed, wild rice or marsh grass, among which cripples will skulk so cunningly as to defy the most accurate marker; but their great forte is where teal, mallard, wood-duck, pintails, and the other fresh-water varieties frequent large flat grassy meadows, intersected by small lagoons, creeks or rivulets in which they feed; or still more, where a slow winding stream, bordered with willows and alder brakes, creeps deviously between swampy banks thickset with flags and sword-grass, furnishing the finest and favorite feeding grounds and breeding grounds for all the varieties of inland wild fowl.

When the young ducks, *flappers* as they are technically named, about three parts grown, are able to make short flights only, with their legs hanging down so as just to bond the tops of the marsh grass, or to dimple the surface of the water, immense sport may be bad in proper localities, which occur every where abundantly from the western parts of the State of New York, through all the Western States to the head-waters of the Mississippi, and the northern extremities of Lake Superior.

Nor are the Southern States, with their unfrozen springheads, tepid streams and vast verdurous lagoons, in this respect inferior. What could be done in the Everglades of Florida by a large party of good sportsmen, not afraid of roughing it, and duly supplied with a proper force of water-spaniels, both in the killing of game and the discovering of new species, is yet to be proved.

Should snipe or woodcock be found lying in the same localities, as is often the case, they will not escape the infallible nose and unwearied activity of the water-spaniel, nor will his long yellow legs and broadly flapping vans secure the hermit heron, nor his clanking cry of defiance or his sharp-pointed bill, fiercely and fearlessly plied, save the brown bittern from the mortal shot-shower.

In beating such a stream as I have described, the shooter should walk some ten or fifteen paces wide of the margin, not following its sinuosity, but proceeding in a direct line from bend to bend, while his spaniels should follow the windings, working out every bush and brake, rummaging all the grass between the shooter and the stream, and—contrary to what is required in every other kind of shooting—hunting behind and not before, or quite abreast of, the gun. By this method the fowl, being flushed quietly by the dog, which they seem often to mistake for a fox or some other animal of prey, and not having seen or suspected the vicinity of man, rise gently, and for the most part fly forward up or down the course of the stream, as it may be, presenting a fair cross shot to the gun. Should they, by an unusual and unlikely chance, rise wild so as not to afford a shot, it is more than probable that they will again drop within a reasonable distance, when being marked down, they may be, in most instances, stalked, so as to insure the getting a close and deadly shot.

With the green-winged teal this result is the most likely to occur, as that bird, if flushed by a brookside, without discovering its arch-enemy, almost always flies quick and strong for some distance up or down the water, and then darts down, like a sharp-flying wood-cock, most generally in a sudden bend or angle of the stream, where there is covert, either of trees shadowing the stream, or of bushes thick on the banks.

In this case it is almost certain that he will lie hard the second time, and allow of an easy shot.

Water-spaniels, though, *as their name indicates,* they shine in pursuit of aquatic fowl, may be broke to hunt for the foot of the various species of American wood-grouse, as the ruffed grouse, the spotted or spruce

grouse of Canada, the red-necked or willow grouse of
Vermont, Maine, the British Provinces and Labrador, in
the vast wooded wildernesses where they abound, and
to chase them when flushed to the tree, in which they
besiege them; keeping them motionless by their sharp
barking, by which also they inform the shooter of their
whereabout, until he can come up, and knock them off
their perch by a felon shot.

For this work, I cannot call it sport, nor those who
pursue it sportsmen, the smaller water-spaniel is the
animal best adapted. I have seen a brace so thoroughly
broke, and so steady, that they were the best dogs I ever
shot over for autumn snipe-shooting, but this is rarely
the case.

Where, however, much inland duck-shooting is to
be had on ground where snipe and perhaps woodcock
also feed—and there is much ground of that nature in
America—no dogs can compete them, as they combine
great powers; of finding game, with vast endurance,
steadiness sufficient to enable them to be shot over satisfactorily—though not that of the perfect pointer or
setter—accompanied by an ability to recover wounded
wild fowl to a degree possessed by no other animal, and
without which it is useless to think of making a bag of
wild fowl on inland waters.

THE NEWFOUNDLAND RETRIEVER.

The last dog with which we had to do, is the last of those which are to be mentioned as employed for the finding their game alive, and recovering it when killed, but which have no share in pursuing or killing it.

Those are the dogs principally used by the shooter, and on them he relies, in a degree second only to his use of the gun, for all his sport in the field and the upland as against winged game.

Those which remain worthy of note, are the retriever proper, which fetches in the dead or crippled game, having had no share in finding him, and the various species of hounds, which are employed in the finding, taking, and killing of large game such as deer, elk, bear, and, perhaps, one or two casual species, not often encountered even in the wildest parts of the country, and which may be held to belong to hunting, as distinct from shooting, in the proper sense of the terms; though, as I have observed before, the distinction is much narrowed in America between the two sports, owing to the

association of the shot gun or rifle with the horse and
hound.

In America the retriever proper is used only in one
part of the country, the vicinity of Chesapeake Bay and
the rivers of that region, which constitute the shooting
grounds of the canvas-back.

In the British Isles pointers and setters are not usually broke to *fetch*, as it is supposed to detract from their
steadiness, and render them likely to break in. For the
moors, therefore, and for pheasant-shooting in covert,
retrievers are employed, especially broken to the purpose, which take no notice of live game, make no effort
to hunt or flush it, but, so soon as it falls—and notice
is given to them to go on and find—will follow the foot
of the identical wounded or wing-broken bird, through
a preserve overflowing with unwounded game of the
same species, without troubling or disturbing any of
them; and will ultimately recover and bring him to bag,
while the sportsman is in pursuit of other victims, far
away with his pointers or his beaters.

Of this species of dog, or way of using it. there is
no trace on the uplands of America, or elsewhere, save
on the salt waters of the estuaries and tide rivers, whose
half-frozen waters swarm in winter with myriads of the
choicest wild fowl, the canvas-back, the red-head, the
scaup, or broadbill, as it is commonly called by American
gunners, and the widgeon, or baldpate, not to enumerate wild geese, brant, and the king of waterfowl, the
superb, incomparable swan.

The usual, and among gentlemen sportsmen, who
shoot for pleasure, not for base profit, the only legitimate way of shooting these delicious wild-fowl, is by lying
in ambush for them behind screens or blinds of rushes
made for the purpose, on points of islands, headlands,
river mouths and the like, over which the fowl fly, in
going to or returning from their feeding grounds, when

they may he shot, by clever gunners, with heavy pieces and large shot, at great ranges and with great sport.

To shoot from batteries moored on their feeding grounds, and still more to sail in upon them when feeding, is properly discountenanced and esteemed unsportsmanlike and infamous, since it causes the birds, which will not endure to be disturbed and slaughtered while on their feed, to collect into great flocks, soar up into the air, and entirely abandon the places where they are thus persecuted.

The flocks of ducks are, it is true, at times *toled* in, as it is called, by the assistance of small curs, trained to play, running to and fro along the margin of the rivers, where the ducks are swimming or feeding, when, strange to say, the wild-fowl are instigated by some sort of insane curiosity to sail up close to the hidden fowler, and, after being shot at again and again, still to rush on their fate, without aim or object, in pursuit of the cur or mongrel water-spaniel which is trained thus to inveigle them.

This animal, however, is a mere cur, and the extent of his discipline and training is limited to running backward and forward after sticks or stones, cast from behind the blind, without appearing to take any notice of the ducks, which, if he pause to look at them, will often swim away or take wing on the instant.

For the recovery of the crippled birds, however, the Newfoundland dog is used, of the truest and purest type; not the huge woolly Labradorean, but the short, small-eared, compact, vigorous dog of St. Johns, easily recognized by his long, stout, waving coat, never curled or knotted like the water-spaniel's or poodle's, by his neat, delicate, rounded ear, and his stern never curled up over his back, but carried pendulous, or stretched out at length when he is in chase, like the brush of a fox, or the flag of a setter.

This dog is a pure spaniel of the largest existing species. He is, perhaps, the most powerful, enduring and dauntless of all dogs. Certainly, and beyond dispute, he is the most sagacious, the most faithful, the most easily taught, and the most retentive of what he has learned of all varieties of his race. When much accustomed to one master, who is fond of them, and who has the knack of teaching and making himself beloved at the same time, they become so intelligent as to understand every word that is said to them, and to act as if in obedience to reason and induction.

They are, in their purest shape, jet black or dingy red; any intermixture of white, beyond a slight frill on the breast, is indicative of Labrador blood. This breed obtains in great excellence on the eastern shore of Maryland, through Patapsco Neck, on the Gunpowder, and up the Chesapeake Bay, where they are considered of unrivalled excellence among the duck-shooters.

These dogs are the descendants of a dog and bitch, the former red, the latter black, which were obtained by Mr. Law, of Baltimore, from an English vessel bound from Newfoundland to Poole in England. They were stated to be a pair of pups procured for the owner of the vessel, of the most approved Newfoundland breed, but of different families, and were obtained by the sailors from the English captain as a matter of favor. Their progeny retains the original color, particularly the red hue of the dog, and all the characteristic excellences of the breed.

"Their patience and endurance," says Dr. Lewis in his edition of Youatt, "are very great when pursuing wounded ducks through the floating ice, and when fatigued from extraordinary exertions, are known to rest themselves upon broken portions of ice, till sufficiently recovered again to commence the chase. We have seen some of the descendants of these sagacious animals on the Chesapeake, engaged not only in bringing the ducks from the water when shot, but also toling them into shore within range of the murderous batteries concealed behind the blind."

The points by which they may be known are, the long, pointed head, small, smooth ears, medium height, compact shape, muscular, short limbs, wavy, long, glossy coat of black or red, not curled, and the wonderful activity, strength, and even speed for which the race is famous.

When they are of the pure breed, they require little breaking and no severity. The water, in the most bitter storm or the severest cold, seems to be native to them. They literally delight and revel in deep snow, wallowing in it as if for pleasure. As to education, they require only to be shown a few times what they are desired to do, before they will acquire, and once acquired, never forget it more; and as friends and companions, they are better even than as servants to man; their gratitude, love, indefatigable desire to please, cannot be surpassed by that of any living being, brute or human; and their fidelity, attachment, truth and devotion, alone of any I have ever seen or proved, defies time and change, is unaltered by unkindness, and survives even the grave.

THE HOUND.

All the different varieties of the hound, which finds and follows his game by nose, seem to be derived originally from the old English bloodhound, sleuth hound, Talbot or Southern hound, all of which were modifications of one animal, the same as that described by Shakespeare in those immortal lines of "Midsummer Night's Dream," which, familiar as household words to all lovers of poetry, deserve to be as well known to all sportsmen, for the admirable description they convey of the old English hound of the Elizabethan era, undoubtedly the parent of all the modern families from the stately staghound down to the minute beagle.

"My hounds are bred out of the Spartan kind,
So fie wed, so sanded; and their heads are hung
With ears that sweep away the morning dew;
Crook-kneed and dewlapped like Thessalian bulls,
Slow in pursuit, but matched in mouth like bells,

Each under each, a cry more tunable
Was never hallo'ed to, nor cheered with horn,
In Crete, in Sparta, nor in Thessaly."

It is not worth the while to inquire whether the Laconian and Thessalian hounds, so often alluded to by Horace, Ovid and other classical writers, were in truth of the bloodhound type, or if they were not rather of the large, shaggy, half mastiff, half sheep-dog type, peculiar still to Albania and Epirus, and adapted to the hunting of the bear or boar, for which purpose they seem to have been principally used.

The first improvement in this old stock was, it would seem, the old improved foxhound of Somerville's and Beekford's stamp, and admirably described by the latter writer in the following passage.

"Let his legs be straight as arrows, his feet round and not too large; his shoulders back; his breast rather wide than narrow; his chest deep; his back broad; his head small; his neck thin: his tail thick and bushy—if he carry it well, so much the better; . . . a small head, however, as relative to *beauty* only, for as to *goodness*, I believe large-headed hounds are in no wise inferior."

This is the stamp of dog after which our forefathers used to ride from the days of Queen Anne to the latter half of the reign of George the Third; and not very different were those which the mighty Nimrods of the day, Mr. Meynell, old Lord Forester, and their contemporaneous worthies followed within these sixty years over the classic ground of Melton Mowbray.

The ordinary time of throwing off in those days was at day break; the fox was trailed by his cold scent from the pheasant preserve or farm-yard which he had been plundering, to the wood where he had laid up, and was run down after a chase of from ten to thirty miles, accomplished in a space of time varying from two to half a dozen hours, the hunters following them at a hard gallop on stout three-part-bred horses, which we should now condemn as too coarsely bred for the carriage, with ample time afforded them to pick the easy places in fences, to ride round by-lanes, and to nick in somehow or other in season for the kill.

What is the cross, or whether there is any, by which the modern foxhound has been brought to his present perfection, cannot, be easily ascertained, as the secret has been well kept by the breeders. Stonehenge believes that there has been a cross of the greyhound, and perhaps of the bull-dog.

Of the former I am not prepared to speak positively, beyond this, that if there be any cross of greyhound blood, it is infinitesimally small, and has left no trace of its existence in form, in coat, in color, or in any thing unless it be speed. It is an error to believe that the greyhound has *naturally* no power of scenting, the true state of the case being that he is regularly restrained from hunting by nose, discouraged from attempting it, and destroyed, as worthless, if he persist in doing it.

The cross, therefore, would not necessarily he destructive of all scenting capacities, and it is notorious that the new high-bred racing foxhound has deteriorated greatly from the old Southern hound, and somewhat from the old English foxhound, in nose. He is less capable of picking out a cold scent foot by foot on a bad scenting day, but on the other hand he comes away with his fox, on finding, with such a dash, and keeps up so wonderful a stroke of speed, with such endurance and pluck, that, in any tolerable weather, the scent has no chance to grow cold, and that, on a good hunting day, no fox that was ever unkennelled can live before him an hour, or any ordinary one half that time.

No horse but one thoroughbred, or, if not tracing

directly to Barb blood on both sides, with at least seven or eight crosses of pure blood, can by any chance live through a run of an hour with fourteen stone on his back within sight or hearing of them, and no horse not the son of a thoroughbred sire, at least, could stay one mile at their pace.

They are truly wonderful animals, with speed equal to that of a slow greyhound, dash and courage equal to any thing, and scent amply sufficient to sustain their other powers.

There may be, as I have said, and probably is, a very remote, perhaps ten or fifteen times removed cross of greyhound blood in them, but I am satisfied that there is no bull-dog, unless what may have come through the greyhound, which we know' has an infusion of that strain introduced by Lord Orford.

The first cross of foxhound and greyhound, which is used on the borders of England and Scotland for fox coursing on the fells, and in the Highlands for pursuing wounded deer, when the true Scottish deerhound is not obtainable, and which is called by the borderers "The Streaker," is familiar to me, and from my knowledge of it, I am satisfied that it would require very many crosses backward into the pure foxhound before we should arrive from it at such animals as Mr. Osbaldiston's, or Sir Bichard Sutton's, or the Duke of Beaufort's, Northamptonshire, or Melton Mowbray, or Yale of Blackmoor, fliers.

The color of the original bloodhound was black, black and tan, or tawny, with very little white, and the pure black breed of St. Hubert was the most highly prized of all. The Talbots varied but little from the general coloring of the bloodhound, but the yellow and black pie was their general color. "The head," says Stonehenge, "is very handsome; ears large, soft and pendulous; jowl square and well developed; nose broad, soft and moist; and eyes lustrous and beautifully soft when in an unexcited state."

The Southern hound, though somewhat lighter framed and not much, has the same general characteristics, but is often, if not generally, blue mottled with patches of black and tan.

The new improved racing foxhound and the modern staghound, differing from the former only in superior height and power, though with equal fleetness, dash, and spiry high-bred carriage, vary from the old strains, not only in their lighter forms, straight limbs, long let-down quarters, slender heads, small ears, and greater celerity of motion with a shriller and less musical note; but in the great prevalence of white, which, more or less pied and spotted with black and tan or yellow pie, is decidedly the prevalent color, at present, of all the favorite families even of the fast modern harrier, which is now little more than a small foxhound, though, perhaps, one shade less removed from the Southern hound.

I am myself inclined to the belief that all the improved modern clogs have been produced rather by the careful selection, generation after generation, of the lightest, best formed, handsomest, and fleetest parents on both sides, than by crossing with clogs of different races and varieties. We know that such has been the case mainly with our improved breed of cattle and sheep, and I do not see why such should be overlooked, as a palpable method of improving families of dogs.

We know that, by constantly, year after year, breeding from the tallest 26-inch foxhounds out of 25 or 24-inch bitches, we have established a permanent family, known as staghounds or buckhounds, of which her Majesty's pack at Windsor are the finest type. These must not he confounded with the Highland deerhound, which is a totally distinct animal, of which I shall treat hereafter.

We know also that raising stock in the same manner from the smallest and lightest foxhounds, which are drafted from regular packs owing to their want of symmetrical size, and physical endurance, we have built up a self-reproducing family of improved harriers. In the like manner—since the formation, slowness, depth of voice, color, and, in a word, all the peculiarities of the Southern hounds and Talbots were comparative—it is easy to conceive, that, when in process of time the clearing up of the forests and other causes rendered a swifter hound desirable, those animals should be chosen from which to raise stock, possessing the points of speed, lightness, and activity, rather than those of strength, endurance, and even of pre-eminent scent. There were undoubtedly also white Talbots and even white bloodhounds, though these wore rare, and it is possible that the prevalence of that color in the fleet modern hounds, may arise from a casual coincidence of color and fleetness in some pure ancestral strain.

I confess, however, that I think it probable that there is a distant cross somewhere—perhaps through the Northern hound, which Stonehenge states, as if with authority, to have been *decidedly* a cross of the Southern hound with the Scottish deerhound—of some slighter and faster strain, which may have imparted color as well as speed.

The harrier—although it also has of late years undergone much the same process of improvement, so that it has become in many instances little more than a dwarf foxhound, increase of speed having been sought at the expense of strength, to the overmatching of the hare and the deterioration of the sport—still retains more of the Southern hound, and shows the blood, both by its colors, the black and yellow pie and the blue mottle, and by its deep melodious challenge.

The beagle, the smallest of the species, now used in

England only to hunt rabbits, is a charming and beautiful little animal, being in fact a mere *pocket* edition of the Southern hound, which it exactly resembles in almost every particular, unless it be the crooklegs, the dewlap, and the pendulous jaws.

It has the color, the soft lustrous eye, the long soft drooping ears, "that sweep away the morning dew," and the cry, though small as compared with that of the great hound, yet tunable, sonorous, deep, and matched like bells.

There is no prettier sport in the world, on a small scale, than to hunt rabbits where they are abundant, with these industrious, active and indefatigable little dogs, and few more interesting sights than a pack of the merry little pigmies in full cry, running literally so that a table-cloth may cover them, and following the devious mazes of their timorous quarry with undeviating instinct through fern, bush, brake and coppice.

Of the improved English foxhound I have never seen any in America, the animals here used partaking largely of the Talbot blood, color and note, and having his qualities of excellent nose, great endurance, indefatigable industry, and the habit of sticking to their scent, day in and day out, until the fox is worn out rather than run down.

The American foxhound as used in pursuit of the fox in Maryland, Virginia, and other Southern States, and of the deer in the Carolinas, Georgia, and wherever deer-hunting on horseback or by driving is practised, is in fact actually the hound, unaltered and identical, of Beckford and Somerville. I am of opinion, moreover, that he is the best adapted bound for this country, where so much of the hunting is in difficult, intricate, entangled woodlands, marshy brakes and deep forests, where perfection of scent is the most desirable of qualities, and where great speed is not attainable, owing to the nature of the ground, and not desirable, owing to the extreme difficulty of following the hunt, which must be kept, in hearing rather than in sight by the sportsman.

I should advise persons choosing this animal to select him exactly for the points laid down by Beckford, as quoted above on page 165; and to be contented with his great scenting powers, industry, and deep resounding voice, which makes wonderfully stirring and sonorous music under the solemn arches of the grand re-echoing forest.

The best colors are black and yellow pied, or blue mottle with black and tan ears, eyepatches and saddles; and a medium-sized dog, strong, muscular, and compactly built, with long back ribs, which, as in the horse, should be well developed and firmly fixed to the hips by strong muscles, long thighs and good strong "stifles"— all of which, as Nimrod properly insists, are essential points—not to exceed from 22 to 24 inches in height, is preferable to a larger dog.

The English staghound, which is never seen in this country, and of which there are but two or three packs kept in England, is from 26 to 28 and even thirty inches, and is a beautiful spiry animal closely resembling the improved foxhound, or in fact identical with him in all points, except that he is exaggerated in size.

The English foxhound ranges from 23 to 25 inches for the dogs, from 22 to 23 for the bitches; but uniformity both of size and speed is especially studied, and the medium height of 24 inches is probably the standard.

The proper height of the old English harrier is from 16 to 18 inches, but the improved or dwarf foxhound harrier often runs to 21. The old harrier is much in use in the northern States, where he is a good deal interbred with the old foxhound, so that he is scarcely distinguishable from him, and is used both for hunting the fox, and for shooting the small American hare. When large, he is often called a foxhound, when small a beagle—the latter animal, in a perfectly pure state, being very rare and indeed almost unknown in America.

When pure they should never exceed 15 inches, and may run as low as 10. 12 is perhaps the most perfect size, and their ears should hang down as far almost as to the elbow.

Of all hounds this beautiful little animal is the best qualified for the pursuit of the small American hare, which is also far better adapted to this sport than the English rabbit, which he much resembles in size, color, and some of his habits, so that he is often mistaken for him by old countrymen, and generally miscalled after him even by Americans. He is, however, not a rabbit, producing young but twice a year, whereas the other breeds monthly; and sitting in a form on the surface of the earth, among thorns, briers or long grass, instead of burrowing under it.

This latter habit it is, which renders its pursuit so far preferable to that of the English rabbit, which, where burrows are near and frequent, goes to earth so quickly as to spoil the sport, and frustrate alike the pursuers and the gun.

There rests only to be named the great Scottish deerhound, perhaps the noblest of all dogs, and one, though rare as yet in America, yet rapidly coming into demand and use in the Western States, for which he is singularly adapted; as coursing the stag, and even the glorious elk over the boundless prairies on fleet horses, or running down the gaunt and grisly wolf, are the noblest, the most exciting, and the most truly sporting of all American field-sports.

The Scottish deerhound, in his true state, is a gigantic greyhound, with hair as rough and wiry as that of an Isle of Sky terrier. It is doubtful whether he is a distinct and aboriginal dog, or merely a carefully improved family of the ordinary, rough Scotch greyhound, which does not exceed the smooth English hound in size and is inferior to it in speed.

Stonehenge believes it to be merely the common rough dog, improved and increased in size by careful breeding; but I lean to the opinion that it is of an ancient original British breed, identical with the famous Alans of the early Norman kings, so celebrated in metrical romance, and not improbably indigenous to Cambria, as the equally noble and gigantic Irish wolf-dog, which was a smooth greyhound of vast size and dauntless courage, was indigenous to old legendary Erin, although both are now unfortunately nearly extinct.

These dogs, the Scottish deerhound I mean, not unfrequently stand 36 and even 39 inches in height, and have been known to measure 71 inches in girth around the chest. Probably 36 inches height and 57 circumference may be held the average size. They have great speed, very considerable powers of scent, dauntless courage, and often actual ferocity. They always run at the head like the bull-dog, and one of them is a match for a red-deer or a wolf, while a brace are said to be able to pull down a bull, and would doubtless show their prowess successfully against that noblest of the cervine family, the great American elk, wapiti deer or wewaskish of the plains.

This splendid specimen of the dog is so nearly extinct in its true form, and so nearly impossible of attainment even in Scotland, that, being absolutely necessary in that country for the pursuit of the wounded harts in the boundless, open, heathclad deer-forests of the highland hills, on which bloodhounds or foxhounds cannot be used, since their baying would banish all the stags from the land, Art has been called in aid of Nature, and by scientific and judicious crossing an animal is obtained closely resembling the original breed, his equal in size and power, and as well adapted for the uses to which he is applied. This animal, now, is for the most part known as the Highland deerhound. It is said that they are now so nearly established as a distinct family, that they are reproduced like for like, for generations.

The usual cross is the Scotch wire-haired colly, the foxhound, and the greyhound. Sir Walter Scott's celebrated and now classical dog "Maida," was the progeny of a Pyrenean sheep-dog and a greyhound bitch; and I have no doubt that a cross of great excellence might be got from the great Albanian or Epirotic mastiff, the *canis molossus* of the ancients, and the greyhound; and should I be successful in a scheme I have long meditated, and am now about to put into execution, upon procuring the animals necessary for originating the cross I contemplate, I shall, before many years, have it in my power to supply all my friends, and all such true sportsmen as shall care to possess them, with a fine type of this noblest cross of the whole dog race.

My method is to put a magnificent jet black St. John's Newfoundland dog, now in my possession, to an equally fine jet black English greyhound bitch; to cross the female progeny of these parents with the large black and tan foxhound, and the female pups of these, in the second generation, again with the smooth greyhounds. The male pups of the first cross I shall put to smooth greyhound bitches, and the pups of these to foxhounds male or female, as the case may require.

I am convinced that by this method I shall procure size, rough hair, scent, courage, and intelligence, equal to that of any conceivable dog, natural or artificial; and four or five years will prove my success or failure.

The first specimen of this breed of dogs I have seen in this country, was a dark brindled gray wire-haired dog, of which I got a sight in Philadelphia in the year 1850, the property of a British officer on his way to

California. He stood above 36 inches in height. There are, or recently were, a brace of very fine dogs in New York, in the possession of Mr. Moore the dog fancier, who can be heard of at the Spirit of the Times. They were valued at $500, and were cheap at that.

Before passing to the field, it will be necessary to lay before the beginner a few instructions for the care of his dogs at home; the feeding, lodging, exercising them, and getting them into or keeping them in condition, without which all is labor lost.

Residents in cities have much difficulty both in lodging and exercising their dogs suitably, especially in summer, when the prevalence of the absurd, useless, brutal and demoralizing *dog laws* are in operation, making it almost impossible to take a dog beyond the precincts of his own guarded yard.

I call these laws "absurd and useless," because it is a notorious fact and an established medical truth, that dogs are not in any degree more liable to canine rabies in July than in January, perhaps less so. Whatever other causes do produce it, heat and thirst do not. Canine rabies is unknown in Grand Cairo and Constantinople, but common in Quebec with the thermometer at 40 below zero.

Besides this, twenty men die every year of kicks from horses, or other accidents arising from riding or driving, and two hundred from firing guns at little birds and cannon at political meetings, for one that dies of the bite of a rabid dog. Cruel of course those laws are, which enjoin the promiscuous slaughter of the most intelligent, faithful, industrious, affectionate, and almost reasoning friend of man. Demoralizing any laws must be, which authorize the payment to wretched street boys, and vagrants, and homeless men, for the cold-blooded massacre of unresisting animals. But it is of course useless to address any argument to the common sense, or any appeal to the humanity of city governments. *De non apparentibus et non existentibus eadem est ratio*[10*]

All that remains to do, therefore, for the town dweller, is to make the best of it, and provide for his dogs as much space, as much air, as much exercise and as much water as may be.

Cleanliness is not only a cardinal virtue, but a cardinal preservative of health and condition. Every dog should have his separate lodging; nothing is better than the ordinary old-fashioned, double, gable-ended dog-house.

It should not have a bottom attached to it, but should be movable, for facilitating cleanliness, and should stand on a board platform. If whitewashed within and without once or twice a year, so much the better. The process will keep down the growth of vermin.

The best bed that can be given to dogs, is carpenters'

---

10   Concerning things which do not appear, and things which do not exist, the reasoning is the same.

pine-shavings. All other beds, straw especially, promote vermin; this seems to prevent them.

The best food for dogs is old Indian meal stirred, with a handful of salt, into water while it is boiling, till it is quite thick, and allowed to become cold; when it should be served with broth, buttermilk, or milk, where it can be obtained. Occasionally, if the dogs are low in condition, a complete blow-out of flesh may be given to them; it acts as a purgative, and they are the better after it. It should not, however, be given above once or twice a year, a few weeks before the opening and close of the shooting season. While at work, dogs should never have flesh, except cooked; and of that the less the better. Broth is all that is requisite, and where milk can be obtained it is preferable to broth. Four sheep's heads a week, will be amply sufficient to make broth for a kennel of three dogs. The bones should never be given. They are constant causes of contention, where there are two or more dogs together; they engender filth and disease, and they are seriously injurious to the teeth.

Dogs much accustomed to flesh are attacked far more severely than others by the special catarrh—the disease known as distemper—suffer from it far more acutely, and are more difficult of cure, since exceedingly low diet is, perhaps, the most efficacious mode of treatment; and when dogs are entirely or principally kept on animal food, it is with great difficulty that they can be induced to take any other.

The water supplied to kennels or single dogs cannot be too fresh, too pure, or too frequently changed. Naturally, dogs are extremely fastidious as to what they drink, far more so than as to what they eat, and although thirst will compel them to drink from any puddle, they suffer much from doing so both in comfort and condition.

Frequent bathing in hot weather is of inestimable

utility and comfort to these hot-blooded creatures, and the way in which even those short-coated varieties, which are supposed to be the least addicted to it, enjoy a swim, and continue half immersed for hours in succession, proves the necessity of it more than could be done by volumes of writing.

No less than pure air and pure water, superadded to wholesome food, exercise is needful to dogs.

For those who live in the country, where space is of little consequence, it is decidedly advisable to let the dogs run at large in a court of twenty to forty feet square, in which are their respective houses, in lieu of chaining each to his several kennel, and where this can be done the animals can get along with less road work.

Nevertheless, dogs are vastly the better in any case for an hour or two of exercise daily on the road. Before the shooting season commences, if they be, as they ought, full in flesh and somewhat high in condition, they are greatly improved by a fast run, after horses or a wagon, of five, ten, or as they improve in wind and hardness, twenty miles.

Such work, particularly on hard roads, hardens their feet, and renders them capable of threefold endurance; expands and invigorates their breathing apparatus, hardens their flesh, and enables them to go through double the amount of labor, without the annoyance or suffering, which dogs otherwise handled would feel in the beginning of a campaign. When dogs are by any accident much infested by fleas, or other vermin, the best way to deal with them is to rub them or smear them over thoroughly in every part, from the tip of the nose to the shoulder of the tail, with soft soap, to let it harden on them, and prevent them from licking it off, by the use of the muzzle. Let it remain caked and crusted all over them for the space of twenty-four hours, and then, washing it off, the vermin will be washed off with it.

For this purpose, tobacco water has been recommended by high authorities, but it is to be used, if at all, with the greatest caution, as it is a deadly poison, even by external application, if an overdose be used.

The feet may be hardened, when not in use, by bathing them constantly in strong brine; but when they are sore, and blistered after work, all applications of this sort should be avoided like poison; emollient applications of lard, or any unctuous substance devoid of salt, are the proper remedies in this condition.

Dogs are extremely subject to cold and rheumatism, both acute and chronic, and they suffer greatly, and are much disabled for work and endurance by the latter form.

Where it is possible, after a hard day's winter shooting, especially in wet ground or in snow, a warm bath is of vast utility and comfort, and on the next morning the dogs will come out "like giants refreshed by slumber," ready for double service. After the bath, or without the bath, in these circumstances, a good, deep bed of clean wheaten straw is a *sine qua non*. They will roll themselves, dry, clean and warm in it, and coil themselves up cosily, to come out new creatures in the morning.

I do not profess in this volume to treat of the medical treatment of dogs at large, or for special disorders. Instructions for such cases will be found elsewhere, in my own larger work, in that of Dr. Lewis, in Blaine and Youatt's Canine Pathologies, and above all in Mayhew on the Dog—which, as the latest, is by far the best treatise on the subject.

Even with any or all of these aids, a young sportsman should be very careful of attempting to treat a dog for any serious case without veterinary advice of an experienced person. He will be apt to err in his diagnosis, to mistake symptoms, and perhaps to apply, as remedies, what are really stimulants to the disease. For trifling and casual ailments or disorders, rest, cool or warm quarters, as the symptoms point to fever or to chilly affections, and plain, wholesome diet, without flesh, will do much.

Emetics, especially violent ones—and that most commonly exhibited by amateurs and quacks, table salt in large quantities, is the most violent, and is often excruciatingly severe in its operation—are generally to be avoided.

Where they seem absolutely necessary, the dog suffering intensely from tumefaction, heat, and tenseness of the abdomen, the best speedy emetic I have been used to esteem tartarized antimony and calomel, in doses varying, according to the size of the dog, from ½ gr. to one grain, given at intervals of half an hour until vomiting is produced. But Mayhew prefers antimonial wine, from a half teaspoonful to a desert spoonful.

Mild doses of Epsom salts is as good a purgative for ordinary cases as can be used; though I find that Mayhew recommends castor oil, 2 drachms, olive oil, 2 drachms— flavored with oil of aniseed and powdered sugar.

A useful formula for a general pill is—

Ext. Colocynth, half a scruple.
Pulv. Colchic. six grains.
Mass. Hydrarg. five grains.

This is the dose for a dog of 6 or 7 lbs.; a Newfoundland dog will require thrice the quantity. This is not a rapid medicine, and it is as much alterative as laxative. The dog will be much nauseated, and will refuse food during twelve hours or upward, at the end of which he will be relieved by not very copious but bilious evacuations. Absolute rest is required during the exhibition of this medicine.

For worms, which often trouble dogs beyond measure, the symptoms being extreme leanness, staring of the coat, ravenous appetite, hot dry nose, and constant irritation of the anus, the best and least dangerous recipe is—

RX Cowbage—Doliehos Pruriens, ½ dr.
Tin filings, *very fine*, 4 drs.

Make it to 4 or 6 pills according to the size of the dog— give one daily, and a few hours afterward the purgative of castor oil, as given above.

Two doses should be sufficient, unless in extreme cases.

For common mange, give 1 oz. of Epsom salts, and apply this ointment, which must be well and thoroughly rubbed into the skin, at three different applications. It must be rubbed in for at least an hour on each application.

Train oil one quart, spirits of turpentine a wineglass full, sulphur sufficient to make it so thick, that it will barely drip from a stick. Let it remain on the clog a fortnight, then wash off with soap and warm water.

For internal poison, large draughts of soap and water, mustard emetic or olive oil, are the best immediate antidotes. For Strychnia, it has been recently discovered that large quantities of liquefied lard are a sure preventive, if given in time; but as it is rarely known that, this poison has been administered until it is too late, I fear the discovery is of small effect.

To extract thorns, nothing is preferable to a strong

pitch plaster, bound upon the spot, and followed by a poultice.

For a snake bite, olive oil well rubbed into the part before a hot fire, and a copious drench given internally, is probably the best application, to which may be added a cataplasm of leaves of the broad-leaved plaintain, bruised with salt and bound upon the orifice of the wound. This is the Indian recipe for the bite of the rattlesnake.

For epileptic fits. Do nothing! neither bleed nor drench with cold water. Wait till the fit ceases, prevent the animal from running wildly away, convey it quietly home, and give injections of 1, 2, or 3 drachms of sulphuric ether—2, 4 or 6 scruples of laudanum, to 1 ½, 3 or 4 ½ ounces of the very coldest spring water that can be obtained. The animal is to be left alone in absolute silence for one hour, and at the expiration of that time the dose is to be repeated. This treatment is to be repeated ad infinitum, until the creature coils itself up and prepares to go to sleep, when one more injection is to be given, and the animal left to itself to recover at its leisure.

This treatment Mr. Mayhew declares to be absolute and almost unfailing, and although I have never tried it, I have no doubt of its merit.

With this I shall pass from the kennel to the field management of dogs, and the various species of game, in pursuit of which they are employed, only advising all persons of mature experience, who determine, or who are compelled by necessity to act as veterinarians to their own dogs, to use Mayhew in preference to all other authorities. He is clearly the most scientific, the mildest and the most simple in his treatment, of all who have written on the subject. All those, who are not maturely experienced, I recommend to take the best advice they can get, as medical men say *pro re natâ;* and above all things to avoid bleeding, and dabbling in energetic remedies and specific nostrums, recommended by grooms, dogbreakers, and old, knowing hands, which in ninety-nine cases out of the hundred will but make bad worse, and will probably kill ten where they will cure one patient.

THE FIELD.

Of the different kinds of field shooting, as opposed to river, lake, sea, or forest shooting, I propose to treat in reference to the season of the year with which each sport commences, beginning with the early spring-time, and continuing until the commencement of close-time, in those States, where any game laws, whatever, prevail; which, unfortunately, is the case only in a few of the Atlantic States, and in the British Provinces, to a certain extent; nor in these even are they, where they exist, observed as they ought to be, even by those who profess to be sportsmen.

The first species of upland, or rather field game, which comes into season in the Northern and Western States—in the Southern States it is a winter resident—is the bird commonly, though not correctly, known as the *English* snipe; this species being distinctly, though only slightly various from the European fowl of which it bears the name. The distinction was first recorded by Wilson, and consists in a permanent difference of number in the tail feathers, and of some discrepancies in cry and habits. Still the similarity is so great that I was at first inclined to believe the two varieties identical, until longer acquaintance with the habits of the American bird has assured me of its decided difference from its transatlantic congener.

This little wader is so generally known to all persons, in all parts of the country, and every where by the same name, that it needs no description; nor do I profess in this work to enter into details of natural history, which will be more fitly sought in works especially devoted to that subject, or to some more extended sporting books; as my own, Dr. Lewis's, and the American edition of Col. Hawker's instructive volumes.

Here I limit myself to explaining briefly to the young sportsman how to hunt for, find, and kill the game in question in fair and sportsmanlike style.

In no two States of the Union does the snipe come into season exactly at the same time, as he is every where a migratory bird, shifting his quarters as the facility of obtaining food, which he can only procure in unfrozen marshy grounds, and the necessity of rearing his young, which he can only do in certain northern temperatures and latitudes, and in wild marshy solitudes, induce or compel him to do.

Every where, however, to the northward and westward, or northward and eastward of the Carolinas, he is, probably, more or less entirely an occasional spring and autumnal visitor; coming the earlier in spring, and returning the later in autumn, the farther south and west the land lies, until he becomes a mere winter resident, departing so soon as the spring sunshine, becoming too warm, gives token of the approaching breeding season, and remaining absent until the freezing of his feeding places drive him southward still, whither he finds waters which are never congealed, morasses never impervious to his sensitive and busy bill.

The seasons of the appearance of snipe in the meadows and salt marshes, where the spring and tide waters meet, which are for the most part the scenes of their first appearance, are to be recognized by the simultaneous appearance of the blue-birds in the vicinity of buildings, of the shad in the river estuaries, by the croaking of the awakened frogs in the pools and quagmires, and by the bursting of the willow buds; all of which indications of the spring occur nearly at the same moment in every various locality from the banks of the Potomac to those of the St. Lawrence.

The frost must be entirely out of the ground, especially in the wet, cold lowlands and meadow-swamps, which are the favorite feeding grounds of this bird, and the spring grass should have come up tender, succulent, and green; the close of winter should have been distinguished by the raw north-eastern equinoctial gale, and this should have been succeeded by warm, genial weather, with an intermixture of soft southerly or southwesterly breezes, and tepid rain showers with April gusts and sunshine; the meadows should not be overflowed with water, nor yet, by any means, be dry or arid, but should be equally divided, or nearly so, between grassy dry tracts, from which the spring rains have long enough subsided to allow the herbage to grow sufficiently tall to yield a dry and comfortable covert, and shallow muddy pools, slants and runnels, in which abound the aquatic insects on which the snipe breed.

When the meadows are in this condition, early, and the weather is settled, fine and genial, the snipe make up their minds, as it would seem, to make a long halt, and refresh themselves fairly, before they again take wing for their northern breeding-places; and, in this case, they attach themselves to the ground, grow fat, tame and lazy; and will sometimes, where they are not harassed by incessant persecution and pot-shooting, lie so hard to the dog, that they can with difficulty be got to rise on the wing.

This occurs, however, only when the birds come on the ground early, and when the weather is fine during the whole, or, at least, the greater part of their stay. On their first coining they are always wild, constantly in motion, restless and capricious, often deserting favorite grounds and shifting to others in no wise superior, without any imaginable reason. If the meadows be in good order, and the weather follows mild and warm, they settle themselves down, often pairing, and sometimes even breeding in the country. I have myself never seen a nest of young snipe, as I have the young woodcock repeatedly, while unfledged and incapable of taking wing; but in July cock-shooting, in Orange County, I have more than once shot young birds of the season, with the pinfeathers not yet fully grown, which must have been bred on the ground.

In wild, windy weather, particularly on their first coming, and when the season is uncertain with interrupted night frosts and hail showers, snipe often rise in *whisps*, as it is termed, or little knots of ten or twenty birds, when they invariably fly wild and high, and often leave the ground entirely, soaring up and going away directly out of sight.

At a later period, when the weather is hot, and when the breeding season is at hand, the birds have a trick of rising perpendicularly into the air, and then letting themselves drop a hundred feet plumb down through the air, with the quills of their wings set edgewise, making a strange sound, which once heard cannot be mistaken, and is known as *drumming*. This is, beyond doubt, an amorous manifestation, like the strutting and cooing of pigeons, the shuffling and wing-fluttering of game-cocks, and the tail-displaying of peacocks and turkeys; nor do I know a sound of worse omen to the sports-man; since, at these moments, the birds are inconceiv-ably wild, calling one another up, until all in the neigh-borhood, or within sound, are wheeling and gyrating in the air like tumbler pigeons, and playing all sorts of fantastic tricks such as well-disposed snipe would never dream of at any other season, sometimes alighting on rail-fences or tall trees, and chattering like hens which have laid an egg.

At such times, there is little or no hope for it, except to wait patiently until the mood be passed or the weath-er change, for unless something of the sort occur, sport under the circumstances is hopeless.

Perseverance, however, is always a merit, and is sometimes rewarded. I once remember, after wholly despairing of sport, getting one of the best afternoon's shooting I ever had, when the snipe, after playing about in the manner above described for hours, until a hun-dred or two were in the air at once in full sight, came in a great flight, sixty or seventy yards high, directly over-head. I chanced to have one barrel loaded with duck shot, and at once let drive at them. Whether the shot struck their wings, or whether, as I think more probable, they mistook the whistling of the charge for the sound of a hawk's pinions,[11] they instantly pitched, scattered over all the country, and lay so well that I made, eventu-ally, a good bag.

When one lives near the snipe grounds it is possi-ble to calculate, with some certainty, on the likelihood of sport, from the nature of the ground, as described

11   That birds frequently do so is certain. If a bullet be fired at a heron, and pass any where near enough that he can hear it whistle, he instantly throws himself on his hack, with his bill pointed upward, exactly as he does when preparing to repel the swoop of a falcon.

above, and that of the weather, after birds are known to have arrived; in addition to which, their cry, as they fly to and fro from feeding ground to feeding ground, or as they come in from the south or north respectively in spring or autumn, on misty, moonlight nights, gives proof of their scarcity or abundance in the meadows.

To persons, living in towns, and visiting the snipe grounds only for a few days at intervals, sport or no sport is little more than a throw of the dice, or a matter of guess-work, so capricious and erratic are the habits of the bird.

The best indications I know of a probability of good sport, when the markets show that snipe are in season—and they alone do show it beyond the possibility of error—are the clearing up of a cold north-east storm into soft genial weather, the commencement of south-westerly breezes, and the subsidence of the waters, if they have been out over the lowlands, the frost being, of course, entirely out of the ground.

Such a combination of circumstances exactly at the nick of time gives good promise of sport; but if it happen too late, it will be of no avail, for the birds will have gone onward, or if it fall early, and be immediately succeeded and interchanged with wild or frosty weather, the snipe will become tricky, and the shooting more than ever casual and beyond calculation.

At times, in the spring, they will lie by day scattered singly all over the high, dry uplands, in fallow fields, hare pastures, even in wood-sides, descending only at night to feed on the marshes, where next morning the sportsman will find the droppings and borings of an innumerable host, but not a feather. When such is the case, pursuit is useless. There is nothing for it but to go home.

Again, in cold blowy weather, with snow squalls, they will lie in bushy covert, among briers and alder brakes, where there are springs of water and muddy pools, or *vlies*, as they are called by the Dutch settlers; and on more than one occasion, I have had tolerable sport, under evil auspices, in easterly wind and pelting sleet or snow squalls, among high wood, on what, at a different season, would be famous summer cock ground.

I mention all these circumstances, as showing where a man should look for his game according to any variation of weather.

No one, of course, in his senses, who lives in near vicinity of the ground, would dream of going out snipe-shooting in such weather as I have named, or of persevering, if the day should change to the bad, or the birds take to drumming. He would, as a matter of course, jog home, give "Dash" and "Don" their messes, hang up his Manton or his Mullin, and say, with Peter Simple, "better luck next time."

Still less would any resident of a city select such weather, or such circumstances, for visiting the country on a snipe-shooting expedition. But with him the matter is widely different; he has come, perhaps, twenty, fifty, a hundred miles from his "*domus et placens uxor*,"[12] for a week or ten days, difficultly spared from business by an effort not this season to be repeated. Therefore, "blow high, blow low," he must make the best of it; and, by knowing in what out-of-the-way, unlikely nooks and corners birds are to be found, if they are to be found any where, in such unpromising weather, he may make a decent bag, when equally good shots and as persevering workmen, not being up to the dodge, will go home empty-handed.

The best day for snipe-shooting, spring or fall, in spite of all that English authorities say—who, writing what is true for one country and climate err not, though they are frequently blamed for error, because readers apply their sayings to another—is *not* a dark,

12   "Home and pretty wife."—*Hor.*

windy, drizzling day. A dark day is never favorable for any shooting on the upland, least of all for the shooting of snipe, which are so exactly similar in the coloring of their streaked plumage to the withered grass and sedges among which they live, and over which they fly in such days unusually low and near the ground—that they can hardly be distinguished except by the glimpses of their white bellies, which they show when they twist.

Drizzly days are never good for any shooting, unless it is some kind of wild-fowl shooting; for no ground bird—this rule is invariable and without exception—will *squat* (without doing which, it never can lie well to the dog), unless the ground or herbage is dry and warm to its breast.

Windy weather, provided that the wind is from the west or south, and not too high, is advantageous for this sport, for reasons to be given hereafter.

A mild, sunshiny, soft, and even hot day, with a gentle southerly wind is, then, of all days, the day for the snipe bogs; and I have invariably found that the hotter the day, if it be humid, with a good deal of gentle air, the closer lie the birds. I have seen the time when they could hardly be kicked up under the dog's nose; nor is this all; for every old sportsman knows that in such weather the flight of the birds themselves is wholly altered, and that, instead of jumping up breast high at one jerk, and then zigzagging away like a flash of lightning, they will flop lazily along, like half-awakened owls in daylight, and, if they have been undisturbed and have long haunted the ground, will often drop again within twenty yards of the dog that has flushed them.

When they do thus, there is no easier bird, even for a tyro; all that has to be done is to let them go away a fair distance, so as to allow for the spread of your shot, to be cool, and to cover your bird before you pull the trigger.

There is one peculiarity in the snipe, that it invariably

rises up wind, and goes away as nearly up wind as possible. The consequence is that a mode of beating for him is proper, is indeed the only proper mode, which would be decidedly wrong in trying for any other kind of game.

One must invariably beat *down wind* for him. If possible, and where there is a long narrow range of meadow, I would make a great circuit, and lose a couple of hours in doing so, since it is by far the better way to enter the ground from the windward, instead of, as one should do in every other sort of shooting, from the leeward end. If not, the whole tract must he worked diagonally, never fully up-wind, and wherever an unusually likely piece of lying ground, soft oozy tender grass, outspread in patches between high dry reed beds or burnt grounds, in which snipe never lie, or rusty half evaporated slanks and pools, or tussocky spring bogs, a circuit must be made to get the wind. If the dog points, the shooter must in every case make a semicircle, so as to get the bird down wind of him, and for this cause, and for others, of which anon, in no kind of shooting is an extremely *steady* dog more necessary than in this.

Many writers, for this reason, recommend as the best dog, for this sport, a very slow, old pointer—as if slow dogs must needs always be steady, or fast dogs unsteady. Neither of the two is the truth.

For young sportsmen, for general shooting, I do, most assuredly, recommend the pointer in preference to the setter, and most of all for snipe-shooting, though for myself I choose, and to all old and thorough workmen I advise, the setter.

Young sportsmen cannot he expected to break their dogs, and all shooting over setters is in some sort dog-breaking; nor even to keep their well-broken dogs, by their own conduct, well broken. A good pointer keeps himself broken.

I am well pleased to find that my preference for,

or prejudice in favor of—I care not which it is called—
the setter, is fully shared by that great authority Colonel
Hutchinson, whose work on dog-breaking is incompa-
rably the best in existence; and for precisely the same
reasons, which I have often previously given, although,
until I have had this volume in preparation, I have never
had the opportunity of consulting him. He likewise
draws the same distinction with myself between steadiness and slowness.

If birds be in abundance, it matters not a straw how
slow a dog may be, nor much whether one have a dog
at all. One may walk the birds up without any dog, and
with this advantage, that they will lie better to a man
than to a man and a dog, as also to a man with one dog,
than to one or two men with two, three or four dogs. But
if the range be very extensive, and the birds very scarce,
lying, perhaps, scattered wide apart, two or three or half
a dozen to the square mile, where is the slow man and
the slow old pointer?

Now a fast dog may and should be both very steady,
and thoroughly cautious. By steady, I mean that, he
must be stanch as steel, and immovable on his point.
For snipe-shooting, above all things, he must not crawl
in, or attempt to decrease the distance from his game,
but must stand stiff, the instant he is sure that his game
is before him. Snipe rarely run under any circumstances, and still more rarely will endure the crawling up of a
timid and tender-nosed dog. Secondly, he must remain
motionless and unexcited, though the shooter, instead
of coming up to flush the bird over his point, should he
chance to point up wind or across wind, turn his back
upon his tail, make a long circuit, and come down in his
face.

He must also, if possible, though few dogs will do
so, advance to meet the gun on a silent beckon of the
hand, without call or whistle. He must, when whistled in,

be willing to follow steadily at heel, without an endeavor to beat until ordered to go on, which is a point of the greatest consequence in snipe-shooting; for a bird which is marked down will often allow a man to walk close ill upon it, which would flush wide of a dog; and, as the snipe never runs above a few feet from the spot into which he is marked, he can, in nine cases out of ten, be found without aid of the pointer.

Of course, no dog is steady, or, indeed, worthy to be called a dog at all, which will not instantly stop, or drop, to the motion of the hand or the report of the gun, without a word spoken; much less one which will rush in and flush his bird from the point, from over eagerness, or break in, instead of down-charging, when a bird falls to the gun.

So much for steadiness, necessary for all shooting, most indispensable for snipe-shooting.

By caution, I understand care not to flush game by either of two errors; by the coming upon it, unexpected, with such speed as to be unable to recover, so as to point before the bird shall be alarmed; or after scenting it, and displaying consciousness of its vicinity, by the drawing in too closely upon it, in order to make assurance doubly sure.

But these points of caution are attainable by all good-nosed and practised dogs, and both are compatible with the highest degree of dash, speed and courage. The neglect of either is a grave error.

The latter can be taught by any, should be taught by every breaker before the dog is allowed to go out as thoroughly broken. It is taught by use of the check cord, by which the dog is jerked forcibly hack from his point so soon as he exhibit the least inclination to run in; by cautioning him with word "toho!" and by punishing him for disobedience.

The former cannot be taught except by long

practice, although some dogs seem to possess it, as if by nature. It is a far more rare quality than the other, and to its rarity is attributable the idea entertained by so many, that speed is dangerous in a dog used in pursuit of wild and easily scared birds, and that slowness is the only guarantee for sureness. Such is not the case. All good dogs, long used to sport and experienced in finding game, know as well, often better than their owners, what is and what is not likely ground on which to find it. Some, as I said before, appear to possess this knowledge by hereditary instinct, as they do that of standing and backing, naturally and without instruction.

These dogs while racing, as they should, at a gallop, whether pointers or setters, over their general range, the instant they come upon ground which their instinct or experience tells them to be likely for their game, will fall into a trot, beat it inch by inch, whipping their sides with their sterns, and if they find the much-wished scent, will point stiff as statues; if not, having beat it out to the end, will go off again, heads up and sterns down, at racing pace, until they come to another likely spot, when they will repeat the same operation, *ad infinitum*.

It follows, as a matter of course, that a person hunting with one such dog will get over two or three times as much ground, with not an iota more danger of flushing a hard-lying bird, as one hunting the much-belauded and recommended of authorities, old, slow pointer; and, therefore, other things being equal, will have twice or thrice the chance of finding game. Again, a person shooting over a brace of such dogs, will necessarily double his chance of filling his bag.

Having entered his ground then to windward, the young sportsman will continue to heat as much as possible down wind. He will himself walk, and encourage his dog to hunt, as fast as possible, over what seems unlikely ground. But if the dog seems bent on hunting any particular spot slowly, he should not cross him—probably the dog has his reasons, and is the better judge. Where the ground looks likely, or where he knows there are birds, he cannot hunt too slowly.

If the dog seem inclined to point, feathering and drawing carefully, it is well to step up toward him gently, saying in a low guarded voice, "Steady! Steady!" or, "Have a care!" When he points, let the sportsman get to windward of his point, come down on him carefully, holding the gun as described at page 88, and be as cool as he can. When the snipe springs, let him shoot it, if he can.

The reason why it is recommended to come down wind on the snipe, is this; that he always rises up wind, and goes away at sharp, short zigzags, tack and tack in the teeth of it, and the harder it blows, the faster he flies and the more he tacks.

By going down wind on him, the shooter forces him to rise in his face, and to go off either to the right or to the left hand, affording him a cross shot, which is always the easiest shot.

The snipe always hangs, when first rising, for a second on the wing before he gets under way, and for that second he is almost motionless. This I consider, unless he be decidedly too near, so that the shot must tear him, or like a single ball, miss him clean, the best time to take him. The old notion of waiting till he has done twisting, and then downing him, is—like that other notion of pulling out your box and taking a pinch of snuff, after the bird rises, and before raising your gun at him—very good to talk about. In nine cases out of ten, to wait until a wild, sharp-flying snipe on a windy day has done twisting, is to wait until he is out of shot.

If he rise above fifteen yards from the shooter, and he will seldom rise closer, he cannot in my opinion be shot too quickly. But it is worthy to be remembered, that with No. 8 shot, the right size, the distance at which the charge covers the greatest circle within which the bird *must* be hit, is thirty yards.

The snipe is a very quick-flying bird except at the instant I have mentioned, or in the case of his being tame and lazy on hot days; it will be necessary, therefore, when he is once under way, to make allowance for him. At fifteen or twenty yards, if he be crossing at speed, the gun should be levelled at least one foot ahead of him; at forty—a full yard. If he be going straight away, the aim should be taken something over him, probably about half the allowance given above; and if he be zigzagging, nearly the same allowance must he made, on whichever tack he may he, as for a cross shot; but to kill, the aim must be taken and the gun fired, almost with the speed of light.

Snipe-shooting, by those who cannot do it, is sometimes called a *knack*. It is so—for it is emphatically the knack of shooting well. In no other respect is it a knack; for it has nothing in it peculiar to itself, nor any thing which disqualifies him who excels in it from killing any other sort of game that flies fast and strong.

Most men who shoot much, have some game on which they most excel, probably, because at some period in their lives they have had more continuous practice on it. To many persons the snipe is a very hard bird; to myself it is the easiest of all; undoubtedly, because, when I first began to learn to shoot as a schoolboy, I used to have a few shots at snipe almost every day of the season, and could knock a long-bill over pretty cleverly before I had ever been allowed to fire at the much slower and easier bird—to the general—the partridge; the snipe in England not being *game* by law, nor as such prohibited to the unlicensed shooter.

Between snipe-shooting in the spring and fall of the year, so far as the mode of hunting, there is no difference, nor is there much in the habits of the birds, except that they never perform the antics described above at page 182, nor are they usually so wild, or so whimsical as to their choice and changes of ground.

They return from the north, where they breed, in different localities, graduating from the north southward, from July until cold weather sets in, not wholly deserting the Northern States and Canada until ice is thick and the marshes impenetrable to their bills.

I have killed them myself in Canada West, so late as the end of November, and have known them shot by a friend and fellow-sportsman, now, alas! no more, on the edges of a perennial streamlet as far into December as the 20th, when all the country round was thick with ice. In Georgia, Alabama, and the Carolinas, they swarm in the marshes and rice grounds, throughout all the winter, and afford unlimited sport to the country gentlemen, and *bonnes bouches* to the epicures of those States, until the advent of spring.

In regard to snipe-shooting, as a distinct branch of sport, there remains no more to be said; but a few rules for general deportment in the field, and for dog-management, may be, perhaps, better stated here than elsewhere; as they are applicable to all shooting, especially all open shooting, and may be laid down once for all.

In the first place, when shooting in company— and here, I will observe, that unless in battue shooting, which is never practised in the United States, every person above two is one too many, unless where two parties, each of two persons, can shoot advantageously, not together, but in concert, as on opposite sides of a river, so as to drive the game backward and forward, from one to the other—it is well that the young shooter should accustom himself to beat the ground, and shoot, on either hand of his companion; as persons are often found who cannot, or will not, shoot on the right hand; to whom, if older men and older Sportsmen, our beginner must yield the *pas*.

The cause of this preference is this; that, of cross shots, the bird which flies to the left is by far the easiest, that to the right, the most difficult, of all shots; and as it is the invariable rule never to shoot at birds, when two are shooting in company, which fly toward the companion, the left-hand beater has the chance of the fairest shots.

In the second place, never, under any circumstances, fire across the face of your companion; or at a bird, which, rising between you, or even before yourself, flies so that it must cross him. When shooting, two persons together, in the open, every animal which crosses to the right belongs to the right-hand shooter, and *vice versa;* and the other has no more right to fire at such, until he to whom it belongs has missed it with *both* his barrels, than to fire at it when falling or after it is down.

There is no greater breach of courtesy and decorum possible, than the violation of this rule. If it arise from ignorance, carelessness, or the over-eagerness and excitement of youth, it may be pardoned; but the person who commits it is likely to be avoided as a most undesirable companion.

He who errs, as many do, wilfully in this respect, from a nasty, selfish jealousy, and the desire of bagging more birds in the course of a day's shooting than his friend, and bragging of it afterward, as is the usual habit of such characters, may be set down at once, so far as sportsmanship is concerned, however estimable be may be in other respects, as no gentleman. Such a partner is to be avoided with as much care on a sporting excursion, as is a gentleman cutaneously afflicted, *more Scotico,* for a bedfellow.

Shots which fly straight away before the face of both shooters must be taken alternately; and it is well to remember that it is always graceful to *give* the shot, especially to a senior.

When a bevy of quail, several snipe in a whisp, or more birds than one of any species, rise in front of two shooters, each man should invariably fire at the outside birds on his own side.

These absolute rules are not, as it would at first seem, mere maxims of courtesy and good-breeding. They are necessary to prevent confusion; to prevent, what will otherwise constantly occur, both men from firing both barrels at the same birds, and consequently getting but two birds, however well they may be shooting, instead of four, for four shots. I have seen this very thing happen fifty times with two jealous men blazing away, all eagerness to outdo each other, at the first birds that take wing; and also have seen half a dozen more birds spring one by one, and go away unharmed, with all the barrels unloaded, after one of these ineffectual *feux de joie;* and I believe that the odds are as five to one in favor of a couple of shooters' making a bag, who adhere strictly to the rules, against a couple who shoot haphazard, without regard to any decencies of deportment, at everything which rises.

If each man shoot over his own dog, as is for the most part the case in America, and one have all the luck of the day, for luck will at times run in favor of one gun and his dog get all the points, it is but courteous to call up the other and offer him the shot.

In covert shooting, especially when birds are scarce, it is always proper to signify to the second party that there is a point, by calling him up in a low tone, exclaiming also "Toho!" which answers the double purpose of cautioning the dog to be steady, and of warning the other gun.

When a bird rises, always, *before firing*, cry, "Mark, right!" or "Mark, left!" as it may be. By observing the two latter points, many birds will be brought to bag which would otherwise get off, either being missed, or affording no chance of a shot to the man who finds them.

Always endeavor to mart down a dead bird or a missed bird. The former by noting exactly some branch, leaf, stone or tuft of grass which you have seen it touch in falling, and then bringing that mark into bearing with some other point, which will fill your memory and enable you to identify the place, when you bring back your eye, after diverting it for the purpose of loading.

This precaution is particularly necessary in snipe-shooting, where every tuft of rushes has so many facsimiles, that unless you have made it safe by bringing it into line with some post, stump, tree or roof, or other distant object on the horizon, you will certainly be at fault to recover it.

Even when using the best retrievers, this point is worthy of observation, and attention to it will reward the pains. Much time will be saved by the shooter being able to put his dog exactly on the spot; and, what is more, the fresh ground will not be disturbed, as it otherwise would be, by the dogs trashing it over and over, in seeking dead.

In marking live birds, let the young sportsman beware of supposing that the birds have alighted, because he has lost sight of them, which he may easily do from any one of half a dozen causes; from their passing behind intervening obstacles, or into or through undistinguishable hollows and swells of the ground; from their flying actually out of sight, or, what is, I think, the most common of all, when the birds are flying low over a background of nearly the same color with themselves, from the marker's eye becoming weary, losing them for a second, and never being again able to recover them.

Few niceties of sportsmanship are less understood, yet on few does more depend, than on this art of marking. I never, in my life, either in this or any other country, saw an untrained person or a countryman, who was not himself a game shot, who had a conception of marking birds down; yet I never saw one who was not confident that he could always do so to a yard.

Every bird has its particular method of alighting, which will be noticed under each head, and the motion which it makes, in order to accomplish this, is so clear, that it cannot by any accident be mistaken by a practised eye. This motion once seen, the marker may be certain that the bird has not merely flown out of sight but has really gone down, and he has only to note the spot, to which this motion has brought the bird.

In the case of the snipe, the peculiarity of action cannot be mistaken. High or low, leisurely or swiftly, as he may be flying, as if he suddenly caught sight of a spot which suited his fancy, and made up his mind on the instant, he makes a short pitch from the direction of his previous flight, with his bill pointing earthward, half closes his wings, and darts to the place he has selected as swiftly and as straight as thought.

In regard to hunting your dogs—observe these rules:

1st. Never do that yourself for which you would punish, or from which you wish to restrain them. If you become eager, and run on to retrieve a winged bird when it is running, you encourage them to do likewise, and do more injury than weeks of breaking and flogging will repair.

2d. Never permit or encourage them at one time to do that for which you rate or punish them at another. Many persons do this; particularly in hieing them after running birds, without considering the mischief they are doing.

3d. Never shoot with any person who will not shoot to rule, as to walking steadily and stopping to load, &c.; much more, never hunt your dogs in company with riotous brutes, which will neither hack, stand, nor down charge. Example is notoriously far more effective than precept, and nothing is unlearned so easily as discipline, or learned so easily as riot.

4th. Never run or hurry up to your dogs when pointing. You increase their rashness and eagerness by doing so tenfold, and tempt them to rush. If the birds are running before them, and they are roading too fast, by hurrying after them you not only excite them yet farther, but run much risk of flushing the birds by the noise you make. Keep your usual pace, or even retard it, advancing so that the dogs can see your motions, with your right hand raised, reiterating the words "Care! Care!" or "Steady! Steady!" in a calm, slow tone, always using the same and but one word of command, for each case.

5th. When the birds rise, whether you fire or not, invariably make your dogs "down!" or "drop!" for a second or two. It tends to make them steady; it gives you time to mark; and if there be a last hard-lying bird or pair of birds, it increases your chance of a shot.

6th. If your dog rush in and chase a hare, or even devour a fallen bird, do not run after him. You cannot catch him, and will only excite him and yourself, and make matters worse. Holloa at him! rate him! whistle to him! but keep your place, till he return from chasing, or become ashamed of tearing the game—he must do so at last. Then make him "drop!" go up to him quietly, put your check-cord on his collar, if he have chased, drag him back to the spot whence he started, flogging him all the way and rating him, and make him lie down in position, and retain him there by the cord for several minutes. If he have broken in from his charge and torn the bird, do the same thing, leaving the fragments of the bird where he left them, and then make him draw gently up to them, and point them, checking him with the cord, and flogging him every time he attempts to touch them.

7th. When you buy a dog, endeavor to learn the exact mode of hunting and words of command used by his former owner, and as far as possible conform to them. If possible, see him hunted by his old master.

8th. Never punish a dog, unless you are certain that he cannot fail to understand for what he is punished.

9th. Never undertake to make a dog do any thing, however trivial, and allow him to get the better of you, for fear of losing time or losing birds. Better to lose a day, and a bag full, than to let your dog discover that he is a master.

10th. Never pass a fault uncorrected. I mean by rating, threatening with the whip, and making the culprit pause and recognize his fault.

11th. Punish with the whip as seldom as possible; but when it is indispensable, use it so that it will be remembered.

12th. In hunting dogs, make as little noise as possible. When it is necessary to call a dog by name, or whistle him up, use exactly the power of voice or sound which will reach his ears, and no more. Dogs, which are always shouted at, come at length to the point that they will turn for nothing but a shout. When it is necessary to turn them, whistle, and wave the hand in the direction you would have them move. The perfection of dogs is to work entirely to the hand, requiring scarcely a minimum of voice.

13th. Make friends with your dog, without absolutely caressing him, so soon as you have done punishing him, and before allowing him to rise.

14th. When he is at point, never allow him to flush the game without your ordering him "On!"—and then instantly "Drop."

15th. When he is down, never allow him to rise till you have ordered him "Up!"

16th. When a bird is killed, signify it to him by note of the whistle and the word Dead!" at which he should come to you. Then give him the word "Seek," or "Find"— when he must draw up and point the dead bird.

17th. When he is pointing dead, never allow him to recover or mouth the dead bird, until you desire him to "Fetch."

18th. When he has retrieved dead, accustom him to deliver dead into your own hand. If he only lay down his birds, he will sometimes do so on the farther side of creeks or impenetrable morasses, and sometimes be will lay down a winged bird, which will instantly run off again and give double trouble.

19th. Never break a sporting rule, in order to recover a wounded bird or get a shot at a live one.

20th. Never lose your temper!

If you can keep the last of these rules, you can without doubt keep them all; and if you do so, though it will be painful and difficult at first, it will gradually become habit and grow into a second nature; and when this degree of excellence is acquired, you will have really become a steady and good sportsman, so far as the field-work of dogs, and may even undertake at a pinch to break a brace for yourself.

And here, before proceeding in its turn to the sport of the next season, though I might, perhaps, have better mentioned it above, I will state, as the most befitting place, that during spring snipe-shooting, the Virginia rail—*Rallus Virginianus,* of which the preceding is a splendid and correct sketch—a distinct variety from the sora, easily recognized by its long recurved bill, and closely assimilating to the English water-rail—is often shot, together with the pectoral sandpiper, which latter is known in Home parts of the country as the jacksnipe.

The Virginia rail lies very hard, and creeps among the grass and rushes like a mouse, to the great discomfiture of the dogs, which can hardly force it up.

When flushed it flies, like the sora, with its legs hanging down, but even more slowly. It is easily brought down, carrying little shot, and is delicious eating.

The pectoral sandpiper is a somewhat smaller bird than the English snipe, light brown on the upper parts, speckled with black and olive, and pure white below. It has a short bill of perhaps three-quarters of an inch, slightly curved downward; feeds in small flocks, but for the most part rises singly with a feeble whistle, lying well to the dog, which points it stanchly, and affording at times excellent sport, on springy upland meadows. It is not in the least degree fishy, and is admirable on the table. I was once, before I knew what was the bird I was shooting, so fortunate as to kill eighteen couple of these capital little birds, with nearly the same number of English snipe, on the Big Piece, as it is called, on the Passaic river, in New Jersey. But that was before birds were persecuted, as they now are, on their feeding grounds, and before shooting for the market had become a branch of market gardening and railroad-business.

BAY-SHOOTING.

At the time when spring snipe-shooting has fully come to an end, winter wild fowl has terminated, also, for several months: indeed, it has ceased to be an object to any save the professional gunner; for, unless in cold and windy weather, it is rare that birds will fly thickly enough, or visit the *stools* with sufficient frequency, to render their pursuit much pleasure—a chilly and laborious pleasure at the best, and one which he must be an ardent and indefatigable sportsman, who follows regularly, unless a dweller cm the coast.

It is true, that when the great swarms of geese have soared sky-high, and long gone *hawnking* away to the northward, to their breeding-places beyond Symsonia and Labrador, that a few brant linger yet about the Long Island bays and New Jersey beaches, and are then deemed by gastronomes to be in the very height of their culinary excellence, "a dainty to set before a king;" but their appearance is so rare, and any tiling like a day's sport so unattainable, that they are abandoned exclusively to the Raynors, the Smiths, and the Veritys of Long Island, and, as they are, whether justly or unjustly, called, it is not for me, who am in some sort a Jerseyman, to say, the pirates of Barnegat.

Just at the moment, however, when all shooting appears to be over, suddenly "from the tepid waters of Florida, the great bay of Mobile, the sea-lakes of Borgne and Ponchartrain, the lagoons, and muddy flats, and alluvial shoals of the lower Mississippi, where they have congregated in countless myriads, while the ice was thick even in the sea-bays of the Chesapeake and Delaware, and while all the gushing streams and vocal rivulets of the Northern and Middle States were bound in voiceless silence," arrive the numerous families of waders, who, their proper name being legion, are indiscriminately and improperly known as bay snipe.

These, like the geese and ducks which have preceded them, farther to the northward than even the intrepid Kane has forced his adventurous keel, are bound Labrador-wise, to lay eggs and hatch countless young in clue season, and every where along our shores they follow onward, host impelling host, and pause awhile to recreate themselves—the Laymen, and such city or country sportsmen as care for the sport, taking a chance at them from Egg Harbor skiffs, with heavy guns and *quantum sufficit* of No. 4 or No. 5 shot, in spite of hot suns and innumerable mosquitoes.

I said that these birds were improperly called baysnipe, and they are so; for the only bird which is nearly connected with the true snipes, is the first or almost the first which arrives among us, the red-breasted snipe, *Scolopax Noveboraccusis,* better, though barbarously known as the "dowitcher," the "quail snipe," and the "brown back," according to the various places in which he chances to be shot. Even this bird, however, is not a genuine snipe, but comes properly under the genus *Macrorhampus*, and has no name of his own in the vernacular.

The other species, generally included under the comprehensive name of bay-snipe, comprise the curlews, three kinds of which visit us in the spring, and return again early in the autumn. The great or long-billed curlew, *Numenius longirostris*, whose portrait is prefixed; the short-billed, or Hudsonian curlew, *Numenius Hudsonicus*, nearly resembling the former, but smaller in size, and, as his name indicates, shorter *i' the neb* than his congener; and lastly, the Esquimaux curlew, *Numenius Borealis*, who is commonly known, heaven knows why, as the jutes and the doe-bird; and who, feeding often on the upland in company with the golden plover, a likeness of whom is annexed, is a bird delicate, succulent, and well flavored on the table, which may not be said of most of the breed, which, to speak truth, are for the most part intolerably rank and sedgy; though there be exceptions, which shall be named with honor.

The golden plover, *charadius marmoratus*, and his brother the black-bellied plover, *Charadius Helveticus*, whom the gunners call the *bull-headed*, follow. Both of these birds are killed on the bays, but are of far superior quality when killed inland, on high sheepwalks and pastures; they must not, however, be confounded with the Bartramian sandpiper, or tattler, the most delicious of all American birds, not even excepting the canvas-back, which goes generally by the name of the "upland plover," while the golden plover figures as the "frost bird."

Two species of godwits are among these wading visitors: the great marbled godwit, *Limosa Fedea*—a regular though rare and shy guest on the sea-shores; and the Hudsonian godwit, *Limosa Hudsonica*, smaller and yet rarer than the preceding. These are respectively known to the gunners, as the "marlin," and the "ring-tailed marlin," and are famous for their watchfulness, which will scarce admit of approach, unless one, by chance, be brought down wounded, when the flock will circle around him, plaintively screaming, and will even allow several shots to be fired into them in succession.

It is singular, that while every bird of all the tribe has its own peculiar name among the baymen and gunners, who make confusion worse confounded by their nomenclative barbarisms, not one by any accident stumbles on its true denomination.

Thus the red-breasted sandpiper, *Tringa Islandica*, which is one of the most numerous and best of these birds, and a general favorite with the gunners, as being easily whistled to the *stools*, and consequently affording great, sport, becomes the "robin snipe," owing to its resemblance to the migratory thrush, or common robin of this country. In winter, the plumage of this bird turns gray above and pure white below, when he becomes the "white robin snipe."

In like manner, the red-backed sandpiper, *Tringa*

Alpina, becomes the "black-breasted plover," and when his plumage is changed in cold weather, the "winter snipe." He flies quickly in crowded flocks, and wheels frequently as if by a signal, when great numbers are often killed at a shot.

This confusion of names is very troublesome to the young sportsman, who has any turn for natural history—for the furtherance of which beautiful study alone, I think bay snipe-shooting worth the pains—and who is naturally nonplussed at finding sandpipers called, as it may happen, snipes or plovers, and other species, which he may indistinctly remember to have seen otherwise described, passing under some barbarous cognomen, defying the skill of OEdipus to decipher its sense from the sound.

The next considerable family are the tattlers, three of which are numerous on all the sea bays in their season—the yellow-shanks tattler, or lesser yellow legs, *Totanus Flavipes*, easily decoyed, and affording great sport when numerous; the tell-tale tattler, *Totanus Vociferus*, a far larger and more suspicious bird, detested by the fowler, who never spares him, on account of his habit, whence his name, of alarming all the marshes and hassocks with his shrill shrieks; and lastly, the seinipalmated tattler, *Totanus semipalmatus*, better known as the "willet," which name is given to him in imitation of his cry, which is said to resemble the words "pill-will-willet," quickly repeated, though, for my own part, I have never been able to trace much similarity between the sound of written words and the piercing whistles of these aerial wanderers.

The willet is one of the best of these birds, and its eggs, much resembling those of the English peewit, or field plover, are really delicious. This is a shy and wary bird in open and exposed situations, but is easily allured to the decoys.

There are many other varieties and families of these birds, turnstones, sanderlings, dunlins—usually known as ox-birds, delicious little fellow's, like flying pats of butter, wheeling in countless flocks over the summits of the curling waves, or feeding along the pebbled shores on which the surges burst, and running back, scarcely in time, as it would seem, to escape the deluge of the spray when it breaks and rolls up the shingle in crisp and foamy ripples—knots, dottrels, avosets, and others. But those I have named above are of the most consideration.

The mode of shooting these birds, is to lie concealed in boats, masked with seatrash and covered by reeds, on the edges of the hassocks where the snipe feed, in the small pools left among the grass by the receding tide. On the margin of these, the *stools* or decoys, admirable representations of the different species, carved in pine wood and painted so as to have deceived the unsuspicious eye of many a deluded greenhorn, are set up, and to them the passing flocks are whistled down by the surpassing skill of the baymen, whose unerring sight instantly recognizes every species, by the motion of its wings and the manner of its flight, when the birds are mere air-drawn specks against the dusky, dawning sky; and whose imitative powers call it down by so perfect a simulation of its cry, that it rarely fails to answer and descend to the wily cheats which tempt it to destruction.

To these decoys are added the killed birds as fast as they are gathered, which are propped up with sticks, after a manner peculiar to the amphibious human natives, so as to complete the mystification and delusion of the survivors.

To me, I confess the sport is a dull one, weary, stale, unprofitable; and the only things that could reconcile me to it, are the chance of obtaining rare and curious ornithological specimens, and admiration for the skill and imitative talents of the baymen.

Sport, to me, in it there is little. If the birds are scarce, shy, and avoid the stools, the reek of the mud-banks and stagnant waters, interspersed with savory odors of departed king-crabs, and such like, the blazing sunshine of an American May or June, reflected from the smooth heaving waters, and, above all, the torturing sting of the mosquitos, are hardly compensated by a few scattering shots, and the "converse high" of my friends, as aforesaid, the Raynors, Smiths or Veritys.

If, on the contrary, the flocks come, as they do sometimes, countless in numbers and in quick succession, there is too much of it. It becomes butchery, not sport.

Sportsmanship proper cannot be said to belong to it, unless—which few persons do except the professionals—one make and set his own stools, *paddle his own canoe*, and whistle his own birds. Then, it must be admitted, there is a high degree of science and of skill exhibited; and where the success is dependent entirely on the science, skill and performance of the performer, it cannot be denied that there is sportsmanship, and the achievement of sportsmanship is of necessity sport.

Beyond this, although there is more or less excitement in watching, expecting, hoping for the passing flights, and triumph more or less in planting a successful volley, the cramped position, the constrained absence of motion, and above all, the want of dogs, greatly detract from the pleasure.

This sport occurs, however, at a time when there is no other; and if one be a resident on the barren, sea-beaten shores, or be wearied to death of the city, and desirous of change at the risk of tedium, why, it is well to try the bay snipe.

The proper weapon for shooting of this kind is a double-barrelled gun of ten or twelve pounds weight, and corresponding gauge, which will do the best execution at flocks. With such a piece, coarse large-grained powder of the diamond grain, from Pigou and Wilke's Dartford mills, and No. 4 or 5 spot, should be used.

Such a gun, however, not being in the armory, an ordinary fowling-piece of 14 gauge will do its work, killing its single shots quite as far, though not telling such a tale with flocks, as the heavier gun. In this case, however, No. 5 is the largest shot that must be used, since the load which such a piece will advantageously carry, will not number pellets enough of a larger size to cover a circle large enough to insure success.

When these birds are flying singly, they often shoot along at a great rate, and it is necessary either to make great allowance, shooting, for the most part, nearly a yard ahead of them, or to keep the gun continually moving in the direction of the bird's flight, even after the trigger is drawn, until the charge has actually left the barrel.

The latter is the old style, and is still practised by the baymen, and by all old-school sportsmen. With flint-and-steel locks it was indispensable, and though the necessity is superseded by the rapidity of fire in the percussion gun, it is by many considered the most telling style for bay snipe and wild-fowl shooting.

I am not prepared to say that it is not so; but it is a serious objection that, when once acquired, this style of shooting is not easily shaken off, but is carried to the upland, where it is of infinite detriment and disservice. It entails a slow, poking, pottering method, utterly incompatible with quick, dashing, clean shooting, and therefore, if therefore only, I would eschew it altogether.

Prodigious slaughter is recorded as having been occasionally done upon these migratory tribes "a noted gunner," says Mr. Gerund, in his admirable work on the birds of Long Island, "residing in the vicinity of Bellport, informed me that he killed one hundred and six yellow-legs, by discharging both barrels of his gun into a flock, while they were sitting along the beach. This is a higher number than I should have hit upon, had I been asked to venture an opinion on the result of a very unusually successful shot. Still it is entitled to credit. Wilson speaks of eighty-five red-breasted snipe being killed at one discharge of a musket. Audubon mentions that he was present, when one hundred and twenty-seven were killed by discharging three barrels. Mr. Brasher, during the month of May of last year, at Egg Harbor, killed thirty-three red-breasted snipe, by discharging both barrels into a flock as they were passing him. This number, although small in comparison with those mentioned above, is large, and exceeds any exploit of mv own, either with this or the former species—the yellow-leg—of both of which I have killed a goodly number, but do not think it important to tax my memory with the number shot on anyone occasion, to illustrate further the gregarious habits of this familiar bird."

These examples, of course, must be regarded as chance occurrences, and are not to be looked for as likely to befall the sportsman of to-day. Still, if he try the sport in the right season, wind and weather favoring, he will not be unusually fortunate if he till a bushel basket with the proceeds of a day's shooting in the bays and on the beaches.

The bulk of these birds have left the seaboard of the United States by the end of June at the latest; in the month of August they return from their Northern breeding places, and remain with us until late in November; being like the English snipe, much tamer and more settled in their habits than in the spring, and consequently affording far more sport to their pursuer. They are, however, for the most part, less troubled at this season than in spring by legitimate sportsmen, owing to the fact, that the real shooting season has commenced, and that game more genuine and more attractive is to be had on all sides.

WOODCOCK-SHOOTING.

In every part of the North American States and Provinces where the American woodcock, lately classed as *scolopax minor*, but more recently erected by naturalists into a distinct family as *micropiera Americana*, breeds and rears its young, law, and custom where there are no specific laws on the subject, have authorized the killing it on the first or fourth of July.

There is probably not a single sportsman in the country, who does not deprecate the practice, and desire to see it abolished; but, in the first place, it appears to be impossible to get legislative assemblies to look upon game laws in any other light than that of class legisla-tion, statutes intended to guard the amusements of the few against the rights of the many, than which no idea can be more erroneous—and no less impossible to com-mand respect or obedience to any law passed on the subject, by the masses.

The fiat of wanton destruction has gone forth

against all the wild inhabitants of the woods, the fields, the marshes, and the waters, as irrevocably as that against the Red Indian. For profit, for pleasure, for mere reck- lessness and the love of useless slaughter, the work of extermination is going on eastward, and westward, from the salmon rivers and trout streams of New Brunswick and Nova Scotia, to the prairies and plains at the foot of the Rocky Mountains.

Many years will not elapse before no species of game, whether bird, beast, or fish, perhaps, no wild ani- mal, not so much even as a thrush or a blue-bird will be left to enliven the field or the forest; and then, too late, when the healthful toil of the sportsman has no longer an object, and the table of the luxurious epicure is deprived of its choicest dainties, America will bewail its shortsightedness, neither more nor less than that of the clown who slew the goose with the eggs of gold.

In the earliest and most favorable seasons, summer woodcocks are at best but half grown, feeble on the wing, slow in flight, easy to be knocked over by the mer- est novice with any sort of gun and any sort of ammuni- tion, over any dog, or no dog at all.

In late seasons, or those wherein June floods have deluged the lowlands and drowned the first broods, the parent birds are busy in July either actually hatching or tending the second brood, so that in this case they are actually slaughtered in the breeding season.

Now woodcock invariably return year after year, if unmolested, to the same wood to breed, as do salmon to the same river. Therefore it follows, that if, year after year, nine tenths of all the birds, old and young, are shot off, as they invariably are in the present system of sum- mer shooting, the breeding stock must in the end be wholly cut off, and the race must become extinct.

Nor is this theory; for it is proved too true by

experience; and over vast tracts of country, where wood-cock swarmed some twenty years since, an ostrich is now a scarce less likely bird, to encounter.

Moreover, the extreme heat of the season, and the extraordinary difficulty of preserving the birds when killed, in fit condition for the table, renders July shoot-ing not only irksomely laborious, but useless.

The only reason that can be adduced for persever-ing in this destructive and foolish law, is the plea, that, if woodcock shooting in July were abolished, there would be no July shooting of any kind. Be it so! we can con-ceive it possible for the most ardent of sportsmen to exist one month in the year, or say two, for February is almost equally barred out with July, without shooting, especially as beating low, swampy woodlands reeking with moist heat and swarming with mosquitoes under a sun at ninety degrees in the shade, is not altogether what it is cracked up to be; though very young men may rejoice in it, and very strong men battle through it, day after day, from sunrise unto sunset.

As it stands, however, law and custom sanctioning it, woodcock-shooting in July will probably prevail, while woodcock can be found to shoot.

The early morning and the latter afternoon, are, so far as comfort both of dog and man prescribes, the preferable time of day for pursuing this sport; though in other respects, as the woodcock, unlike the quail and ruffed grouse, feeds and lies up for rest on the same ground, and in moist shadowy woodlands is more or less on the move, and to be found all day long, it is a matter of no consequence at what hour they are hunted.

Than a July woodcock, when he is first flushed over dogs, there is no easier bird in the world to kill, the only possible difficulty arising from the thick coverts in which he often lies, and the fulness of the summer verdure.

The old birds flap up lazily, hovering their

half-grown broods, and, unwilling to desert them, will often drop again within twenty feet of the muzzle of a gun which has just been discharged at them; and the young rise like owls, often fly almost into the shooter's face, so that they might he knocked down with the gun, and from pure inability to sustain a long flight, generally can be found again if missed within thirty yards. It is not once in twenty times that they will quit the covert in which they are bred, and fly across the open to a neighboring woodland.

When they lie in thick covert, it is well, as soon as the dog points, that one of the shooters should select an open spot or glade, where he can command the bird when he rises; as it is more than probable that he, whose point it is, will hardly get a shot at the bird, unless he be a very quick workman indeed in thick covert. There will be no great difficulty in this, as woodcock, early in the season, lie extremely hard, and will not ordinarily take wing until they are actually forced to do so.

Colonel Hutchinson, in his admirable work on dog-breaking, recommends that every dog should be trained to advance towards his master and flush his bird, on a signal given him by a beckon, or inward wafture of the hand, and instances the great advantage to be derived from such a habit, both in wild snipe-shooting in the open, and in American cock-shooting in heavy covert.

I have only to say, that I have never seen a dog broken to this movement. I will not say that it cannot be done, for I am well aware that, by a patient, persevering, clever, steady breaker, there is scarcely any thing, short of speaking, which an intelligent and good-tempered dog may not be brought to do; and there is no doubt, but that, by implicitly following the Colonel's directions, this is one of the things that can be taught; but there can be little question that it is one of the most difficult points to which properly to educate an animal, since, when he is once accustomed to be so waved onward, he will unconsciously become so impatient, that he will be sorely tempted to anticipate the signal, and rush in.

For my own part, looking above all to the paramount necessity of keeping the dog steady and stanch. I have leaned to the habit of *never* allowing my dogs themselves to flush their game, under any circumstances.

When at point, I have always gone in, or gone up to them, and then made them road on foot by foot, myself keeping step with them, until the bird has sprung, seeing to it that they then instantly "drop!"

This course has its disadvantages. One certainly loses some shots by it, and has to take others just as they come; whereas otherwise one may select his own ground, so as always to be sure of a fair shot. But on the other hand, one avoids the great danger of leading his dog, step by step, into error, and teaching him to commit a fault.

The moment a dog, as it seems to me, comes to expect that he shall *flush* the bird himself, and to regard *flushing* as the ultimate end, I fear he will speedily become so over-eager in this respect, as to shorten his point, and perhaps at last neglect it altogether, when his master's eye is not on him.

Every one knows that the best and steadiest dogs, when by chance they get out of range of the gun in large woodlands, and come on the point, where they are not seen, become so impatient after standing awhile, that, when the gun does not come to their relief, they will flush their game, and go on hunting as if nothing had happened. This is one of the drawbacks to hunting pointers and setters in covert, for every time they get out of sight and do this thing, as they must do it, or stand at point half the day until by chance discovered, they are rendered so much more likely to do it again; and they often come at length to such a degree of cunning, as invariably to flush every bird, running over it without taking the slightest, notice, when not in sight of the master; though, when under his eye, they will point everything none more stanchly.

For this reason, also, I consider it the duty of the gun always to be up with the dogs, and never to allow them to hunt wide or independent.

I have seen men pride themselves on being able to sit down on a post of the fence, while their dogs were beating a fifty-acre cornfield, in the idea that, if they should point, it would be easy to get up to them before the game should rise. I have also seen dogs hied in, like foxhounds, to beat heavy coppice or covert, while the shooter walks quietly along the bank, on the look-out to shoot the woodcock as they top the hushes. This, I submit, is legitimate, and beautiful spaniel work, but is utterly ruinous to pointers and setters.

A friend of mine, and otherwise a good sportsman, once told me with exultation that his setters would beat the heaviest and most impenetrable woodcock cripple, flushing and driving out every bird to him, as he walked along the outside, like spaniels, and yet would hunt steadily and point stanchly in the open. He was much astonished at my telling him that I did not hold such dogs worth the rope that should bang them. Yet such is my deliberate opinion.

I do not consider that to bag the most game *any how,* is the greatest sport, or the object; but doing it in beautiful style, with the animals showing their qualities and performance in the highest possible degree; and to get them to do this, one must occasionally sacrifice a broken-winged bird and lose a fair shot.

The great injury which accrues to dogs from getting off into the woods alone, and hunting on their own account—as some old dogs are exceedingly fond of doing, never missing an opportunity to steal away when they can do so unobserved—arises from this fact; that after they have found and pointed their bird, they must of necessity flush it themselves, and go on hunting, without dropping to charge, until they find another, when the same process is repeated.

Nothing can prevent the best dog from being in the end irretrievably ruined by this practice; and I confess it to be my own opinion, even in contradiction to so distinguished an authority as Col. Hutchinson, that no dog should *ever* be allowed or encouraged to flush or to hunt where his master is not close up with him, and able to overlook his every movement, and shoot at every bird he points, or which rises wild of him.

Some persons recommend that no bird shall ever be fired at, but shall be allowed to go away, which the dog carelessly or wantonly flushes; which is only a corollary from my axiom, as tending farther to impress on the dog the culpability of flushing. I do not consider this extreme measure necessary, but I think it corroborates my view of the subject.

There is no doubt that, as a dog can be broke to point "dead," and then "fetch" when ordered to do so, so can he be broke to point, live game, and "flush" at word of command. In one respect, however, the analogy fails here. For when the game is killed and pointed "dead," it is nine times out of ten immediately under the eye and control of the shooter, whereas the cases of finding the live bird in sight are exceptional.

I therefore advise all young shooters, who desire to become good shots and good sportsmen, always to go into covert, even the worst covert, even the worst covert, with their dogs; to keep as close to their dogs, and make the dogs keep as close to them, as possible; never to allow their dogs to flush, but always to put up their game for themselves; never to let their dogs do wrongly, without rebuke; and above all, never to do wrongly themselves, for the sake of bagging a bird or two the more.

For every easy shot that the beginner will lose, he will be the gainer by so much as he learns to kill a difficult shot; and as the American woodcock, in the open, flushed over dogs, is as easy a shot as any that flies, so even thick covert cannot make him a very difficult shot.

The only advantage that I can perceive in summer woodcock-shooting is, that it does unquestionably teach one how to kill snap shots, and to bring down birds, firing at them unseen, by calculation, in a style which can hardly be acquired in any other school.

Summer woodcock almost invariably fly straight, rising gradually till they have topped the bushes, if in close covert, and then go away nearly in a horizontal line, until they choose to alight. Their method of doing this is peculiar; they never gradually decline, lowering and lowering their flight as they near the earth, like the quail, nor pitch down at an acuter angle from their original line of flight, like the snipe; but invariably make a short, quick zigzag turn to right or left, and then dart downward in an instant, and run off swiftly five or six yards, before they settle either to feeding or to lie up.

The knowledge of this trick is essential to marking correctly, and to finding the bird when marked in.

In thick coverts, always cast the eye forward to the next weak or open spot in the direction of the bird's flight, and higher or lower, as he is declining or rising, whether to get a snap shot at a live bird, to mark one supposed to be hit and falling, or to follow up one which has gone away unhurt.

I have recovered many dead birds, which my companions have asserted not to be killed, by satisfying myself that they did not cross some weak open place immediately ahead of their course when last seen; and I have killed many, by waiting until they should cross some such opening, in otherwise impervious covert, and then letting them have it, just in the nick of time.

In summer, birds fly so slowly, and the ground is so close in which one ordinarily shoots, which renders it impossible ever to make long shots, that to give much allowance for flight is unnecessary; an inch or two in snap cross shots is the utmost that can be given. It is, however, sometimes advisable to avoid tearing the birds all to pieces with the shot, to lay the muzzle a little wide of them, so that they shall be on the edge rather than in the centre of the circle of missiles. A very small blow brings down a summer woodcock, and it is rare indeed that one rises a second time after being wounded.

As to choice of ground, much depends on the country, and much on the season.

In the southern part of New Jersey, in Salem and Gloucester Counties, where there is no autumn shooting of any consequence, the birds lie in the wide open meadows among rushes, bogs, waterflags, and the plant commonly known as skunk-cabbage, where there is not a bush or brake within miles, and are rarely found in the woods. In some districts, especially in dry weather, one must look for them in the thickest, deepest, and most tangled brakes of alder and even briers, where there is a muddy bottom; in others, they will be found in moist grassy meadow sides, where there are springs and rivulets, and patches of willow, alder, and other water-loving shrubs, and this is the prettiest ground in which to find them. Of this nature was the finest portion of my favorite old shooting grounds in Orange County, New York, and Sussex County, New Jersey, although that magnificent range contained lying of all sorts and feeding until late in winter.

Again, in mountainous districts they love the swales and little valleys, both at the base of the hills along the water-courses, and those smaller hollows through which the little upland rills percolate through stones and gravel, leaving a rich alluvial deposit of black vegetable mould, rich with ferns and water plants.

Lastly in level countries, near large rivers, as on the banks of the Wall Kyll in Orange County, and of the Passaic in the Big Piece, and at Chatham, they haunt wide open woodlands, where the great pin oak or maple trees stand fifty feet apart, and all the rich alluvial soil is free from underwood, but covered with succulent short grass.

In very wet seasons, when all the low woodlands have been submerged and drowned with water, woodcock will be found on hill-sides among second growth and saplings, especially I think of chestnuts, contiguous to wet bottoms and swampy feeding ground. Thick maple swamps in flat lands adjacent to wide meadows, and large, slow-flowing streams are always favorable; and I have found them in impracticable white cedar swamps, among underwood of rhododendrons and calmias, which the multitude call sheep-laurels.

Hot, dry weather, is the most favorable for July shooting, as it forces the birds to congregate in numbers in all the wet, shady places, so that they are easily and surely found.

Wet weather is the worst, as they can live and feed every where, in highlands, in lowlands, in ploughed fields or pastures, in any and every, likely or unlikely, place equally well; so that they can only be found few in number and dispersed over large tracts of land, making the search for them an absolute toil, in lieu of a pleasure. In hot, dry weather, when they abound, they will often run out, especially in the middle of the day and toward afternoon, late in the season, into moist low-lying cornfields by the woodsides, in which, when found, they are the most difficult shooting in the world, as they always fly down the rows without topping the corn.

Many persons believe that when the woodcock disappear, as they always do in August at the moulting season, not reappearing in numbers until the cold season commences in October, they merely retreat to the cornfields. I am satisfied that this is not so; a few may linger in such places, but of the great mass there is unquestionably a short summer migration; and, although I have heard *tall* stories of great sport had in cornfields, I have yet got to see it.

For the rest, when woodcock are not to be found in one sort of ground, they must be looked for in another, and are sometimes found most plentiful in what we should probably, at first sight, pronounce the most unlikely.

Patience and perseverance are the only sure means of obtaining ultimate success, and after all the best teaching in the world, a few grains of hard-earned experience are worth the whole of it. This is the great charm and delight of field-sports, that the longer one pursues them, the more he learns of their theory as well as their practice; and that the more he learns, the more he finds that be has yet to learn.

Each new fact discovered points some new principle to be investigated, and paves the way to some yet newer discovery; so that of them it may be truly said, with but a little variation, what Enobarbus said of Cleopatra,

> "Age cannot wither them, nor custom stale
> Their infinite variety."

In proof of which it only needs here to say, that when we again come to speak of the woodcock in the maturity of his birdhood, in the lusty days of autumn, we shall speak of a different biped altogether, and one who, instead of being an easy victim to every owner of a five-dollar popgun, will give work to a nimble finger, a sure eye, and a trusty gun, and confer lustre on the sportsman who can bring him to bag unerringly, in style.

All the rules given above in regard to decorum, and deliberation in shooting, and avoidance of danger through rashness and unsteadiness, hold good here; and in no shooting is it more necessary to hold straight than it is in summer cock-shooting, when your mark is there but for a second, and then gone.

It has been and probably will always continue a matter of doubt and dispute among sportsmen, what becomes of the woodcock at the period of his moult, which occurs—happily for the continuance of the breed, since otherwise they would be exterminated within a single year—immediately after the first month of summer shooting; say early in August; after which they vanish from their *usual* haunts, and are to be found neither in upland nor in lowland, until the *early* frosts bring them back full grown *and full feathered* in time for autumn shooting.

My opinion remains unchanged on this subject, since first I wrote on it, above twenty years ago, that there is an actual migration of the birds yet farther northward. That some few birds linger in wet spots and in moist cornfields is true: but to maintain that all the thousands of cock, which are found here in the fall, remain all the season under our noses in the maize fields, is simply absurd. Those who desire to investigate the subject may look to my Field Sports, vol. 1, p. 191.

GROUSE-SHOOTING ON THE PRAIRIES.

Of Grouse, there are six distinct varieties in the United States and British Provinces, although but three of these are ordinarily shot by sportsmen, or brought into the market. They are the ruffed grouse, commonly known east of the Delaware River as the partridge, and south of it as the pheasant; the spotted, or Canada grouse, known as the spruce partridge; and the willow grouse, known as the red-necked partridge. These three birds are all wood-haunters, and the two latter species are found only in the northern parts of Maine, the wilderness of the eastern British Provinces, and northward so far as to Labrador. The first, or ruffed grouse, has a wide geographical range, being found in all the wooded regions of North America, from Lake Superior and Texas to the Bay of Fundy. It is a fine bird on the table, but rarely affords much sport over setters and pointers, as it is a wild, shy, rambling species, and has a knack of running far ahead of the dogs, when pointed, and of rising entirely out of shot. It flies strongly and swiftly, taking wing when disturbed with an impetuous whirring rush, that is apt to disturb the nerves of a novice; and, as it for the most part takes to the tree, on being roused, it cannot generally be found a second time. The method of shooting it, usually practised by the inhabitants of districts where it abounds, is to flush it with curs or spaniels, which chase it, yelping in pursuit, until it takes the tree, and then bay at the trunk, until the gunner comes up and shoots it sitting. No sportsman, of course, condescends to such butchery; for which the only excuse is, that in thick cedar and tamarisk swamps, where it frequents, it can hardly be shot fairly. Occasionally, where underwood is heavy and the country level, they will lie to the point; and in ravines, by hunting with three guns, two of which keep well in advance of the dogs on the ridges, while the third hunts along the hollows, shots may be got. I have never, however, found it pay to hunt for them exclusively, as they are the most rambling of all birds, not adhering, like quail, to the fields and feeding grounds in the vicinity of which they are hatched, but wandering over leagues of wood and mountain, so that the pack which is seen to-day at sunset, may be twenty miles off at noon to-morrow. The erroneous legislation on the subject of this species, still farther diminishes the possibility of sport. By the twentieth of August the young broods are fully feathered, above three parts grown, and in all respects as fit for the gun as young quail two months later. At this time they are found in coveys, under care of the old birds, and where they lie in open hanging woods on hill-sides, with an undergrowth of cranberries, fern and winter-green, a kind of ground to which they are much attached, they might afford fine sport. The law, however, in the Northern States, prohibits the killing of them until the first of November, when they have dispersed themselves, and are only to be found singly, and as wild as hawks.

It is needless to comment on the childish incongruity of game-laws which allow woodcock, a weak bird, which requires the utmost protection, to be shot half-fledged in July, and will not permit the ruffed grouse, a strong wild bird, admirably able to protect itself, to be killed, until it is almost impossible to kill it at all.

To hunt it with any chance of success, exceedingly stanch dogs are requisite, which will point dead the instant they strike the scent; for if they attempt to road up to the game, it is certain to run, and rise out of distance.

In general autumn shooting, No. 8 shot, which is that most recommended for all game, will bring it down from a close-carrying, hard-hitting gun at 10 yards; but where no other game is expected, I should advise No. 6, or Eley's blue cartridges.

Few birds get on the wing more rapidly, or fly more swiftly than the ruffed grouse; and when they have got full headway, and, having been put up at a distance, come sailing past the shooter, very much allowance must be given, or the shot will surely fall behind them.

The best ground on which to look for them is the skirts of upland woods on the edge of grain and buckwheat stubbles, or crags and knolls of red cedars, which are to be found interspersed amid cultivated fields.

On mountain sides, and in pine woods or laurel brakes, I regard it nearly lost time to look for them. It is much like seeking a needle in a hay-mow, and, if found, it is heavy odds against killing.

The spruce partridge, and red-necked partridge, are out of the question; as they afford no sport.

The other three varieties are now purely Western birds; for, although the first species did formerly exist abundantly on the brush plains of Long Island, in the pines on the seashore of New Jersey, and on the scrub-oak mountains of North-eastern Pennsylvania, where perhaps a few scattered broods may still exist, they have become, to all intents and purposes, as a bird for sporting ends, extinct.

These species are, the pinnated grouse, or prairie hen, which is identical with the heath hen, as it was called on the barren lands of Long Island, and the grouse of the Pennsylvania mountains and New Jersey pines; the sharp-tailed grouse, found nearly on the same line of country as the preceding variety, but somewhat farther to the West; and the great sage grouse, or cock of the plains, which is only found in the regions of the Artemisia, in the neighborhood of the Rocky Mountains, and on the verge of the American Salt Desert.

The pinnated grouse is that best known—that which affords the best sport and the best eating; the sharp-tailed grouse, however, is shot with it to the westward of Lake Michigan, though not, I believe, to the eastward of that noble sheet of water, and is scarcely inferior to it.

The great sage grouse is not shot at all as a sport, and is only killed rarely by the voyageurs who cross the dreary wastes, in which alone it has its abode, and the adventurous hunting parties, who from time to time invade its wild fastnesses.

The pinnated grouse abhors wooded country; is rarely, if ever, found in tall timber; carefully eschews low, wet lauds; and haunts in preference, high, dry, rolling prairies, where there is little water. Indeed, it is believed that this bird never *drinks*, but takes all the liquid which it uses by picking the dew or rain, drop by drop, from the herbage or bushes on which it has fallen. This curious fact was first discovered by a gentleman, who kept a hen bird for some considerable time in a cage, and observed that she would never take water from a cup, though if any were spilled over the bars of her cage she would eagerly pick it off.

This is a beautiful and noble species, the full-grown

male weighing nearly two pounds, and being proportionally vigorous, bold, and strong on the wing. It is decidedly the finest gallinaceous game, if it may be so called, of America, and affords the greatest sport to those who are so fortunate as to reside where it abounds.

In the barrens of Kentucky and the prairie regions of Ohio, it begins first to be found in numbers, increasing as one proceeds westward, wherever there is open country, throughout Michigan, Illinois, Missouri, Arkansas, Wisconsin, Minnesota, Upper Louisiana, and Texas, and far away to the wild regions of the Columbia River.

About the 20th of August, these birds are ready for the gun. By that time they are nearly full grown, and are not easily distinguished from the adult birds by their plumage, or even by their weight, although by their power of wing and length of flight they may easily be distinguished.

During this month they lie hard, although, at times, when the weather is hot and dry, with little or no wind, they are so wild as to task a good gun.

The excessive heat of the weather, however, on those treeless plains, which is almost insufferable, and is often fatal to dogs, during the summer, renders the shooting a toil rather than a pleasure.

Early in September, however, the heats begin to moderate, and the sport becomes fine. At times it will happen, that early in this month there are sharp cold and strong winds accompanying it on the prairies, and in such weather the birds will rise for many days together entirely out of range.

They never should be fired at with smaller shot than No. 6—when they can he brought down with No. 7 or 8, it is proof positive that they are too young to be shot at all—and after September, No. 5 is the proper size, and a cartridge in the second barrel is advisable.

The finest shooting of the year, is in the latter part of the month of September and the beginning of October, when the mornings are cold and frosty, and the middle of the days mild and warm. The birds will then lie sufficiently well to afford great sport. They will not, it is true, allow dogs to draw or road close up to them, but their scent is so strong that a good pointer will stand firm at twenty yards' distance. And firmly and stanchly he must be taught to stand, if one would have sport. The slow, poking dog, that roads on till he is close in with his game, will not do a moment for this work. One *must* have fleet, high-couraged, wide-ranging dogs, that will point as stiffly as rooks the instant they strike the scent. Setters would doubtless be better than pointers for this sport, and Russian setters the best of all, as their speed, courage, endurance, and dauntless perseverance, as well as their hardness of foot, give them vastly the superiority, but for one fatal deficiency—their inability to exist, much less hunt without water.

In many of the best grouse districts it is even necessary, as it is in the vicinity of St, Louis, to carry out water in wagons for the use of the dogs. This no setters could endure. Their sufferings are painful to behold, when they cannot both drink and bathe at least every half hour in hot weather; and if they be unable to do so, they speedily lose their powers of scenting, and if unrelieved, would soon die.

For dry prairie lands, therefore, during that part of the season in which grouse can be shot to the dog at all—for after November, when the cold weather fairly sets in, they cannot ordinarily be approached within rifle range—highbred, swift pointers of the new improved stamp, are the best dogs for the sportsman's use.

The best way of hunting these birds, is to begin on the stubbles and cornfield edges in the morning, while the coveys are on the feed, and to drive them out and mark them on the open prairie, where they will scatter widely, often allowing themselves to be pointed singly, and rarely rising above two or three together. They flush strongly on a sharp pinion, and get under way in an instant, but they fly as straight as a bee-line, whether crossing or going away from the gun. The majority of the shots at birds in September are within thirty yards, and it is rarely that one is required to try a shot at above forty. At either of these distances No. 5 will stop nineteen shots out of twenty out of a really good close-shooting gun, if it be held straight. If not, the fault of the shooter, and not the wildness of the game, is blamable.

In October, the grouse becomes wilder, yet there are still many calm, warm days, with a light and pleasant breeze, when the birds will still lie and afford sport; though at this time of the season cartridges in both barrels are decidedly commendable, and even these will sometimes fail to stop an old cock grouse, when he gets under way at fifty yards, and goes away before the wind with a crow of defiance, as who should say, "Catch me, if you can."

Many persons use ten-pound guns of 9 or 10 gauge for grouse-shooting; but, unless they are men of great size, strength and endurance, I by no means advise the adoption of so formidable a weapon. An ordinary sized piece of 14 gauge, 30 to 31 inch barrels, and 7 ½ to 8 lbs. weight, with 1 ½ oz. of No. 5, will stop any thing short of a tearing old cock bird at any distance short of fifty yards, or at that, if it be an out-and-out good London gun, and beyond that there is no certainty with any gun.

Such a gun, I can safely assure any one, even if he be a strong man, and a stout, enduring walker, in addition to the other traps, ammunition, and the like, which he will have to carry, even if he be provided with an attendant to take charge of the game—which, by the way, is indispensable, since it would be something of a puzzler for one to find himself weighed down with a back load of thirty or forty brace of two lb. prairie-fowl—will be found quite as much weight as it will be either profitable or pleasant to carry during an all-day tramp over a rolling prairie in the month of August, or even on a warm Indian Summer day of brown September.

The instructions for hunting pointers in the open, as given before, are all especially applicable here. You can hardly get them to range too high or wide, as they are constantly in full sight, provided they will stand stiff and firm, until you can get up to them, and that they back in first-rate style, without the necessity of shouting, rating, or whistling to them.

Grouse are a shy, wild bird, at best; and in no bird of sport do finely broken dogs, that will beat their ground silently and steadily as you wish them, at a wave of the hand, drop, stop, or come to heel, at a motion without a word or whistle, tell more effectual a tale than on the prairie.

If your dogs be perfect and thoroughly trained, there is no objection to using two or oven three brace together, where there is range enough; but I should myself prefer, however strong my kennel, to use a single brace in the forenoon, and after luncheon, when the first dogs were becoming dull, if not tired, to start fresh with a second team. In the afternoon, the birds will be found again on the feeding grounds, whence they were driven in the morning; and where there are pea-fields, great sport may he looked for with confidence until nearly sunset.

The sportsman must remember that he has to deal with a strong, hardy bird—though he is said less frequently to carry away his death-wound than any member of his family, some of which, the quail especially, will fly off for a mile or more on an unflagging pinion, and literally *die* in mid air—and one which springs and is off like a flash of lightning. He must shoot, therefore, on the first sight, and that a sharp and quick one, yet coolly. For if he hope to kill, the muzzle must he laid so straight, that the object at thirty yards shall be exactly in the centre of the scattering charge. The dispersed pellets of the outer circumference will but sting him ineffectually. If he be crossing you, a yard's allowance in advance of him will not be too much at forty paces, and if you fetch him so, a beautiful sight it is to see him skate down at a long tangent, and rebound stone-dead from the dry earth of the prairie.

BIRDS NOT TRUE GAME.

So soon as summer woodcock-shooting and bay snipe-shooting are at an end in the Northern and Middle States, and just about the time when grouse-shooting is beginning in the West, two other kinds of sport come into season, which, though they can scarcely be called, in the strictest sense, game-shooting, have yet many votaries, and afford much amusement, beside supplying the table with two of the choicest delicacies known to America.

The upland plover, as it is generally called, not being a plover at all, but a tattler, of the same species with the yellow-leg, the willet, and some others, was first classified by Wilson, who gave it the name of his venerable friend Mr. Bartram, who has conferred much benefit on the science of natural history in America, and well merits the distinction. The Bartram's sandpiper,

Totanus Bartramius, unlike most of its relatives, is rarely, if ever, found on the sea-shore, frequenting upland downs, sheep- walks, and large short-grassed pastures in the interior, feeding on grasshoppers, and other small insects, snails, worms, grass seeds, and many wild fruits and berries, and becoming excessively fat, tender, and succulent.

It is often found in company with the golden plover, which is frequently confounded with it under the name of the frost bird, and which, in those feeding grounds, becomes greatly improved in flesh and condition.

The upland plover is, in the opinion of judges with whom I fully agree, the most delicate and delicious of all wild birds. It is often so fat that the breast bursts open on its striking the ground when shot, and the meat is the richest and most succulent that can be imagined. Its peculiar excellences are, that it never clogs; it is never greasy, nor has that rank, half-oily, half-fishy flavor, which is common, more or less, to all birds which feed on the salt marshes, and which is not entirely absent from the golden plover, even when he feeds on the upland.

The Bartram's sandpiper is about the size of the common pigeon, though far more gracefully and slenderly made, with extremely long pointed wings, and a slight recurved bill. It is a shy, wary bird, and can hardly be approached on the open plains or downs which it frequents, within gunshot, unless under cover of some artifice or quaint device. I have occasionally walked up to it, near enough to kill a few by aid of Eley's green wild-fowl cartridges, on the large open pastures in the vicinity of Bristol, Pennsylvania, known as Livingston's manor; but this was regarded as unusual good fortune, and the experiment is scarce likely to be rewarded with success.

This bird has a soft, plaintive call or whistle of two notes, which have something of a ventriloquial character, and possess this peculiarity, that when uttered close to the ear, they appear to come from a distance, and, when the bird is really two or three fields distant, sound as if near at hand.

They are found more or less abundantly on Hempstead Heath, as it is called, although not a sprig of heather ever grew on its bare and grassy surface, and on all the open, down-like hills of Long Island. In the neighborhood of Newport, Piliode Island, it is very frequent, and perhaps in that region, more than elsewhere, is pursued by the sportsmen, who visit that pleasant watering-place in summer.

It is usually shot from chaises, as the easy, two-wheeled gigs of that part of the country are called; and there is much art in driving up to them, much more, indeed, than in bringing them down when once within shot.

The shooter sits in the bottom of the gig, with his left leg advanced on the step, ready to spring out and fire the instant the chaise stops and the bird rises—the two movements being simultaneous.

The driver, as soon as he perceives the bird, which looms up large on the bare pasture, drives rapidly round him in gradually decreasing circles, keeping his eye steadily on him, and watching every motion, so as to calculate how close he can get before he will be alarmed and take wing. In this is the great tact and skill of the whole performance. A good driver will land his gun to a certainty within ten or fifteen paces of the sandpiper, and pull up his horse, describing a sort of short semi-curve away from the bird, which allows the shooter to spring out on his right foot clear of the wheel, with his back to the horse's tail, and to get a fair shot as the bird takes wing.

This sandpiper, as is the case with most of his family, rises at first with a slow unfolding of his wings and a sort of momentary hover, during which it is easy to bring him down; but the next instant he is off like a bullet, and it requires a quick eye and a sure judgment to stop him, whether crossing the gun or going from it, when he is once under full way.

Another mode is to stalk him with a pony, trained to feed gradually up to him, while the shooter stands concealed by his forelegs and shoulder in a crouching position, ready to shoot when within distance. Other persons, market shooters principally, and those who kill for gain as contrasted with sport, are content to build bough-houses in the pastures which they haunt, and to lie perdu awaiting their approach, while their confederates, in two or more parties, keep continually moving to and fro, so as to put them up, and keep them in motion, hoping that they will fly over or alight within gunshot of their concealed enemy.

I have never heard any one who could call the Bartram's sandpiper, and I have been informed that it cannot be done; nevertheless, I cannot understand the wherefore, nor do I see why, when the bough-house method of ambushment is adopted, *stools* or decoys should not be adopted as for the shore birds of the same family. I think it would succeed.

The chaise-method, however, is regarded as the genuine and correct manner of the sport, and is the only one which the genuine plover-shooter deigns to adopt. After all, it appears to me to be rather a cockney sort of shooting, not worthy to be looked on as a field sport, though it may answer to while away the monotony of a watering-place day, and drown the deep disgust which must rise in every sober breast, at sight of the doleful doings of the young Americans and Americanesses in their diurnal polka ballrooms. It is but a knack, at best; and were it not for the surpassing excellence of the plover on the table, he would, I fancy, be generally suffered to go free·in the field, and his pursuit would be held "tolerable, and not to be endured."

Almost simultaneously with plover-shooting on the upland, commences rail-shooting on the reedy flats of the rivers on which this curious and delicate little bird breeds to the northward.

The sora rail—*Rallus Carolinensis*—winters far to the southward, and on the breaking of the spring comes on to make its nest wherever there are flats and marshes on the margins of tide rivers, alternately submerged and left bare by the rise or subsidence of the waters. In such places it rears its young in vast multitudes, and is ready for the gun early in August, before which period they are rarely to be seen, although long anterior to it they can he heard clucking over all the marshy meadow's, and among the reed beds in which they abound. Their favorite haunts are the wild rice flats on the borders of many of the tide rivers of the Atlantic seaboard, as the James River in Virginia, the Susquehanna and Delaware, and their tributaries, the Raritan, the Passaic, the Hackensack, and some other streams of New Jersey, on which they literally swarm during the season, feeding in company with the reed-birds and marsh blackbirds in countless swarms, and becoming so fat that they can hardly fly, on the seeds of the aquatic rice, or oat, as it is otherwise termed.

The rail is singular in habits; it can run like a mouse among the stalks of the wild rice, and although it has a strong scent, which dogs will readily own and eagerly follow, it cannot be forced by them to take wing, with all their exertions; so much so that, when the flats are dry and the tide out, one may beat with the best setters or pointers in the world until he is weary, and that, too, where there are birds in millions, without raising half a dozen in a day.

They fly very slowly and heavily, when they do rise,

with their legs hanging down, and rarely go above twenty, or five-and-twenty yards before they drop, affording the easiest shots that can be imagined. So exceedingly slow, indeed, and heavy is their flight, that if one have been much used to shoot sharp-flying birds, snipe more especially, he is not unlikely to miss them at first by shooting before them, or over them when rising, instead of behind or below them, as he is apt to do with any sharp-flying game.

The only method of killing rail, with any success, is from boats, driven over the flats and through the reeds while the tide is rising, as fast as the power and skill of the man who pushes the sportsman with a long punt pole can accomplish. The higher the water, and the greater the speed at which the skiff is propelled, the more the sport. The birds will only take wing when the tide is rising, and then only when the boat is forced upon them with such rapidity that they can neither run nor swim away from it. When they have no other choice, they flap up just as the gunwale is run over them, fly awkwardly and lazily away for ten or twenty yards, and then drop again, if not knocked over, which can be done with the merest touch of the shot.

Unless they are killed dead, however, they are rarely recovered, as when wounded they dive to the bottom, and hold on to the weeds and water-grass till life actually leaves them. All the skill in this sport lies in the pusher, and with him, in fact, it depends whether the gunner has sport or no; for he has not only to push the boat, on which depends half the battle, but to mark the birds which go down, whether dead or without a shot, to a yard's distance, and if killed, to retrieve them.

All that the shooter has in fact got to do, is to stand firmly in the boat as it runs over the smooth, moist weeds, which is a knack easily acquired with a little practice, and to shoot as slowly and as coolly as he can.

The birds get up so close to him and fly so slowly, that he cannot, if he were to try, be too slow or deliberate with them. The further they get away, the surer he is not only not to miss, but to bring them to bag without smashing or disfiguring them. As to missing them, after the shooter has once learned to stand up in a Delaware skiff, and has got his sea legs on board, it is impossible; at least for any man who can, under any circumstances, kill any tiling.

The only things to do are to stand steady, shoot slowly, and load quickly; by observing these three rules, the merest beginner, if he have a good poleman, can rival the best and oldest sportsman in the land.

The right gun is the lightest you have, and that which scatters most. If any one were to think of having a piece built on purpose, it should be one of 26 or 28 inches barrels and 11 or 12 gauge, and one should use out of it about 1 ¼ drachm of powder and ¾ oz. of mustard-seed shot. The handiest way to load, which cannot be done too fast, as the birds often keep rising in a constant stream, is to have the shot loose in a wooden box or bowl, with a charger lying in it placed on a thwart in front of you, with powder-horn and out wadding beside it, and a loading rod at hand to save the trouble of drawing and returning the ramrod. A small light landing-net is convenient, fixed on a long handle, for retrieving the dead birds which have fallen in the water, without altering the course of the boat.

It is well to have a larger gun in the boat, either a common fowling-piece or a double duck gun, of 10 or 12 lbs., as well for shooting at the vast flocks of reed-birds which frequently cross the boat, as for picking up chance shots at green or blue-winged teal; at both of which birds, as well as at the gallinule, or common water-hen—a bird of a closely allied family, which is frequent in the South, 14 and a cut of which is prefixed to this paper, though it is less common to the northward and eastward—the rail shooter frequently gets a chance.

Prodigious bags of these easily killed and dull flying little birds are frequently made, particularly on the Delaware River, in the vicinity of Chester, and about the mouth of the Schuylkill River, in which localities as many as 175, and even 200 birds, have been killed by a single gun, and during a single tide, which does not, at most, give above two and a half or three hours' shooting.

Still, notwithstanding all this, and despite the admitted excellence of both rail and reed-bird on the table, I think the pastime but a poor one; and if it were not that there is little else to do at that season of the year, and that it does serve to keep the hand in, one which would be, to the full, as much honored in the breach as in the observance.

All sorts of absurd stories used to prevail about this little bird, whose slow flight and lazy habits appear to render it impossible for it to make long over sea migrations. It was sapiently held, and I believe still is, by the longshore Jerseymen of Gloucester and Salem counties, that it turns into a frog in the winter, and sleeps till spring in the mud. It is, however, clearly proved that it is a regular bird of passage, often boarding ships at sea under stress of weather.

AUTUMN SHOOTING.

With the latter days of October or the beginning of November, quail-shooting, as it is termed every where to the eastward, and partridge-shooting every where to the westward, of the Delaware, commences.

Woodcock are still abundant on the proper grounds, particularly among hanging woods of second growth, of chestnut interspersed with evergreens, on the hill-sides, adjacent to water, and in low level maple swamps and alder thickets.

On different ground, but still on the same ranges, on the higher slopes, where there is a mixture of crags and cedar brakes, with deciduous trees and cultivated buckwheat fields and corn stubbles, the ruffed grouse is frequently to be found.

The smaller hare, or rabbit, as it is usually and falsely railed, at this season lies in the same beats, making his form sometimes among the brambles and weeds near the side of the boundary stone-wall of some wheat or rye stubble, sometimes among the pumpkin leaves and bare stalks of a maizefield, oftener among brush-heaps where underwood has been trimmed up and piled, constantly in dry brushy coppices, and never—where an English sportsman would first look for him—among the ridges and furrows of a fallow field.

The larger hare, which turns white in winter, is becoming rare, and is now found in but few localities. In the Eastern States, about the Catskill Mountains, and in Canada, it is plentiful. It is, however, but little pursued or shot by sportsmen, though it would afford excellent sport before beagles, and is killed principally for its culinary value, which is great—whether it he converted into soup, or confectioned into ragouts; for roasted, it is dry and unsavory, even currant-jelly and herb-stuffing being added in the estimate.

When all these species of game, the latter alone excepted, are found together, as is often the case in good ground during the autumn, the shooting is the finest that can he imagined; the uncertainty what animal is about to show itself before the point, and diversity of practice required for stopping whatever it may be in the finest style, adding infinite variety and excitement to the sport.

Of autumn shooting, however, quail may be regarded as the most legitimate object, the other varieties coming in incidentally, and being killed as they come, the ruffed grouse and hare more particularly, without being, as a general thing, directly sought for of set purpose. It is not exactly so with woodcock, though it is not advisable to endeavor to find these early in the day, in autumn shooting, for, if one do so, he is likely to miss the quail while they are on the feed, and when that is the case, his chance of making a bag will be a poor one.

On starting out in the morning, which it is unnecessary to do so early as many persons imagine, unless one has a long distance to drive or walk before reaching his ground, the first thing is to know the ground, and then to consider how to beat.

I should consider eight o'clock in the morning to be quite sufficiently early to begin beating for quail, especially as the season advances. It is not well to disturb birds in their roosting-places, before they have moved, as in that, case they are apt to go away in a body without dispersing, and to lay up for the day, thoroughly alarmed, in some cunning, out-of-the-way nook, in which it is a hundred to one against finding them.

Until the dew is sufficiently exhaled to allow the birds to squat without wetting the plumage on their breasts, it, is useless to expect them to lie to the dog; and if there have been a white frost, while that is in process of exhalation there is not a chance of the scent lying.

It is not, however, on this account desirable to wait until the grass is dry, or the hoar-frost all completely exhaled; for, were that the rule, on some days in November one would have to wait until tomorrow. As soon, therefore, as, judging from the morning, quail are likely to be on the move, it is high time to be after them, since, if they fail to lie at first so as to afford a shot, they can probably be marked down, if not exactly to the spot, at least so nearly as to render it almost certain that they can be found again.

The first thing in beating ground for quail, is, if it be by any means possible, to begin driving the whole range of country, which you desire to shoot, from the leeward extremity up wind, so as to give the dogs the advantage of having the air in their noses, which at least triply facilitates their finding and pointing the birds in good style; and also to increase the chance of getting a fair shot, since quail usually prefer flying down wind to facing it, especially if it be blowing a strong breeze.

Where, from the direction of the wind, and the distance of the extreme part of the intended beat, it is not practicable to drive the whole range from the leeward, it will still be advisable to enter all such fields as seem likely to hold game, and *invariably* all spots, whether high timber, coppice, low brake, or bog meadow, into which game has been marked down, in such a manner as to let the wind face the dogs, even if it be necessary to make a circuit in order to do so.

The likeliest ground on which to find quail in the morning, while on the feed, is wheat stubbles, buckwheat stubbles, and cornfields, in which the maize has been topped in order to admit the ripening of the grain, and particularly such fields as lie adjacent to dry bog meadows, beds of bulrushes or cat-tails, as they are commonly called, from which the water has been drained or exhaled, and low spots full of rank grass with briers, low bushes, and wintergreens or cranberries, such being the places in which they love to roost.

The edges of the fields, along the hedgerows, in the angles of the snake-fences, or by the wall-sides, where sumachs and coarse weeds grow rank and tall, if the farmer be a careless one, and on the bushy verges of large woodlands, the bevies will generally be found. These places should, therefore, be the first beat, and then the middle of the fields, in which the birds comparatively seldom lie.

When the dogs find their game, it is easy for a good sportsman to judge by the attitude and action of the animal, what game it is, whether wild or tame, stationary or on the move. If the pointer stands like a statue, with his stern outstretched and rigid, his whole frame quivering with nervous excitement, his eye glaring and his lip slavering, the game is close before him. If he waver, wag his stern wistfully, and look back at his master, he is doubtful whether the game have not gone, or is not far away. If he crouch low, and show an eager and almost uncontrollable desire to crawl forward on his belly, there is surely a running bevy before him.

In the first case, all that is necessary is to take such a direction in coming up to him, as will enable you to command a fair shot as the birds rise, and as will probably drive them in the direction of the ground which you propose to beat hereafter, and in which you would prefer to have them. That is, of course, covert of some kind—the easiest you can select, or brakes which you know or shrewdly suspect to contain woodcock.

On getting abreast of the pointer, if the birds do not rise, encourage him by a gentle chirrup, and the word "On," in a low whisper; when he should lead you step by step, you keeping exact pace with him, your forward foot parallel with his shoulder, never heeding him until he has brought you to the very tuft, brake, or bush in which one of the birds—that which he first scented—lies.

If the bird do not then spring—he probably will do so, however, even before this time, on the first disturbance before the bevy has been broken, although in the heat of the day, after being shot at, they will often squat until literally trodden upon—the dog should not be pressed or urged to jump in upon the birds, but the shooter should kick the brake with his foot, or stir it with the muzzle of his gun. If he have an assistant with him to carry the game-bag and spare ammunition, it is his duty to throw a stone or beat the bushes with his stick, and *instantly to crouch to the earth*, when he *hears* the birds rise, otherwise he will often be in the way of the gun, and deprive it of a fair shot.

If a single bird rise, the sportsman's work is clear enough—particularly if it be, as it generally is, the old cock, who leads the bevy. Kill him at all hazards, if you can. The other birds will alight three fields sooner, if he is not there to lead them over the tree-tops far away. If, by good fortune, a clever double shot brings down both parents, the old cock and the old hen, the rest of the bevy may be counted on as dead sure.

If the whole bevy rise at once, on no account shoot at the bulk of it, or at a central bird. To do so, is probably to wound and cripple half a dozen, and bring down none.

Coolly select the outside birds on your own hand, those that go to the right, if you are standing to the right, and *vice versa*, leaving the balance: to the skill of your companion; if they rise very close at hand, let the first bird go fifteen yards before you raise your gun, then cover him, pull your trigger, cover another, and fire as quickly as you possibly can. If you have held straight, your brace of birds will be dead at about twenty and thirty yards' distance; at which range the No. 8 shot will have had space to spread fully, without losing force, and will kill its object clean without any risk of tearing it to pieces. The next thing is to mark the birds carefully; to do this, fix the eye on them steadily as they skate away, gradually lowering their flight—never take the eye off them for a moment; if they sink into a dip or hollow of the ground, cast your eye forward in the line of their previous flight, and if they reappear beyond it, you will catch them again. If not, you may beat for them in that vicinity, judging by their elevation above the ground when you last saw them how much farther they will have gone. If the wind be high, and they are flying with it, make plenty of allowance for that. They will often skate before it across two or three fields, and over as many fences, especially if they lie down hill, and if there be good lying ground beyond.

If they enter a wood, they are almost sure not to leave it on the other side, and you can guess with some accuracy how far they have gone into it, by the height at which they enter it, though something will depend on the nature of the lying on the inside. If there be a verge of tall grove-like timber trees, with no underwood, for some distance, and then heavy coppice, they will probably have alighted close within the edge of the bushes, and run a few yards forward before squatting.

If the wind be high, and they have entered the wood before it, they will often fly quite on to the extreme leeward side, particularly if it be the thickest portion, or if it have a bushy skirt running out into meadow land or stubbles, or again, if it have an old dry brush fence.

Indeed, if at any part of the wood there be such a fence, or if there be fallen trees with large prostrate tops, these should always be looked to with much pains or caution. A low-flying bevy will often drop to them; a running bevy will almost invariably stop in them; and if there be either ruffed grouse or hares ill the wood, it will be in such places.

I must again here caution the young sportsman against imagining that he has marked a bevy of quail, because he has lost sight of them. All that he can do in that case, is, judging by their flight, the state of the wind, and the nature of the neighboring ground, to approximate the spot for which they have made, and, by the aid of his dogs, in due season to discover it.

If he see them drop, that is another thing. Their mode of doing so is unmistakable. Quail never dart abruptly down, and very rarely, if ever, wheel round before they alight, but gradually lower their flight until they are close to the ground, when they throw themselves up with a particular motion, bringing their feet, and tails down first, and clap their wings over their backs. When they are seen to do this, they are down— and no mistake!

It is worthy of remark, that for some time after quail have dropped and squatted, they yield no scent whatever, and cannot be pointed even by the most excellent dogs on the best scenting days. It is a question, though it matters not to the sportsman, the fact being once established, whether this retention of the scent is voluntary on the part of the bird, or a peculiarity of which it is unconscious. I am, however, well satisfied that the former is the case; for at such times as it gives out no scent, the quail will not take wing at all, however narrowly the thicket or covert, of whatever sort it may chance to be, is beaten by dogs and men.

This peculiarity is especially to be noted; for to follow birds immediately to the new hiding-place, is worse than time thrown away. They will not be found until at the end of half an hour or upward, when they shall have begun to run, and if at all scattered, to call; and while the sportsman is fruitlessly toiling after these, such other birds as are feeding in the vicinity, having got through their morning meal, will have betaken themselves to the small isolated spots in which they bask and lay up during the heat of the day, and in which, unless stumbled on by accident, the best dogs will fail to find them.

The proper method, therefore, by which to have great sport in the afternoon, is to persist in beating the stubbles, feeding grounds and wood-edges, so long as the birds are on the ramble and the feed, and to take such shots as one may get, in the mean time, until the scattered birds shall begin to call, and there seem no more fresh bevies to be found. Then follow up those which have been flushed during the morning, either to the precise spots into which they have been marked, or as nearly as can be judged to the place, and proceed to beat for them with the utmost care and patience, picking up bird after bird, and never sparing to turn and return, if it were a dozen times, until every quail has been accounted for.

In this part of the sport, if the country be well

stocked, it will be hard fortune, indeed, if one do not fall in with fresh bevies; which, for the most part, lie up during the basking time of the day in precisely the same ground to which they fly for shelter when disturbed; and if this be, as it almost invariably will in rolling country, where the bevies are found on the upland slopes and hill-sides, in the swamps and hollows, it will be bad luck, indeed, if a good sprinkling of woodcock and a few ruffed grouse, do not come in to swell the bag.

The quail is, probably, the hardest bird in the world to kill quickly, certainly and cleanly. He gets under way with the speed of light; before the wind he goes like a bullet from a rifle, when he has once fairly got on his wings; he flies as fast in the thickest covert, which he affects, as he does out of it; he takes a heavy blow, and that planted exactly in the right place, to bring him down; and, above all, he has a habit of carrying away his death-wound, flying as if unhurt, until his life leaves him in mid air.

He has another knack, which disappoints the sportsman of many a snap shot, when not pointed, of lying close while one is passing him, until the back is fairly turned on him, and then off and away, with a startling whirr of his pinions, leaving nothing by which to judge of his direction, when the shooter has wheeled in great trepidation and anxiety, but a few sprays of the underwood still shaking, in the breathless calm of the woodland, where his rapid flight has stirred them.

With reference to the hunting of dogs on quail, I have no other instructions to give than those laid down before in reference to snipe, except that in covert it is necessary to keep a doubly watchful eye on all their movements, to be constantly on the guard that they shall not steal away, out of range, which if they do, they will unquestionably run riot; and, if one desire to have good sport at present, and to preserve his dogs good for the future, to work well up to them with the gun, and by no means to lag behind, however hot the afternoon, however thick the covert, however hard the work.

The right charge is 1 ½ oz. of No. 8 shot, with a cartridge of the same weight and number in the second barrel, and this will tell a tale on the hares and ruffed grouse which one may chance to encounter.

With regard to the latter bird, the difficulty of bagging him, if not much exaggerated, is entirely misstated, and attributed to false causes. It is true, he is amazingly fleet and powerful on his pinions, when he is once fully under way, and shooting down wind with his wings set and motionless. At such times one must aim a full yard ahead of him, at thirty-five or forty paces, and then if your gun be not a close carrier and a hard hitter, he will laugh you and your shot to scorn.

It is true that he rises with so prodigious a flutter and rush, that he shakes the nerves of young shooters, and nine times out of ten gets away unharmed. It is true, that when flushed once, he mostly takes to the tree and cannot be found again; and, to conclude, it is true, that he is the wildest and shyest of all wood-hunting game, and that his habit of running three or four hundred yards away, as fast as he can ply his legs, from the spot where he is pointed, and then flying off at a bee-line, renders it difficult indeed to get a shot at him.

But therein is the difficulty; not in shooting him, when one has the chance of a shot. For when he rises within range, although he does so with a fearful fuss and flutter, if one keep cool, and be not flurried, he hangs heavily at first on the air. displays a wide mark of rustling loose feathers to the aim, and is far from requiring an unusually hard blow to bring him. When he comes, great is the fall of him, and great the rejoicing over him in the dining-room and the kitchen; for if he be hung till he be thoroughly tender, quickly and discreetly roasted, and eaten off hot plates with bread sauce and fried bread crumbs, his *tout ensemble* is undeniable, and the *fumet* of his thighs and back-bone a thing worthy the knowledge of Apicius. For marking the ruffed grouse, the same rule holds good as of the quail; but, in all my experience, I have not seen this bird marked a dozen times, so wildly does it fly.

The woodcock, moreover, is now in full vigor, in full plumage, in prime condition, a large, plump bird, with a ruffed neck, a fair gray forehead, and pink legs, weighing from eight to nine and a half ounces on an average, and sometimes exceeding the latter weight by one or even two ounces.

He is, also, as different a bird to shoot now, from what he was in July, as if he were of another rare. Even before setters, instead of flapping up lazily like a half-awakened owl by daylight, he springs sharply with a clear ringing whistle, darts upward through the tree-tops, and often makes two or three quick zigzags like a wild-flushed snipe, before settling on his flight. Among saplings I have seen autumn cock twist worse, and have found them more difficult to kill, than the wildest spring snipe I have ever shot, especially if they have been raised by a beater, or by spaniels, when they will dart hither and thither like bullets through the leafless trees. It is only quick and slashing snap shots that will fetch them, and sometimes the very best shots will unavoidably miss, from the bird dropping suddenly three or four feet with a jerking twist at the very point of time when the trigger is drawn; so that, no matter how true the aim, the charge must go over him.

In marking him, the same rules are to be observed now as in summer shooting; but whereas he then rarely flew fifty yards, or went out of sight, he will now soar away half a mile, leave the wood he is flushed in, and perhaps fly across a valley or a dozen open fields, and drop on a ferny hill-side, or in a single willow bush by some lonely spring.

Nothing can be said, with certainty, I believe, concerning the lying of woodcock in autumn, except that they are never, so far as I am aware, found, as they are in some districts during the summer, in perfectly open meadow-land. Generally they seem to frequent drier and higher woodlands on the hill-sides and slopes in autumn, among second growth and saplings, or what the country people usually call sprouts. Still, I think, on the whole, the finest autumn woodcock shooting I have ever had, has keen in maple swamps, and wet brakes adjacent to bog meadows, identical in fact with their summer feeding ground. I should say, that the only sure rule is to beat every various sort of ground until you do find them; the later in the season the more they affect warm, well-sheltered coverts, where there are living springs and streamlets which never freeze. In such places they frequently linger till sharp frosts set in, and in these I have found them, on more than one occasion, in countless swarms, evidently congregated for the purpose of emigration. I have observed that this was always near the full of the moon, and that, on the day following the occurrence of these assemblages, there was not a bird left in the country.

Hare-shooting with regular sportsmen, is little regarded as a separate sport, though it well deserves to be so; it is in fact, for the most part, shot by such only, when it is now and then kicked up out of a brier bush over a dead point, in the course of a day's autumn shooting.

In many parts of the country, however, where either of the varieties, the little American hare or rabbit, and the great northern hare, which turns white in winter, are abundant, the farmers are in the habit of turning out in large parties with hounds, toward Christmas, and driving the woods as in European battues, when at times much sport is to be had.

Wherever hares are plentiful, it would well repay the ardent sportsman to keep a couple or two of small beagles on purpose for this sport, which is much prettier and more advantageously pursued than the famous English rabbit-shooting, which it much resembles; inasmuch as the hare never, like the rabbit, frustrates both dog and gun by taking to the earth, since it burrows only in the breeding season, and even then, I believe, rather uses some natural cavity in the ground, under a stone or in a hollow stump, than excavates a hiding-place for its own use.

There is not much art in hunting these timid little animals; one has only to be out betimes with the busy little beagles along the wood edges, which abut on meadows or grain stubbles, while the dew is on the herbage; or in the green woodpaths among the coverts which they love, such as bushy barrens, with bare spaces intervening among scrub oaks, dwarf pines and laurels—to find their trail as they come in from feeding.

The merry little hounds will soon push them up, and will stick to them stanchly, following them through all their mazes with unerring industry, and making the low woods vocal with their small but sonorous melody.

One may easily keep up with them if he pleases, for their speed through the covert does not exceed a man's fair jog-trot, and it is beautiful to see them work and east themselves, and feather to the scent, and spring to their companions when one opens on his game; but the way to kill the most hares is to stand still, pretty well concealed by some pine bush or stump, keeping every limb perfectly motionless, with as many open glades around you and under your eye as you can command, nearly in the spot from which the *same* was first started. He is perfectly certain to return, once and again; for it is his nature ever to run in small rings, endeavoring to deceive his pursuers by foiling his own track, rather than to outstrip them by speed. I never knew an instance of either variety going straight away, or of the beagles being above a quarter of an hour out of hearing. Indeed, they are rarely so long absent. Their cheery cry at the return will tell the sportsman when and in which direction to look for his game; but he must look sharp, or he will be apt to find, to his astonishment, by seeing the hounds carry the scent past his face within ten paces, that the small gray rascal has stolen before his eyes unobserved, under cover of—it is wonderful how—little brush or low herbage, or jumped across an opening while his eyes were momentarily averted.

Again, if he do not keep himself perfectly motionless, his time is thrown away. A hare before hounds, and sometimes even a deer, if the wind be not fairly in his nostrils from the enemy, will run straight up to a man, standing in full view in the open, if he move not hand, head nor foot, as if he were a post, perhaps mistaking him for such. But let him wink but an eyelid perceptibly, and it will be off at a tangent, like lightning. It is singular, indeed; but his voice not only has less effect in deterring the animal or increasing its speed, than the show of any movement, but actually causes it to stop and listen.

A sharp whistle, or the simulated bleat of a fawn, will cause either the one or the other of these wary animals to stop short in full career, within point blank range of the gun; and the hare, at such an interruption, will sit up on end, with one ear cocked forward and the other backward to catch the smallest sound.

The hare has the power and the habit, it seems, in a great degree, of turning its large and prominent eyeballs so as to turn its range of vision, when pursued, as it does its ears, almost directly backward; and it must be something very abrupt and decided in the way of sound or sight, directly in front of it, which shall attract its attention.

This does not appear to me to extend to such a length in the American as in the European hare; which latter, when flying in terror from sounds behind it, as in a battue, seems to be wholly blind to everything in front of it, and has been known to run actually into the mouth of a dog, and to break its neck by coming into collision with one of its fellows flying in similar consternation, along some winding woodpath.

Though it is, however, easy enough to get shots at the hare running before hounds in covert, it is by no means so easy to shoot him; and many men, who can follow a wild duck cutting the air at the rate of ninety miles an hour—which, by the way, is his ordinary measured speed—with a heavy duck-gun, and bring him down to a certain, will be puzzled and foiled completely by a hare dodging in a brake, or glancing across a wood road, seen for a second, and lost as soon as seen. Here no following is possible, and the man who expects to kill his hare by shooting at him, might as well shoot at the moon, in the hope of bringing it down with a charge of a double B. To kill him the instant he shows his nose out of the brake on one side of the footpath, up with your gun and blaze away, like lightning, at the edge of the bushes on the opposite side. If you take your level at the right height—that is to say, *low* enough—when he has disappeared across the path in the shrubbery beyond, and you have reloaded and recapped your gun, you will find him dead, shot in the forepart, lying just where he fell, having turned one summersault after the shot struck him.

A single couple of beagles is all that is absolutely necessary for this pretty and enlivening pastime; but it is needless to say, that the more there are in the field the merrier is the cry and the greater the sport.

Wherever there are extensive ranges of scrub-oak barrens, pine barrens, or any tracts of low bushy underwood, there is little doubt of finding the smaller hare in abundance.

He is plentiful in the woodlands of southern New Jersey, and in the old fields and worn-out lands of Maryland, Delaware, and Virginia.

In the pine forests of Maine the larger hare is abundant, and with two guns and ten couple of the right sort of hounds, I could desire no better sport than to hunt him on some fine bright September morning.

WILD FOWL SHOOTING.

Wild fowl shooting in America may properly be distinguished into three classes: the Chesapeake Bay shooting, to which, as the finest of all, both in the quality of the game killed and the greatness of the sport, the palm must be assigned; sea-shooting, over decoys, which, though tedious, and requiring much exposure to wild wintry weather, is a favorite amusement with enthusiastic sportsmen; and lastly inland duck-shooting, which, in the places where it is to be had in perfection, is a most exciting and delightful pursuit.

The game killed, in these three different kinds of sport, are as different as the modes adopted of bringing them to bag.

In the Chesapeake Bay shooting, in which I include, of course, all the rivers which debouch into that fine sheet of water, all more or less frequented in winter by innumerable legions of wild fowl, the birds most commonly met with and most eagerly pursued, are the wild swan, *Cycnus Americanus*—a species peculiar to the American Continent; the canvas-back duck, *fuligida valisneria*, so named from the wild celery, which is its favorite food, whence it derives its delicious flavor; the red-head, *fuligula ferina*, next in excellence to the canvas-back, and little inferior to it when killed in the region of wild rice and wild celery; the American widgeon or bald-pate, *anas Americana*, and the scaup, broad-bill, blue-bill, or black-head, as it is variously denominated in various localities, the latter being its Chesapeake alias, *anas Marila;* these being considered the choicest, and those which improve most by the food of that region.

These birds, with the ordinary wild goose, *anas Canadensis*, do not generally appear in these waters until the middle of November, when the cold has already been severe at the north, and ice is beginning to make even in those warmer regions.

The smaller ducks, such as the buffel-headed duck, *anas albida*, the ruddy duck, *anas rubida*, and the long-tailed duck or south-southerly, *anas glacialis*, make their appearance somewhat earlier in the season; but they are little regarded, and seldom pursued by sportsmen.

Of the larger ducks, all of which feed on the same grasses, and acquire so nearly the same flavor that they are not easily distinguishable even by epicures, the canvas-back is the first, the red-head, or, according to some, the widgeon is the second, and the scaup, or black-head, the least deserving of the lot.

It is worthy of remark, that within the last few years the English widgeon, and the English green-winged teal, *anas Penelope*, and *anas Grecca*, both of which are distinct varieties from the American kinds, distinguishable by small though plain and immutable marks, are becoming frequent among us, working their way, as it would seem, from the north-east south-westerly, having been, until within the last twenty-five years, unknown on this continent.

The annexed cut represents the English widgeon, the principal difference between which and the American bird is, that the former has the whole of the wing-coverts pure white, tipped with black, whereas in the latter the primary coverts are brown and the secondaries only white. This distinction is well preserved in the cut, as also the variation in the shape and coloring of the head and bill.

The English widgeon was first noticed by Mr. J. N. Lawrence in Fulton market, having been shot on Long Island, and the discovery was communicated by him to Mr. Giraud, who has embodied it in his admirable work on the birds of Long Island. Since that period, however, it has been killed so frequently as to merit a place among the birds of America.

The existence on this continent of the English green-winged teal, which wants the peculiar lunated bar of white, bifurcated at the inferior extremity, crossing the scapulars, which is so conspicuous in the males of the American species, I was myself, I believe, the first to establish; having remarked the fact—which had induced me, in the first instance, to suppose the distinctive bar a mere casual variation, not a specific distinction—that

I had unquestionably shot many birds in this country, without that mark, to Mr. J. C. Bell, the distinguished naturalist and taxidermist of New York, who had then no knowledge of the bird as belonging to this country, but who informed me only the other day, that recently many specimens have been brought to him. It was previously known to exist in Nova Scotia.

It is worthy of remark here, that many varieties of wild fowl, formerly confined to extreme northern and southern latitudes, are, of late, greatly extending their ranges, and meeting, as it were, midway between their natural abodes. Several Arctic fowls, which were formerly never seen westward of Cape Cod, and others of which the farthest eastern limit was the Cape of Florida, now meet, as it were, on the neutral ground of the Jersey bays and the Long Island shore.

The method of shooting wild fowl on Chesapeake Bay, is to wait for them as they fly up and down, in proportion as the flats on which they feed are submerged too deeply for their use by the rise of the spring tides, behind screens erected for the purpose on the points and islands over which they must necessarily pass, and thence shoot them on the wing.

The sport often had by parties at these points, which are for the most part rented by clubs of sportsmen or by individuals, and very jealously preserved, is magnificent. The shooting, however, is peculiar, and exceedingly difficult to those unused to it, who are apt to miss all sorts of fair shots, though good marksmen on the upland at other game. This is owing to the fact, that many of the shots have to be fired almost perpendicularly in the air at flocks passing directly over the sportsman's head—a difficult shot at the best to kill, and one in which it is doubly difficult to make a large allowance for the distance and the speed at which the fowl are flying. This is, moreover, very deceptive. Duck of all kinds, although their flight appears slow and lumbering with a vast expenditure of flapping, fly infinitely faster than is commonly supposed, as is evident from their having been minuted by telegraph while passing points and promontories on the sea-coast, and found to travel, when on their ordinary comings and goings, at the rate of ninety miles an hour. Of all the missed shots at ducks flying past or over the gun, nineteen-twentieths fall far behind the object.

Another point worthy of notice is this, that the breast of all wild fowl is nearly impenetrably cuirassed against shot by the dense Cushion of down which envelopes it, and that a blow behind is rarely on the instant effective to bring down the fowl. So that unless the charge take effect in the head and neck, well before the wing, or a pinion be broken, the shot is generally thrown away. It is, therefore, scarcely possible to fire too far in advance of a single bird, crossing or passing over the gun at from forty to sixty yards' distance.

The guns most generally used are double-barrels of twelve or fourteen pounds' weight, and about 8 calibre; I greatly advise, however, the use of two single guns, each of fourteen lbs. and 5 gauge, which will carry a quarter of a lb. of shot with ease from the shoulder, will chamber BB as easily as the others will No. 2—will recoil less, and will do their work at flocks far more effectively at long or short ranges.

These guns, moreover, are infinitely safer, and are handled as readily, if lightened toward the muzzle by removing the ramrod and ramrod pipes, using a detached loading-rod instead, and if needful, improving the balance of the piece by loading the butt with lead. A little practice will soon enable a sportsman to use two of these guns quickly enough to discharge both into the same flock, and if he succeed in doing so, great will be the havoc he will make.

Another method, much employed in this paradise of duck shooters, is to *tole* the clucks, as it is called, while they are feeding along shore, quite out of range, into shooting distance of the ambushed fowler, by means of a dog[13] trained to gambol to and fro along the margin of the stream, in such a manner as to attract the attention of the fowl, which are so easily excited to a sort of insane curiosity by his movements, that the same flock have been known to swim in half a dozen successive times, each time receiving a murderous volley, and leaving the waters Strewed with their dead and wounded, without appearing to take permanent alarm. The black-head is, of all the ducks which frequent those waters, that which is *toled* the most readily, and the bald-pate the shyest.

The shots obtained in this manner are, of course, sitting shots, the birds sailing in from forty to seventy yards' distance from the shore; and it is necessary to remember, that nothing is so deceptive as shooting over water; that as the gunner lies in ambush, he is almost precisely on the level of his object, and that it is the natural effect of these causes to produce an overshooting of his mark. If the piece be levelled directly, as it seems, at the middle of the flock, the whole charge will almost surely pass far above them. The correct way to aim is to see the whole of the nearest duck in full relief above the sight; this level will in all probability rake the entire breadth of the mass of ducks, and even if the charge strike on the near side of them, the ricochet will be far more fatal than a plunging shot.

Paddling up to the birds in canoes on the feeding grounds, sailing into them, or firing with heavy swivels from punts, are strictly prohibited, as they cause the fowl wholly to desert places where such practices obtain, and

13 The action of the dog is described above, under the head of Retrievers, at p. 156

are esteemed—and that deservedly—unsportsmanlike, and unworthy of gentlemen.

For all fowl shooting on salt water, where the saline particles of the atmosphere disorganize the gunpowder from their affinity with the saltpetre, large coarsegrained cannon powder is preferable to the finer article, and the best of all is Hawker's ducking powder, prepared by Curtis and Harvey. This, with the best of Starkey's central fire-caps, will insure the discharge of the gun even in a sea-mist.

For the rest, I think fowl shooters almost invariably overcharge with powder, and use shot of too coarse a grain. The shot is amply large, which will break the pinion of the game at which it is fired, at seventy yards. All extra weight is thrown away, with a positive loss in the number of shot lodged in the same space.

SS in green cartridges are all very well for wild swan shooting, and in 4 oz. cartridges for a gun of 5 calibre, it will be difficult to say how far they will not carry, and kill. I should dislike marvellously to be in the fair range of one at half a mile. BB is proper for geese or brant, but for all other fowl, for the largest shoulder-guns 1 or 2 is amply large for any range; and from guns not exceeding 10 gauge, No 3 or 4 will do more execution. Equal measures, not weights, of shot and powder, are, in my judgment, the best proportions for all guns.

Sea-shooting of wild fowl, as it is practised on all the bays as they are improperly called, being in truth shallow, land-locked sheets of water or lagoons, lying along the greater part of the Atlantic seaboard of the United States, from Florida so far north as to the eastern extremity of Long Island, between an outer beach or sea-hank of sand or shingle, thrown up by the action of the surf and undertow, and the main land, is for the most part of one character.

It is prosecuted either from boats, concealed in nooks cut out of the sedgy points or islands of sedge and hassock, with which these waters abound, and partially covered with reeds, sea-weed, salt meadow hay, and other trash; or from what are technically called batteries, narrow, shallow, coffin-like boxes of wood, just large enough to contain one person lying flat on his back, provided with a margin of boards nearly horizontal, but slightly inclined upward at the outer edge like the brim of a soup-plate, which, resting on the surface of the water, support the box itself, so that it cannot absolutely sink, but is submerged by the weight of the concealed shooter until its edges are level with the sea on which it rests. The flat boards or margins above described, are covered with sand, pebbles, small shells, and sea-weeds, so that it resembles a little shoal peering above the water, or a lot of floating wrack and trash, and is not suspected by the fowl.

This treacherous contrivance is moored exactly on the flats where the fowl feed, the gunner is conveyed to it in a boat by a partner, who, as soon as he is perfectly ensconced and invisible, with his heavy guns and ammunition, and provided with his fleet of decoys of all kinds and sizes, exactly representing all the varieties of fowl which he may expect, riding at anchor around him,

within half gunshot, rows off to a distance, and plies bus-
ily about the bays, disturbing all the flocks he can discover on the feed, in the hope that, as they fly over, they
may descry the decoys and fly to them.

When the roar of his confederate's gun informs
him that execution has been done, he rows to the spot,
gathers up the cripples, and withdraws again as before
to beat up the neighboring flats and shallows for fresh
teams of victims.

The slaughter committed from these batteries is
often prodigious; but so irksome, if not actually painful is the cramped position in which the sportsman is
compelled to lie, that, to my thinking, it scarcely can be
called sport.

Unsportsmanlike, in one sense, it certainly is to the
last degree, that it harasses the birds to such an extent,
by the very fact that they are slain unseen and unsus-
pecting on their very feeding grounds, where most they
desire to be quiet and unmolested, as in the end, if long
persisted in, to make them entirely abandon the flats on
which it is practised, and betake themselves to other and
safer localities.

For this reason the use of these batteries has been
generally prohibited by law; but on Long Island, as all
other statutory provisions for the protection of game,
this salutary enactment is utterly disregarded, and the
birds arc decimated daily throughout the season, where
they ought to be the most protected, and are accordingly becoming annually fewer, wilder, and less easy of
access.

On the Jersey waters of Squam Beach, Barnegat,
greater and lesser Egg Harbor, and other places of
equal resort by wild fowl, the use of these destructive
machines is proscribed by public opinion of the gunners themselves; and these men being a bold, hardy,
lawless, and some say, half-piratical race, half-fowlers,

half-fishermen, and more than half-wreckers, who are apt to enforce the laws of their own enactment by the strong hand and with the aid of their Queen Anne's muskets and a handful of heavy shot; the prohibition of batteries, as also of sail-boats provided with swivels, is on the whole enforced with tolerable regularity.

On the waters of the Chesapeake Bay, the law again provides against the use of batteries, as also of sail-boats, and punts with swivels; but here also it is the strong hand of the lawful and sportsmanlike gunners which alone carries out and vindicates the operation of the law; and it is not without desperate, and at times even bloody affrays, that the poachers are prevented from carrying on their ruinous trade.

In those waters, however, the shores for the most part belonging to comparatively few and wealthy proprietors, the points and islands being, as I have observed, ordinarily rented by clubs of sportsmen, and the excellence and actual *value* of the game being of sufficient importance to render its protection an object, the laws are rigidly enforced, preservation is effected, and notwithstanding the countless multitudes which are yearly destroyed, they do not appear very materially to decrease in number.

The other mode, described above, of shooting from boats moored among the hassocks in the bays, is not liable to this objection, as the birds are shot, not while in the act of feeding, but always on the wing, as they are passing up and down from one flat to another, accordingly as this is submerged too deeply, or that left wholly bare, by the rising or falling of the tide.

This, it seems, does not molest or disturb them to such a degree as to cause their abandonment of the neighborhood, and only operates so far as to render them shy and fearful of the points whence they are peppered, causing them to fly down the middle of the bays and channels, without passing over the land, if they can avoid it.

This it is which gives scope to all the gunner's ingenuity, both in the selection of his points in reference to the wind which may be blowing, and the knowledge of the feeding grounds, in order that the fowl, as they are driven up from the outer beaches by the rising tides to the inner marshes, may he jammed down by stress of weather upon the station which he has chosen; and in imitating the call of the various species of which he is in pursuit, by which he often succeeds in seducing them down from their secure elevation, to seek company with his painted wooden decoys, and find a speedy death.

The birds which are most easily called down are the Canadian wild geese, the noblest and best of all the tribes taken in this fashion, whose loud and sonorous hawnking is admirably simulated by many of the amphibious natives of the duck-haunted bays, and not a few amateurs.

The most impracticable of them all is the brant, the gabble of which, somewhat resembling the distant clamor of a pack of hounds in full cry, is generally said to be inimitable to any useful end.

The skill to be acquired in shooting these birds— for getting shots at them, the amateur gunner is compelled to rely on the skill and cleverness of his guide or boatman—consists only in shooting sufficiently in advance of the passing flocks, or in keeping the gun in such continuous motion, following up their flight, that the shot shall not fall behind them.

No retriever or dog of any kind is required for this sport in the other sea bays, but in the Chesapeake the best Newfoundland dogs are used, and are, indeed, imperatively necessary.

In regard to guns, ammunition, and the mode of charging, especially in the avoidance of overloading

and the use of too large shot, the rules prescribed heretofore will be found applicable.

The species of fowl usually killed and most prized,
in the Atlantic bays and lagoons, are the wild goose,
anas Canadensis; the brant, *anas bernicla:* the scaup or
broad- bill, of two kinds, greater and smaller, *anas marila;* the dusky duck, *anas obscura;* the red-head, *fuligula
ferina;* occasionally the canvas-back, *fuligula valisneria,*
which is but a third-rate fowl where it cannot obtain the
wild celery and inferior to both the varieties last mentioned; and the ring-necked duck, *fuligula rufitorques.* In
addition to these, the coarse and fishy sea-ducks, known
as coots, namely, the scoter, the velvet-duck, and the
surf-duck, and sometimes the harlequin-duck, the pied-
duck, the ring-duck, and even the eider-duck, are visitants to our bays and beaches. Their flesh is, however,
worthless, and unless for specimens, or, in the ease of
the last named, for its down, they are literally not worth
the powder. The mergansers, commonly known as shell-
drakes, fall under the same category, as do also the south-
southerlies, which, however, for the most part, take far
too good care of themselves to venture near enough to
the stools to tempt the gunner's forbearance.

The little dippers, or buffet-headed ducks, are held
in small estimation from their inferior size, and on salt
water they are neither so fat nor so succulent as when
killed on inland ponds and streams, where they are
highly and deservedly esteemed; and the same is the
case with the blue-winged teal, when it is found on the
bays, as it is at some seasons.

The winter is the best season for the prosecution of
this sport, and the severer the frost, and the rougher the
winds and waters, the better tile chance of success. It is,
therefore, no holiday work, no light matter to be undertaken as a frolic, by rheumatic or otherwise delicate folk,
who are apt to catch cold if they sit in a thorough draft,

and shiver at a strong breeze through a key-hole. It is
hard, earnest, downright work. It requires a man, who
not only *can* rough it, but who loves to rough it, for its
own sake—who can endure cold, wet, fatigue, and the
weariness of long waiting, not only with patience but
with pleasure, and at last feel himself well rewarded if he
make a good bag, and not altogether unrewarded, if he
make a bad one. If he cannot bring himself to this, he
would far better stay at home by his cosy fireside, and
pretty wife or pleasant friend; and, if he be past forty-
five years old, I do not know but he were wiser to do so,
whether or no.

    The third and last variety of fowl shooting is inland
duck-shooting, whether on the large fresh water lakes
and rivers of the interior, on the vast half saline, half
fresh meadows, where the tide waters meet the springs
and rivulets which drain the uplands, along the margin
of meadow-watering brooklets, or on wide, marshy, and
at times submerged tracts, such as the drowned lands
of Orange County, New York, the snipe meadows of
New Jersey, the saline districts of Western New York,
and thousands and tens of thousands of similar regions,
north, west, east and south, throughout the United
States and British Provinces.

In all these localities in the autumn and the spring, there is to be had immense sport; the varieties of duck generally killed, all of which are excellent, especially where there are wild rice lakes, as in Canada and the Western States, are the mallard and duck, *Anas Boscbas;* the pin-tailed duck, *Anas acuta;* the blue-winged teal, *Anas discors;* the green-winged teal, *Anas Carolinensis,* a likeness of which adorns the last page, showing the lunated bar across the scapulars, which distinguishes him from his European cousin-german; the golden eye, *Anas dangula,* which is abundant on Lake Champlain; the summer duck, *Dendronessa sponsa;* the buffet-headed duck, *Anas albeola;* and the dusky duck, *Anas obscura;* which last must be added, although properly it is a marine rather than a fresh-water duck. The canvas-back, redhead, scaup, widgeon, and ring-necked duck, all properly and chiefly sea-ducks, are found on the western rivers, the great lakes, and the head waters of the Mississippi and Missouri, where also wild geese, wild swans, and a second variety of that noble bird, unknown elsewhere, the great trumpeter swan, *Cycnus Buccinator,* with an alar extent of no less than ten feet, abound on the waters and morasses. There is also a variety of brant, known as Hutchins' brant, and a large winter duck, nondescript I believe, until I described it myself after a visit to the great Georgian bay of Lake Huron in 1849, found in great numbers in the same regions of which the snow goose, *Anas hyperboreus,* and the white-fronted goose, *Anas crytliriopas.* are occasional autumnal visitants.

The methods of hunting wild ducks and wild geese on inland streams and marshes are threefold: First, to beat the marshes and reed lands along the margins of slow- running, sedgy streams, with one or more well broke, mute water-spaniels, trained to hunt close and to retrieve. This is a beautiful and scientific sport, the best mode of pursuing which, as well as of breaking dogs for it, is described at length under the head of water-spaniels and retrievers, at pages 152 and 153.

The second method, one much practised on the streams flowing through woodlands into the great northern lakes, is to take a stand at nightfall or day-break, at some spot over which they fly, near the river's mouth, going out to the open lake or returning to their roosting-places in the inland morasses. The flights last not above an hour, or a little over, morning and evening; but during that space of time two or three guns may occupy themselves incessantly, and their bearers will probably return well loaded.

The third and last method, is to paddle slowly and silently in a hark canoe, through the shallow ride lakes of Canada and the West, with or without a brace or two of water-spaniels swimming constantly about the barque, to flush the living and retrieve the dead.

The presence of the spaniels will add much to the interest and perfection of the sport; but except as to retrieving the cripples, many of which will other-wise escape, I know not that they will add much to the amount of the bag; for in those places, at the proper sea-son, the name of the ducks is absolutely legion, and they rise in such clouds before the canoe out of the thickly set wild rice, that the worst shot can scarcely fail to fill his vessel. The first thing to be acquired for this kind of shooting, is the ability to move and shoot out of a birch canoe, without upsetting it, a thing by no means easy to be done, and to be gained only by practice.

For shooting them, no other instructions are required than those already given in regard to wild fowl in general—to fire quickly on the first sight, and to allow well for the speed of cross shots, or rising shots, although going straight from you.

The best gun for inland duck-shooting is the kind described above, and of which John Mullins, of New

York, is strongly recommended as a maker, of about 10 lbs. weight, 10 gauge and thirty-four inch barrels, barlocks, and plain case-hardened steel mountings; such a piece will throw 3 oz. of No. 2 shot, if required—but in nine cases out of ten 4, or 3 at most, will be amply sufficient—with telling force over an ample area, so as to kill surely at sixty yards. In the Appendix, I annex a letter from this responsible maker, containing the scale of his rates for guns of different classes and calibres, which may be found useful to distant readers.

THE FOREST AND THE PLAINS.

Of all those grander wild sports of the extreme North and West, the moose and cariboo hunting of the British provincial forests, and of the hyperborean regions of Maine; the elk, buffalo, and antelope hunting of the western plains and prairies; the bear hunting of Arkansas and the Southwest; nay, even of the deer and turkey hunting of the regions wherein those animals are still to be found, survivors of the innumerable multitudes which formerly roamed unmolested from ocean to ocean; there are no rules, positive, which can be laid down, no instructions which can be of much use to the young sportsman. Where the rifle, or the double gun with buck-shot is the implement, beyond the mere directions how to take aim, load, and fire to the best advantage, nothing can be taught.

Of all things wholly unteachable by writing or oral instruction, unless upon the spot, with practice and example to illustrate precept, the most impracticable is woodcraft.

How to find or follow the trail of an animal, itself not discernible to the sharpest unpractised eyes, in the seemingly untrodden grass, or on the leaf-strewn surface of the pathless soil of the wilderness, cannot be taught by words written or spoken.

How to judge by the foot-prints, half seen, of bear or deer, as a woodman will do at a glance, whether the animal which left the sign was young or old, fat or lean, going to or returning from his lair, how long he has gone by, and whether it avails to follow him or not, can only be learned by long experience, attentive observation, and a course of pupilage, on the ground, under thorough and competent teachers.

In the same way it is evident that one cannot give directions how one shall steal up, unseen and unheard, within rifle shot of a herd of deer, a gang of elk, or a watchful moose or cariboo. This may be told, and this is about all, that you must invariably advance on all wild animals which it is desirable to stalk, *up wind.* If you attempt to go down wind on them, their unerring scent will frustrate your every endeavor, and render it impossible to approach within half a mile, much less within gunshot of the quarry. It is wise also to stalk game so far as it is possible, owing to the state of the wind, with the sun on your back and in their eyes.

Wild fowl on the water are more easily stalked, where the ground will allow it, from below upward, and mountain-dwelling animals from above downward, owing to the fact that these are apt to be expectant, under ordinary circumstances, of enemies coming upon them from higher, those from lower ground.

Deer are killed by three different methods: driving with hounds to guns posted at such passes as the hunted animals are likely to make for when afoot before dogs; pursuing on horseback, across country, with packs of hounds, having it in view to shoot them with buck-shot, whenever the rider can approach them nearly enough to do so; and still-hunting, or stalking them in the forest, or on the plains, without the aid of dogs, relying on the eye and intelligence of the sportsman alone.

Fire-hunting from canoes by night, and lying in ambush at some solitary drinking-place or salt-lick, I cannot regard as legitimate sporting, though both are undeniable ways of getting venison, when one happens to be in want of it; because I conceive there is no sport, where there is no skill exhibited, no doubt of success, and no chance of escape left to the quarry either by flight or resistance.

Neither do I dwell upon shooting deer over pointers—for not describing which, I have seen myself recently grossly and abusively commented upon by a vulgar, illiterate, anonymous western clown, writing under the signature of "Quid," from Quincy, Illinois, in the columns of the New York Spirit of the Times, who neither spells correctly nor writes grammatically, and who resorts to the contemptible meanness of making false quotations from my works in order to magnify himself and make a case against me. Of course, both I, and—as I presume—my friend Dr. Lewis, who comes in likewise for a share of this nameless slanderer's abuse—must feel highly gratified to learn that our writings are read by such fellows as "Quid" with "disgust and loathing." Mine, at least, are only intended for men who feel like gentlemen and act like sportsmen.

But to return from this brief digression, I have not described deer-shooting over pointers—not because it is any thing new or unknown that a pointer or setter will stand upon deer if he get a chance, or that, if he get a chance point at one, a sportsman would and could shoot him with buck-shot—but simply because the places where such things can be done systematically, if any where, are so rare as to be out of all rule of example; because, neither I, nor, I will venture to say, one in ten thousand of all the deer hunters in America ever dreamed of going out, of set purpose, to beat for deer with setters; and because, if there be any place where this can be done, there are other modes which would afford five times the sport.

In a word, however, I utterly disbelieve that Mr. Quid, either at Quincy, Illinois, or any where else, ever got fifteen points at deer, and killed half the number, as he implies, in a morning. This is, however, but the ignoble work of breaking a butterfly on the wheel! Let Mr. Quid go!

In these three kinds of deer hunting, all that the beginner has to do, is, if placed at a stand, to hold himself perfectly silent, perfectly motionless, perfectly observant and attentive, neither to smoke cigars, nor go to sleep; neither to fire his gun at any thing but the deer, nor to let the deer go past without firing at him. In a word, let him keep his mouth shut, his eyes open, and his head clear, trust in Providence, and be patient.

If he be riding to hounds, let him choose out the best rider, and the person best acquainted with the country whom to follow, let him stick upon his horse as well as he can, hold him hard by the head with the snaffle, keep his spurs out of his sides, put his head straight at whatever fence he means to take, refuse no necessary, and ride at no unnecessary, leap, and when he fires, grip the horse firmly with the knees, and bear his weight on the stirrup of the side *toward* which he fires, rather than on the other, since, if the horse swerve, it will be away from the shot, not toward it. If he be riding at speed on parallel lines with the game at which he shoots, little allowance will be necessary, as the gun and its object advance at nearly equal rates.

In still-hunting, which no one, a novice, of course, dreams of doing, except in company with an experienced guide, the only thing to do is to follow silently in his wake, imitate all his motions, observe all that he observes, and whatever else one may; ask for explanations, not at the time, but by the camp fire, when the hunt is over; keep cool, and when the critical moment come, if come it may, take as good an aim and shoot as quickly and as straight as he can.

Elk and moose hunting, and yet more, cariboo hunting, partake all of the character of still-hunting—except the pursuit of the former when it is made with greyhounds or deer hounds on the prairies—with the addition of difficulty and hardship of running many miles on snow-shoes in pursuit of the vast and cumbrous animals over the frozen snow crust of the wintry wilderness, and camping out many nights in succession, under the inclement sky of the high northern latitudes, with the thermometer at 40 degrees, or more, below zero.

Buffalo are sometimes stalked, but more usually ridden down by mere speed of horses without the aid of hounds, and shot in full career with carbine or rifle, by the hunter galloping side by side with them. The horsemanship is the great art to be attained, and skill is needful both to gallop at speed safely over the broken and interrupted surface of the wild plains, and to sit firmly and securely, when the horse swerves or sheers off, as he is taught to do, the instant the shot is fired, to avoid the sudden charge of the infuriate beast.

The best place at which to fire in any large animal in motion, is immediately behind the bend of the shoulder, where the fore-arm is articulated with the shoulder-blade, at about two thirds the distance from the withers, measured downward to the elbow. If the ball, or charge of buckshot be lodged here, it will infallibly strike the heart. The head should never be aimed at unless in a standing shot, by a certain and steady marksman with a ball in his gun.

For large game shooting, the rifle should not carry a smaller ball than 32, and I greatly prefer 16 to the lb. A deer which will carry off a bullet of 60 or less to the pound, apparently unharmed, and die of it in a week afterward in misery, and unprofitably in the lonely wilderness, will either fall to the shot with broken bones, or bleed to death in a few leaps, more or less, from the large wound inflicted by an ounce ball.

For buffalo hunting on horseback, the new breech-loading carbine, described at page 76, is the implement of all others, for ease of loading, quickness of firing, and the tremendous penetration of its large acorn-shaped ball.

All sporting rifles should be fitted with fowling-piece stocks, and back-sights moderately open at the top, for catching rapid aim in snap shots, though at the bottom they should be filed into mere hair-line clefts, for the purpose of drawing a fine bead, when desirable.

Remember, after firing, the first thing to be done is always to reload. No practice is so had as to go up to a beast, when it has fallen, with an unloaded weapon. If the animal be of a dangerous nature, it is doubly perilous so to approach him, even if he appear to be dead. The first infliction of a wound often produces a stunning sensation, and a sort of stupefaction, which passes away on the fear or rage produced by the sudden advance of an enemy. I have more than once seen deer spring up, go away, as if unhurt, and effect their ultimate escape, in this manner, after lying for some seconds as if killed outright; and the stories of accidents incurred from wounded carnivora through the like want of caution are innumerable.

Turkey shooting, which alone remains, can, I must

maintain it, in spite of the prejudices of my western friends, hardly ever be had under circumstances which constitute it a sport; for the bird will rarely either lie to setters, or flush to spaniels within shot; and to lie under shelter of a covering log, and call it up by imitating the yelp of the hen bird, and then shoot it with a rifle, is, for the reasons I have given above, though an effective way of procuring an admirable species of game, no genuine sport.

I have heard of this bird being hunted with beagles by sportsmen mounted on slow, active ponies, through the fine open forests of Canada East, where the ground is unencumbered with brushwood and coppice, and where the giant trees stand so wide apart that one might manoeuvre a regiment of cavalry among them; and by this means, it is said, they are forced to take wing, and afford fair flying shots to their pursuers, or are driven to tree after a short and exciting gallop, when they can either be shot sitting on the branches, or driven out to the gun, accordingly as the sportsman inclines to fill his bag at all hazards, or to give the game a chance for its life.

In my belief, it is not in sportsmanship, as it is said to be in love and war, where all that wins is reputed fair. It is not in the mere killing of numbers, much less in the mere killing at all; it is not in the value of the things killed, though it is not sportsmanship, but butchery and wanton cruelty, to kill animals which are valueless and out of season; it is not in the inevitable certainty of success—for certainty destroys the excitement, which is the soul of sport—but it is in the vigor, science, and manhood displayed —in the difficulties to be overcome, in the pleasurable anxiety for success, and the uncertainty of it, and lastly in the true spirit, the style, the dash, the handsome way of doing what is to be done, and, above all, in the unalterable *love of fair play*, that first thought of the genuine sportsman, that true sportsmanship consists.

And that it never may be degraded into aught else, is the ardent wish, as it shall ever be the teaching, of Frank Forester.

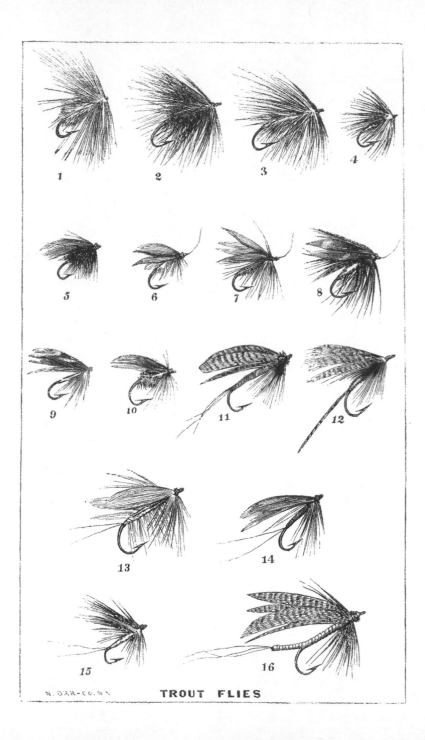

N. ORR-CO. N.Y. **TROUT FLIES**

GAME FISH, AND THE BEST MODES OF FISHING THEM.

YOUNG SPORTSMEN.

RIVER FISH AND FISHING.

Of the following pages, which will, I think, be found to contain all that is needful, both in theory and practice for the instruction of the young angler, much of that which relates to tackle, implements, the most approved baits and the precepts for their use,—most, indeed, which is not connected entirely with the varieties of fish peculiar to this continent,—is selected from that excellent and most practical little work, Stonehenge's Manual of British Rural Sports. I have no hesitation in using these extracts, since although the trout, the pickerel, the perch, and indeed all the fish of America, with the exception of the carp, which is a direct importation, differ from the similar and similarly named fish of Europe, still the method of taking them is identical. Trolling is trolling, and fly-fishing fly-fishing the world over; nor have I ever any where else met instructions for both, so practical, so plain, and so replete with all that can be taught by precept, and may be matured by experience into perfect science, as in extracts which I here submit, partially altered, it is true, and adapted, where alteration and adaptation were necessary, to the state of the art piscatorial in America, but still in the main attributable to the clever writer and compiler, whose *nom de plume* is so well known as an authority on English sporting matters.

The brief description of the leading American fishes, which are of interest to the angler, are arranged according to the best authorities, and the instructions for such modes of angling as are peculiar to our waters are original, and will, I hope, be found useful and authentic.

It will be observed that I have not, in this volume, entered largely into ichthyological questions, or discussions concerning the natural history and breeding of fish, which subjects will be found treated at large in my work on the fish and fishing of the United States and British Provinces of North America, and in other books devoted wholly to the topics of natural history, and the fauna of the continent. The paper on trolling for lake trout, which is quoted from the pages of my work above referred to, is from the pen of an excellent fisherman, who is much accustomed to the sport and the waters which he describes, and who kindly prepared it for the Appendix to the second edition of my volume.

The Common Salmon, *Salmo Salar,* stands at the head of American fish, as affording the best sport to the angler, and the greatest treat to the *gourmand;* its flesh being rich in flavor, and of a beautiful red color. It is a fish of large size, sometimes attaining to the weight of 50 or even 60 pounds, and of beautiful proportions. The head is small; upper jaw longer than the lower; vomer furnished with teeth; body slightly arched on the back, which ought to be broad and muscular, and gradually tapering to the tail, which is broad, and ends in a crescentic curve. The color of the salmon when in season, is a purplish-black on the back, softening into a silvery-gray on the sides, and ending in a pure white on the belly. When out of season, these colors are represented by a dull brown on the back, reddish or pale-brown on the sides, and reddish-white on the belly. The male has several small, irregular, and copper-colored spots on his sides. These in the female are larger, darker, and generally round or lunated. The male is also more slender, The scales are middle-sized, and are easily detached. The average length is from two and a half to three feet. Salmon feed freely on fish and mollusea, but digest their food so rapidly, that when opened their stomachs are generally found empty. Their growth proportionate to the quantity of food which they can procure; and hence when they increase in size in a marvellous manner, during a very short period. the successive stages of development of this fish are now supposed to be as follows:—the fry are hatched chiefly in the spring and early summer, and grow very slowly till they are about a year old, up to which time they are called *salmon fry,* and are several transverse bars on their sides. When these disappear, and the fish becomes uniformly silvery in color, it is about to commence its first migration to the sea, and is called a *smolt.* After the smolt has remained in the sea a few months, it returns to its native river, if possible, and is then greatly increased in size, generally weighing two or three pounds, or even considerably more. They are now called *grilse*; and after a second time descending to the sea, where they again rapidly add to their size and weight, they attain the full dignity and name of salmon. The female salmon deposits her ova in the gravelly beds of mountain streams, where she ploughs a groove with her tail, and is assisted by the male in the whole operation. The size of the salmon does not entirely depend upon the age, but on the nature of the river in which it is bred; some rivers never produce large salmon, whilst others are remarkable for fish of great size. The salmon was originally found in all North American rivers eastward of the Delaware. It now hardly exists west of the Kennebec and Penobscot, and even there is becoming yearly more scarce. In the British Provinces, and in California and Oregon, it still abounds.

Sea Trout, *Salmo Trutta.*—According to Mr. Yarrel, this fish is distinguished from the common salmon by the gill-cover, which differs in the following points:— The line of union of the operculum with the sub-operculum and the inferior margin of the sub-operculum, is oblique, forming a considerable angle with the axis of the body of the first. The posterior edge of the pre-operculum is rounded, not sinuous. The teeth are also more slender and numerous. The flesh of this fish is very similar in flavor and color to that of the common salmon, with which it is very generally confounded; and the two are sold indiscriminately by the fishmongers as ordinary salmon. In habits, haunts, &c., they are also alike. It is common in the St Lawrence, and the rivers of Nova Scotia and New Brunswick.

The Common Trout, *Salmo Fordinolis,* is distinguished by the length of the lower jaw being greater than that of the upper. It weighs from half a pound to four or five, or even, in rare cases, up to eight pounds;

and its ordinary length is from 10 to 18 or 20 inches. In shape it is not quite so elegant as the salmon, but it is, nevertheless, a very beautiful fish. The snout is more blunt, and the jaws are thickly supplied with teeth inclining inwards, and very sharp. In color it is dark brown, mottled with yellow on the back, pink on the sides, in season, and silver-white below. It is marked on the sides with several distinct round spots of a bright red color, each surrounded by a halo of pale gray; its fins are tricolored, bright red, bordered with black; and an anterior margin of pure white. Trout vary so much in different rivers, that no one description will minutely apply to all, but the above will give the general characteristics of the species. The trout feeds like the salmon, and in habits resembles that fish in all respects but the migration to the sea. He is generally found in swift and gravelly streams, and rejects those of an opposite character, though he is occasionally to be met with there in consequence of the artificial and compulsory interference of man. The spawn is deposited in the same way as that of the salmon; but as the young do not migrate, their successive changes and growth cannot be so clearly made out. The spawning time begins in September, in some few cases, but it is not commonly in full operation till October or November, after which it may be said to be completed. The trout is in full season from March to July, but the time varies in different rivers so much, that it is impossible to lay down any decided rule. When in high perfection its spots are peculiarly brilliant and distinct; the head is small, the body being plump and thick, and the belly silvery. Of Lake Trout there are several species, the great lake trout of Superior and Huron, *Sahno Amethystus*; the Siskawit, and the common lake trout, *Salmo confinis*, besides other, perhaps casual varieties.

The Mascalonge and Pickerel.—Of these voracious

fish there are many varieties, in almost all the lakes and rivers of North America. The former species is confined to the waters of the St. Lawrence; the latter is common to all the lakes and fresh rivers of the Eastern, Middle, and North-western States. It is closely allied to the English pike, and is a very ugly-looking fish, the head being large, the jaws long and savage-looking, and armed with several hundred teeth; the tail is lunated; the color is a pale olive-gray, becoming deeper on the back, and marked on the sides with several yellowish spots or patches. Sometimes the pickerel reaches an enormous size, instances having been known in which it was taken more than three feet in length. The food of the pickerel consists of fish, frogs, rats, the young of water-fowl, or, in fact, any thing in the shape of animal food. They spawn in March and April, among the weeds of their favorite haunts.

The Chub, Roach and Dace are common in all American streams, but are little fished for except by boys, and are worthless on the table.

The Common Carp, *Cyprinus Carpio*, is the type of a family which have all a small mouth without teeth, but possessing a bony apparatus in the throat as a substitute. They have only one dorsal fin. The common carp is not a native of Great Britain, but was introduced by the monks to serve the purposes of the table during their fasts. In length it is usually from one foot to one foot six inches. The back is arched and thick; color yellowish, approaching to brown over the back, and to white under the belly. The mouth has a short beard on each side, both above and below; on the sides are some blackish specks; fins, brown; tail, brown, and forked. Carp feed on worms and insects, and are very prolific, living also to a great age. They are a very wary and cautious fish, and very uncertain in appetite, being sometimes ready to take a bait, at others obstinately refusing every temptation. The carp is now common in the Hudson, having escaped from the store ponds of Captain Robinson, who imported it from Holland, and having been protected by law until It became abundant.

The Bass.—Of this fine family there are four species peculiar to the waters of the rivers, lakes, and sea bays of North America, besides a purely salt-water species taken on the outer sea-banks, known as the sea bass, *Centropristes Nigricans*. These three are the striped bass, *Labrax lineatus*, a noble migratory fish, varying according to age and condition from half a pound to seventy pounds weight, and frequenting all the waters of the Middle and Eastern states, from those of the Chesapeake to Boston Bat. He runs up the fresh rivers from the sea in pursuit of the shoals of shad and smelt, on the roe of which he feeds greedily, and frequents the fresh waters until late in the autumn, when he retires to the sea bays and inlets, where he remains imbedded in the mud of those calm and brackish lagoons until the return of warm weather.

He is a handsome, active fish, bluish brown above and silvery white on the sides and belly, marked with seven or nine longitudinal stripes of chocolate brown, those above the medial line terminating at the tail, those below it fading away and disappearing above the anal fin. Like the perch he has two dorsal fins, the anterior one having nine sharp-pointed spirous rays. He is a gallant fish and bold biter.

The two next species, the Black Bass of the Lakes, *Gristes Nigricans*, and the Rock Bass, *centrarchus ceneus*, are originally peculiar to the basin of the St. Lawrence, though they have been purposely introduced into many other waters, and have introduced themselves, *via* the canals, into the Hudson and other rivers connected with those great Canadian waters.

The black bass is taken from half a pound to eight

or nine pounds weight, though its ordinary run does not exceed, if it reaches, three or four pounds. It has a double dorsal, like the preceding species, the former with nine sharp spines, the latter with one spine and fourteen soft rays. It is of a bluish black color above with bronzed reflections, and below of a bluish white. It loves clear cold limpid lakes and swift rivers; it is a delicious fish and a bold biter. It abounds in Seneca, Cayuga, and Crooked Lakes of New York, and in all the great northern lakes, though it is not found to the north of these.

The Rock Bass, *centrarchus census*, peculiar to the same waters, is a smaller fish, rarely exceeding a pound or a pound and a half weight.

Its color is dark coppery bronze above, with green metallic reflections, the sides coppery golden, with several rows of dark oblong spots.

Its dorsal fin has eleven spines and twelve soft rays. It is abundant in the lakes, in the Hudson river, and in many adjoining lakes and rivers into which he has been casually or intentionally introduced.

The Growler, *Gristes Salmoneids.*—This fish considerably resembles the black bass, and arrives at nearly the same size. It is of a deep greenish brown color, and has ten spines in the first dorsal and fourteen rays in the second dorsal fin. This fish is known as the salmon in the Susquehanna, which river is not visited by the true salmon, as the white salmon in Virginia, and as the Welchman in the inland waters of North Carolina. It has been taken in the waters of Western New York, though not frequent in them, but abounds in many of the Western States.

The Pike Perch or Sandre, *Lucioperca Americana,* deserves mention as an admirable fish on the table, and a favorite with the angler, both for its beauty, strength, and boldness of biting. It is a true perch, and has nothing of the pike but its elongated snout, whence it derives its name. It has thirteen spines in the first dorsal, and one spine and twenty-one soft rays in the second. Its general color is yellow, beautifully mottled with purplish brown, zigzag lines above, and pure silver below. It rises to nine pounds weight, is a fish of the western waters, loving quiet pools under mill-dams or at the foot of rapids, and retires in the summer into the depths of the clear cold lakes, or quiet shadowy places in rivers, amid water grasses and weeds.

There are many other varieties of fish, of greater or less value to the angler, found in all the waters of the continent, from the abominable and gigantic catfish down to the diminutive breams, shiners and killy fish, which afford so much sport to boy fishermen, but with the exception of the perch and eel, there are none others which require especial notice.

The Perch, *Perea Americana,* is a very handsome fish of medium size. Body deep, with high-arched back; head small, with sharp teeth in the jaws and the roof of the mouth. The edges of the gill-covers are serrated, with a spine on the lower part. Colors as follows:—Back, deep olive-green, with broad black bars, gradually becoming white towards the belly. It has, however, many varieties and shades of color, sometimes being found, especially in the large clear spring lakes of the inland country, of a rich golden yellow, barred with dusky bands. There is a small variety known as the "sunfish," or "pumkin seed," mottled with various colors, and a great favorite with boy anglers. The dorsal fin is furnished with spinous prolongations, so sharp that it can scarcely be handled with impunity by the angler. It thrives best in large tidal rivers, where it seeks the point at which the water is usually brackish, and grows there to an extent never seen elsewhere. It is a slow-growing fish, requiring many years to arrive at its full size. The perch spawns in the months of March and April. It is a gregarious fish, and is very tenacious of life.

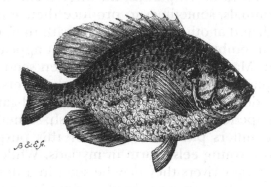

The Eel, *Anguilla communis.*—Of this fish there are several varieties, but they differ so little as to require no particular mention. They do not exist above the Falls of Niagara, which they cannot ascend, being migratory fish descending to the sea, where they grow to a vast size, and ascending annually to spring waters. In length they are from 1 to 3 feet; color, on the back sometimes a dark olive brown, at others light brown; belly, always white and silvery, especially in the silver eel, a variety peculiar to some rivers. Head flat, and jaws more or less oblongated, but the lower jaw always the longer; eyes very near the mouth, and small, with a reddish iris; gill-opening set far back, and close to the temporal fin. The eel is now ascertained to spawn in the sea, for which purpose it descends from its usual haunts and visits the ocean. It has the power of overcoming all obstacles, because it can leave the water, and by its serpent-like form, travel over or round any flood-gate, or mill-dam, in its course, whether up or down stream. It generally chooses dark stormy nights for this purpose; and its migration downward takes place in the months of August, September, and October, during which time eels are taken in large numbers by the millers throughout the country, who set their pots at the chief water-courses. Eels are generally considered to be viviparous, but they seem, like many other animals, sometimes to produce their *ova* already hatched, and at others to eject them with their contents still in an embryo state. The young first appear on the coasts in March and April, and are then seen in enormous quantities. They soon ascend the rivers, and by various devices they surmount the flood-gates, &c., which impede the progress of other fish; sometimes the English millers put straw ropes for this purpose, up which the young eels swarm in myriads. While ascending the larger rivers they may be seen in a double column, one close to each bank, swimming with great power and speed. These young eels are from half an inch to an inch in length. The eel is a very voracious fish, and will feed upon all kinds of garbage, and upon small fish, frogs, rats, &c; it may be said to be the great scavenger of our rivers. Eels feed chiefly by night, and they lie chiefly by day in the deep pools of rivers, or under stones or stumps of trees, or among the weeds or other impediments to the current of water, which they seem in all cases to dislike.

This, which is the essential part of all fishing-tackle, consists of a reel-line, varying in length, strength, and size,
according to the nature of the fish which is sought after;
of a reel to wind this upon, also varying in accordance
with the line; and of a smaller and finer foot-length
attached to the line, which is usually composed of silkworm gut, hair or gimp, and is armed with one or more
hooks, variously baited.

Reel-lines are made of horse-hair, from the tail, of
silk, or silk and hair mixed, of Indian-weed, and of silkworm gut. It is usual for the amateur fisherman to purchase these lines, which are made by a small machine,
but sometimes the angler prefers making them himself,
and if at all handy, he in ay do this with great advantage
by an easily acquired method, which is much superior to
the twisting-machine, because it admits of the introduction of fresh hair with much greater facility.

Silk and hair-mixed lines are those usually sold,
and they are the best for general purposes, because they
wind so well on the reel, and are strong and durable.
They are made of all lengths, and may be purchased at
any of the tackle-makers. Indian-weed or grass lines are
also sometimes used, but they do not stand sudden jars,
being inclined to snap. A plaited silk line is now made
without hair, and is very generally adopted. It is much
more free from kinking or ravelling than the other lines.

The reel is generally used by the angler, partly for
the convenience of carrying the line safely, but chiefly
in order to allow of rapid extension or drawing in of the
line which is wound upon it. Multiplying-reels, in which,
by the introduction of machinery, the barrel is made to
travel several times to the single revolution of the handle, were formerly much used, but they are now in great

measure replaced by the more simple plan of having a large barrel or drum on which to wind the line, instead of a small central spindle. By the use of this large drum even a salmon line may be taken in as rapidly as can be desired, and the line lies much more evenly and free from any kind of hitch, with the great advantage that it will give off the line readily to the end.

The foot-length, or the extreme portion of the line, is composed of finer materials than the reel-line, in order to escape the eye of the fish. It is generally made of pieces of gut, knotted together, and altogether comprising a length of from three to eight feet. Sometimes it is of single gut throughout, but generally of two or three thicknesses of twisted gut at the end next the line, then of two, and finally of one piece of gut. This material is the produce of the silkworm, and is the unspun substance intended for silk, but made into gut instead by the art of man. The silkworm, just before spinning, is broken in two by the hand of the gut-maker, who, by drawing the pieces apart, obtains gut of any firmness, according to the length to which he pulls it. Considerable knack is required to make it uniformly round and free from weak places, which should be searched for carefully in selecting gut for the single lengths. Horse-hair is sometimes used for this purpose, and in some instances gimp, consisting of silk protected by wire. All these various sorts will be treated of under the respective kinds of fishing in which they are employed.

Hooks are pieces of bent steel wire, barbed at the point, and of various sizes and forms. They are made according to the respective patterns which are fancied by the English, Scotch, and Irish makers. The round bend hook, is that which is most used in England, the Limerick pattern being chiefly in vogue in Ireland, and the Scotch anglers using, some of them the former and others the latter: while many Scotchmen use what is called the sneck-bend, differing slightly from both of the above, in being made of a more square shape. The round bend hook is numbered from 1, the largest salmon size, to 14, the smallest midge. The best Irish hooks, made by Philips of Dublin, are classed in a different way: F E is intended for the smallest trouting-fly; F, the next; then F F; then, again, F F F. After this come C and C C; then B and B B. The C's and B's have intermediate or half-numbers, and above B B the hooks for salmon are known by numbers, beginning with B B, which corresponds with 9, and going on regularly up to No. 1.

Various articles are required for uniting these portions of the line—viz., silk of different degrees of strength, cobbler's wax, spirit varnish, and small scissors, &c.

The joints used are—first, *whipping;* second, *knotting.* Whipping consists in drawing successive circles of silk, well waxed, tightly around the two objects laid in apposition; as, for instance, two portions of the line, or the line and hook. This is finished off by slipping the end of the silk through the last circle and drawing tight, and, if necessary, repeating the operation again and again; this is called the half-hitch. Knotting is effected by several modes, the most common of which is the water-knot, which is managed as follows—Lay the two pieces of gut or hair together, one overlapping the other three inches or more, then hold one end in the left hand and form a simple slipknot upon it, turn the other end to the right and do the same thing, then draw the two together, and the knot is complete; be whipping with fine waxed silk this knot is made still more firm. The advantage of this knot is that it will never give way to a direct pull, and yet may always be undone without difficulty.

The accessories to the line are the float, and the shot or leads. These are used in bottom-fishing only, and are intended to keep the hook at a certain distance from the bottom. The float is either of quill or cork, and is fixed upon the line by a ring at one end and a sliding-quill at the other. The shot are partially split and then brought together again upon the line. In this way, by plumbing the depth of the water, and adjusting the float so as to keep the bait at a certain depth, the object of the bottom-fisher is attained.

Box-swivels and hook-swivels may be readily understood from their name, and are used in spinning tackle, in order to prevent the line from twisting.

Gimp is composed of silk or other material strong enough to resist any straining force applied to it, and protected from the teeth of the fish, or from sharp stones, by fine brass wire neatly wound round. It is made of various sizes and strength.

The rod is the machine with which the line is conveyed to the place where the fish is the most likely to take it, and with which the various manoeuvres prior to his capture are effected. It is made of several pieces united by joints, and these are of varying size, length, and materials, according to the kind of fishing to which it is to be applied. It is also sold to suit all purposes in one, by changing the top joints, and it is then called a general rod; but though this may suit the pedestrian tourist who wishes to avoid carrying more than one rod, yet it interferes a good deal with the efficiency of both, and especially does it fail as a fly-rod. It is, however, well enough suited to the beginner. The extra pieces are contained in the butt, which is hollowed out to receive them. The specific varieties of rods will come under consideration in each section devoted to the particular sport for which they are intended, but I may enumerate them here as the general rod, the trolling rod, the trout fly-fishing rod, and the salmon fly-fishing rod. The materials of which these are composed are ash, hickory, lancewood, and cane, which are united together by brass ferules. Whalebone is also sometimes used in the top joints of fly-rods, but these are made so much better by the tackle-maker than by the amateur, that it is useless to go into the description of their manufacture.

The earth-worm is the most primitive and simple of all baits, and is that which is generally first used by the juvenile angler, because it is easily obtained, and applied without difficulty. There are several varieties of these worms, known to anglers as the *dew-worm*, *lob-worm* or the *marsh-worm*, the *tagtail*, the *brandling*, and the *red-worm*.

The dew-worm, or large garden worm, is of considerable size, varying from 6 to 12 inches in length when extended. The tail tapers somewhat, but in the squirrel-tailed variety it is flattened. In color this worm is of a dull brick-red, approaching to a crimson towards the head. These worms are obtained either by digging, or by searching for them quietly at night with a candle and lantern on the lawns or paths of the garden. In dry weather they are always out when the dew is falling.

The marsh-worm, or blue-head, is found in moist and undrained localities, where they may be obtained with a candle and lantern in large, numbers during the fine summer nights. In color they are of a light dirty or brownish purple. These worms should be kept in damp moss with a little earth mixed with it. A variety of this worm, found in land only partially marshy, is called in Scotland the black-head or butt on-worm, and is more tough, and therefore better calculated for standing the rough treatment which it must undergo in swift and wide streams. It is an excellent bait for trout.

The tagtail is common in good strong clays, which are well manured for turnips, mangel-wurzel, &c. It is a small worm of about 2 or 3 inches in length. Head larger, and of a deeper blue than the body, which is a dingy red; tail, yellowish.

The brandling is a small worm found in artificial composts, and in rotten tan, or other decaying vegetable matter, of a dirty red color, approaching to brown.

The red-worm is about the same size as the brandling, which it resembles in all respects but color, that being in the red-worm exactly what its name implies. It is found in the banks of ditches and sewers. The *gilt-tail* is a variety of this worm, but larger, and of a paler color towards the tail.

All these worms should be scoured,—a process which consists in starving them, by placing them in damp moss, neither too wet nor too dry. The worms here are not only deprived of their usual food, but in their efforts to escape they mechanically compress their bodies between the fibres of the moss, and in that way completely empty themselves of their fecal contents. Before putting them in the moss, Mr. Stoddart recommends that worms should be placed in water for a few minutes, after which they should be suffered to crawl over a dry board, in order still further to cleanse their skins. They may then be transferred to the moss, as described above. The worms should be examined from day to day, and those which are unhealthy or injured should be removed. When the worms are quite sufficiently scoured, they should be stored for use. Three or four days is the average time required for scouring.

Worms are preserved in the following manner:— Procure some fresh mutton suet, cut it fine, and boil it in a quart of water till dissolved; then dip in this two or three pieces of coarse new wrapper large enough to supply each variety of worm, which should not be mixed together. When these are cold, put them into separate earthen jars, with some damp earth and the worms which are to be kept, and tie over all a piece of open and coarse muslin.

Shrimps are much used for angling in tide waters, and are good baits for perch, if used alive.

The cockchafer is a common bait, but is not of much value in angling, except for chub.

Dung beetles, of various kinds, are also employed, and some anglers use them after removing their wing-cases. They should be placed crosswise on the hook.

Grasshoppers form good baits for some fish, and are much used for chub in particular. They are met with after the beginning of June till the end of September. The greener and larger they are, the better they take.

Butterflies and moths are also sometimes efficient baits, but their artificial representations are more commonly used.

The ephemera, or natural May-fly, is used as a bait during the period when it comes forth in countless myriads. By baiting with this fly in May and June success is often attained, putting two flies on the hook at the same time.

Caddis-flies are also used in the same way as the ephemera.

Humble bees, blue-bottle flies, gnats, and ant-flies are held in estimation by many anglers, as well as the harry-long-legs, and the common house-fly.

Many larvae or grabs are used in bottom-fishing, and are of great service in that department. Of these the principal are—1st, *flesh maggots*; 2d, *beetle larvae;* 3d, *caddies;* and 4th, *caterpillars.*

Flesh maggots, or gentles, are obtained and scoured in the following manner:—Procure any kind of flesh, or the body of any small animal. If there is any difficulty about this, the liver of a horse or cow answers remarkably well. With a knife cut some deep gashes in the substance of the liver or flesh, and hang it up in a shady place, but near the haunts of the blow-fly. In a few days the maggots will attain a lively state of existence; but they require about a week to reach their full development to the green or soft state, and another week to reach their maturity, when they are large and fat, with black heads. The various stages are adapted for different fish. Blowflies are abroad from May to the end of November, or even to the middle of December in mild seasons. The scouring of these gentles is effected by placing them for a few days in a mixture of bran and fine sand, slightly damp. By this process they are emptied of their contents, and rendered tough in their skins. When the object is to preserve them in this state for many days, they must be kept in a very cool place, such as a cellar, or they even should be buried in the earth. Without attention to this precaution they are almost sure to assume the chrysalis condition, in which stage they are useless as baits. A low temperature and exclusion from air and light retard this development; and by burying the carcass of a small animal after the larvae are a day old in a cool place, and confined in a box containing a mixture of dry cow-dung and fine earth, the gentles may be preserved in their larva state during the whole winter. The place selected should be protected from severe frosts, which would kill the gentles, and therefore an outhouse is well suited for this purpose, or any space in the garden well sheltered by a thick shrub, such as the sheep laurel.

The larvae of the various beetles are called by anglers, the *white worm grub*, the *cow-dung grub*, the *cabbage grub*, and the *meal worm*. The first is the larva of the cockchafer, and is found in loose loamy soils, especially near the horse-chestnut. It may be easily found by following the plough. The second, as its name implies, is found in cow-dung, and is the larva of several of the beetle tribe. The third is found in the stalks of old cabbages, and often about their roots, and is the larva of two or three varieties of the beetle. The last is found in the meal-tub, is much- smaller than the three first-mentioned varieties of grubs, and is not so good for angling purposes as the gentle.

These grubs may all be preserved by simply placing them with some of the earth in which they are found, in any receptacle, keeping them afterwards in a cool situation.

Caddies are the larvae of the ephemera, or May-fly, as well as the stone-fly and the caddis-fly. They are easily found beneath the stones, weeds, &c., of shallow brooks, and may be stored by putting them in water, with some sand, in a cool place. By placing them in a perforated box, they may be suffered to remain in a running stream, where they continue to grow and thrive as well as in their native haunts. They are not, however, much prized as angling baits.

Caterpillars, or the larvae of the butterfly, are either smooth or rough. The former are not much used, and the latter are so thoroughly imitated by the artificial fly called the palmer, that they are scarcely ever employed. There is no doubt that in angling natural products are better than artificial, if they are equally capable of enduring the rough usage required to drag them through the water. In this respect it is that the artificial palmer beats the hairy caterpillar, its original; and hence the latter is almost wholly driven out of the angler's list of baits.

Salmon-roe is a very favorite and killing bait for trout, and is found to be so destructive that its use is often considered to be a species of poaching. I cannot understand on what principle this odious stigma should be cast upon its adoption, because it may be employed, like any other bait, in open clay; and the only objection to it winch can be urged is its very great success. No one would call an unerring shot a poacher, simply because he kills more than his neighbors; then why should the bait which is more successful than any other labor under this imputation? It appears to me that every one is straining to effect a certain purpose, viz., the killing of the greatest number of fish, and yet when a certain mode of attaining this object is at hand, its adoption is forbidden because it will insure what all are aiming at, and by open means too. However, as I cannot discover any real foundation for this crusade against the salmon-roe, I shall include it in the list of baits, and describe its preparation and mode of application to the hook. The roe itself should be collected as near the time of spawning as possible, and should either be preserved whole, or be made into a paste at once. If the former, the best way is to keep it in a jar, with alternate layers of wool. The roe should be carefully separated from its enveloping membrane, and should be sprinkled with salt, as also should the wool. When the jar is filled, it should be tied down with a bladder, and kept in a cool and rather moist place, such as a cellar.

Salmon-roe paste is made by boiling the roe without its envelope for 20 minutes, then bruising it in a marble mortar until it forms a uniform mass. After this add to each pound of the roe one ounce of common salt and a quarter of an ounce of saltpetre; beat them all up together, and keep in a jar tied down with bladder.

Paste may be made in the same way of shad and smelt roe, and are very killing bait for bass.

Shrimp paste is made exactly in the same way, after removing the shells.

Bread paste is also used as a means of taking fish, and is made from new bread, well kneaded, and with or without the addition of honey. It is either used in the white state, or it is colored with vermillion, lake, or turmeric. Sometimes stale bread is used, but it requires more kneading, and the addition of gum water, or mated greaves, or some more adhesive material. It is often flavored with the roe of salmon, or other fish: the size of the portion used must vary with the fish angled for. Cheese is also sometimes made the foundation of paste, either by itself or mixed with broad: by constant kneading it becomes perfectly tough, and withstands the action of the water for a, long time. A peculiar kind of paste called *patent paste*, is made by washing away all but the pure gluten. A paste of flour is first to be made in the usual way, then by successive washings in cold water, by degrees the process is completed, care being taken not to dissolve the gluten itself by mixing it up with the water; and to avoid this, after each successive washing, let the paste drain for a few minutes. This paste will keep for any length of time, if protected from the action of the air by wrapping it in sheet-lead.

Ground-Bait.—The object of this very general accessory to the angler's art is to collect an unusual number of fish to a given spot, and at the same time to do this by offering them a quantity of bait of the same kind as that which is afterwards to be used on the hook, but of an inferior quality to it. Thus, if intending to fish with earth-worms, bait with unscoured worms, and fish with them well scoured. Worms in clay-balls are a good ground bait, because they are not all at once presented to the fish, but appear gradually as the clay dissolves. Mr. Salter, who is a good authority in bottom-fishing, recommends the crumb of a quartern loaf to be cut in slices two inches thick, and soaked in water till thoroughly saturated, then squeeze it tolerably dry, and add bran and pollard, kneading all together till a firm mass is the result as tough as clay. *Soaked greaves*, which are commonly known in the United States as *craps*, being the refuse of flesh used in sausage-making, mixed with tenacious clay, are a very useful ground-bait; and may be made into large masses, and thrown into the water in lumps of two or three pounds weight. *Gentles* mixed with sand are also used, but they should be unscoured, and coarse old carrion gentles for this purpose are the best, as the fish will be attracted by them, but will take the scoured gentle on the book in preference.

Dead fish as baits are usually so arranged on the hooks as to spin or rotate on their axis rapidly, by the action of the current, or by drawing them through the water. This is an unnatural motion, and unlike any movement of any known inhabitant of the river; nevertheless, it takes well with many fish; and, judged by that unerring criterion, may safely be approved of and adopted. Minnows, trout-tails, bream, shiners, and other small fish, are thus used; but the preference is always given to the two first when they can be procured. There are various modes of baiting with minnow's and these small fish, and almost every fisherman has his particular whims and oddities here as well as in other matters connected with fishing. Nothing could more completely disprove the necessity for the adoption of any peculiar mode of baiting than the immense variety in the plans of the most successful anglers. Some use one hook, some two, some three, and others even four. Some—as for instance, Mr. Stoddart—bait tail foremost after removing the head; others always take care to present the head to the trout or pike. The great thing to be attended to is to make the bait spin well, which can only be done by producing a slight curve in its body, and by making the line draw it on one side more than the other. In this way, with one or two swivels, which prevent the line throwing any impediment in the way, the bait rotates rapidly if well applied, and the fish is deceived to his ruin. When two hooks only are used, the extreme one is larger than the other—usually Nos. 3 and 5, English sizes—and they are whipped on the same piece of gut or gimp, at an interval of a hunt half an inch clear between them. A baiting needle is required for most of these hooks, but here it is not necessary, as the larger hook is passed through the mouth and out at the root of the tail, so as to leave the barb free. When this has been done nicely, the minnow assumes a bent form, corresponding with that of the hook, and if properly put on, it will spin or rotate when rapidly drawn through the water. But for this purpose its mouth must be closed mechanically, and this is effected either by a leaden cap which slips down over the line, or by the second hook being passed through both lips, and thus holding them shut; or sometimes, in addition, by a few stitches with a fine needle and thread. Colonel Hawker recommends a hook or two to be allowed to float loosely and openly by the side on a stout piece of gut, but I cannot advise their adoption. The usual mode of employing the third hook is to whip it on to a piece of gut about an inch long, and then to include this gut in the whipping of the second or smaller hook, which it should also match in size. This third hook then, lies closely adapted to the side of the bait, but not floating loosely, as advised by Colonel Hawker. The two first are applied exactly in the same way as when two hooks only are used, when the third will lie flat against the side of the bait, and retains its position there by the stiffness of the gut or gimp. This last form is used for the application of the celebrated parr-tail as a bait, which is much used in Scotland; and is strongly recommended by Mr. Stoddart, one of the highest authorities on the subject. He advises all the fins and tails to be cut off, and the head and shoulders to be then obliquely sliced off with a sharp knife. When this is done, the tail- end is to be used forward—that is, nearest the rod, and is then made to appear as the head of a fish. In this mode the shiner, bream, or other small fish may be prepared, when the parr is not to be found; and they answer well for large trout or pike. But nothing takes so completely and generally as a good minnow of the proper size, requiring no paring, and fitting the hooks exactly, so as to allow the one to project slightly through the tail, while the other closes the mouth. Borne other modes are described as useful variations in adapting dead fish-baits, but I believe the double or treble hook, as above, will suit all purposes where the bait is required to spin rapidly, whether it be the entire fish, or part, as already mentioned. The shiner, bream, or roach may be divided in the same way as the parr, and will spin remarkably well when used as he recommends that little fish to be employed; as will also the perch itself when deprived of its back fin, or any of the smaller fish which are attractive to the pike. All these various hooks require swivel-traces, single or double, which will be found described under the head of pike-fishing.

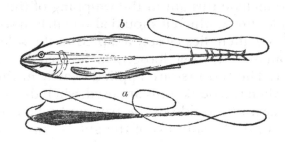

Minnows are also mounted on gorge-hooks: see woodcut, in which *a* represents the hook itself, and *b* the fish and hook ready for use. Gorge-hooks are either single or double, the latter being represented in the annexed woodcut. In baiting this hook, after it has been whipped to a piece of strong gut looped at the other end, take a needle used for the purpose, and by its means draw the gut and hook through the mouth and body of the fish, bringing the needle out at the root of the tail, and leaving the hook buried in the body of the minnow, with the bend and barb of the hook on each side of its mouth. After the needle has been brought out, re-enter it on the other side, so as to include a piece of the flesh of the tail in a loop of the gut. If this is neatly done it will be found, after drawing the gut tight, that there is no disposition in the fish to slip off the hook, unless very flabby; in which case a single turn of light silk tied tightly round the root of the tail, is sure to make all safe. Besides these modes some others are used in pickerel-fishing, but as they are peculiar to that department, they will be treated of under the head of Pickerel-Fishing.

Dead bait-fish may be preserved for use, as well as other small baits, by keeping them in salt and water, or pyroligneous acid and water; but the latter, I believe, gives them a flavor which fish do not like. Sugar also will answer the purpose, or any kind of spirit, as whiskey or gin; but by far the best material is oil, which will keep them sweet, and also stiff, for a great length of time, if they are just raised to the boiling temperature, by immersing the vessel containing the oil and fish in boiling water for a few minutes. More than this renders them tender, and liable to break. All fish bait should be killed by a blow on the head as soon as taken.

Live fish form a very common lure for the larger kinds of fish, and they are used by inserting the hook in some part of the body not necessarily vital. This is called roving, and is practised with any of the smaller fish, such as minnows, shiners and the like, in capturing trout, perch, pickerel, &c. The hook is merely entered in the back close to the fin, and the barb is suffered to protrude above that appendage and with the point of the hook directed towards the tail of the fish. The line must be shotted so as to sink the fish to the required depth, and it may be used with or without a float. Some other methods of fixing the hooks have been recommended, by which the hook is entered in one part, then made to traverse the fish under the skin, and finally brought out at the mouth; but they are so abominably cruel that I must decline having any thing to do with their description. All field-sports are too much mixed up with an undercurrent of cruelty; but where there is a choice, no man of any ordinary feeling will hesitate in selecting the least severe modes of taking game.

Frogs may be used exactly in the same way as the minnow, by passing the hook through the skin of the back. They must be well shotted, to keep them down, and must be raised to the surface every four or five minutes, to allow them to respire.

Bait-fish are procured for the purpose of using them as baits, either by angling for them, and carefully removing them from the hook, and then placing them at once in a vessel of water, or by taking them with a large hoop-net or fine casting-net. The last plan is that usually adopted, but it requires some little practice for its use, and nothing but an ocular demonstration will give any idea of the mode of employment. Any fisherman will, however, initiate the tyro for a trifling consideration. With the hoop-net they may be taken, by sinking it by means of weights to the bottom of the brook; then, after enticing the minnows by means of small pieces of worms dropped over it, the string is suddenly raised, and the minnows are caught in its meshes.

Bait-fish may be preserved alive by placing them in a perforated tin or wooden case, and sinking them in any running stream, in which mode they retain their health and liveliness for an indefinite period. They may also be kept alive for a long time in any clean vessel by changing their water frequently; but in this way they are not so healthy as in the above plan. When wanted for use, a small bait-kettle is used with a perforated lid, and capable of containing from one to two quarts of water. This should be kept under the shade of a tree or hedge while the fishing is going on, as the heat of the sun soon raises the temperature of the water to such a height as to destroy the life of the fish, or so nearly so as to cause their death soon after putting them on the hook.

Minnows are now manufactured so as closely to resemble the real fish in appearance, but most of them fail in imitating the consistence and softness of the original, and consequently do not take nearly so well as their appearance would lead one to expect. The Archimedian minnow spins beautifully, and so do some others constructed on similar principles, and all will take good fish, but certainly not so well as the real minnow. In many localities, however, these are very scarce, and there the substitute is certainly useful. Mr. Flinn's flexible minnows are far the best, as they are soft and yielding to the grasp of the fish; they are made of gutta percha, painted very closely in imitation of the minnow, gudgeon, &c., and are of sizes suited to all fish, from the trout to the salmon. The Archimedian, on the other hand, is hard and inflexible, and though it spins well, and is to the eye all that can be desired, yet from its hardness to the touch it is very apt to deter fish from a close approach, and is not so successful as Mr. Minn's imitation. Mr. Blacker, also, has recently introduced a modification of the "devil-bait," with the addition of a pair of Archimedian fins; this is said to spin well, and to take good fish, but I know nothing personally of its properties.

Artificial flies are so numerous, and their importance is so great, that a great part of the angler's time
is generally occupied in mastering a knowledge of their
various forms, and the mode of tying them. All of them
are composed of three essential parts: first, the hook;
second, the gut or loop to attach the hook to the line;
and third, the various articles tied on the hook for the
purpose of imitating the natural fly. The angler will
have no difficulty in procuring his hooks and gut, both
of which, however, he ought to select with great care;
but he will experience some little vexation and disappointment when he attempts to tie an artificial fly, especially without the practical instruction of some older
craftsman.

Hackles and Palmers—The mode of tying the
peacock-hackle, *fig.*1, which is one of the simplest of
all files, is as follows:—Begin by whipping the hook on
the gut, leaving a loose end of the silk hanging from
the shoulder where the whipping is to be commenced.
When the whipping has proceeded to within two or
three turns of the bend, include within its folds the ends
of two or three peacock-herls, which are to be left projecting beyond the bend, and after making these turns
fasten off. Then take a red cock's hackle, and smooth
the fibers of it well; with a pair of scissors trim these off
at the point, leaving the shank bare for about an eighth
of an inch; next include this within two or three turns of
the silk left at the shoulder; directing the hackle towards
the gut and fastening of the silk. Then, taking the bend
of the hook between the finger and the thumb of the
left hand, lay hold of the herls with the right, and wind
them carefully round the shank of the hook up to the
point where the hackle is tied, where they are to be
include in the silk which is still left there and then cut
off. The body is now complete, but the legs are still to be
imitated by the hackle, which should be carefully wound

round the hook above the herl; arranging the fibres, as it is wound, by means of the picker, and fastening off at last by means of the silk which is still projecting, and left for the purpose. Now cut off the silk at both ends, lay on carefully a very little varnish at each end, and the fly is complete. All palmers and hackles, *figs.* 2, 3, and 4, are made on this principle, substituting various feathers for the cock's hackle, and various dubbings for the peacock-herl.

Simple Winged-Flies.—Sometimes a pair of wings are tied on at the same time as the hackle-point, and afterwards the hackle is wound round the shank, and thus serves to keep the wings from lying flat against the hook when in the water. (See the black gnat, hare-lug, yellow sally, oak-fly, caperer, &c.)

The Black Gnat, *fig.* 5, is tied in the same way as the peacock hackle, using a smaller hook. No. 13, and fine black silk. A small black ostrich-herl forms the body, and a piece of the starling's wing-feather the wings. A very fine black cock's hackle is used for the legs.

The Hare-lug, *fig.* 6, is composed of a body consisting of a dubbing from the back of the hare's ear, making it thin and neat towards the tail, and pretty stout near the shoulder. The hook is of the same size as in the black gnat, and the wings are the same. After these are tied, pick out a little of the clubbing to make the legs.

The Yellow Sally, *fig.* 7, is tied exactly like the hare-lug, with the substitution of yellow or buff mohair or fur for that of the hare, and the addition of a fine yellow cock's hackle for legs; wings from a feather from the inside of the thrush's wing. Hook No. 12.

The Oak-Fly, *fig.* 8.—The body is made of brown mohair and a little hare's ear-fur towards the tail. Legs of a bittern's hackle, or partridge feather, or a furnace-cock's hackle; wings of a woodock's wing-feather. Hook No. 8,

The Caperer, *fig.* 9, is made up as follows:—Body of rich brown floss-silk; legs of a fine red or brown hackle; wings of a woodcock's feather. Hook No. 9.

The Winged-Palmer, *fig.* 10, a good common autumn fly, is made on the same plan as the peacock-hackle, but of a smaller size, and with the addition of a pair of wings made from the outside-feather of the thrush's wing. The end of the body is finished with a few turns of orange silk. Hook No. 9 or 10. It is the cock-y-bondhu of Wales.

Winged and Tailed-Flies.—These are made like the last set of flies, except that at the time of whipping on the hook the fibres are included which are to consti-tute the tail. The body is then formed by the dubbing, floss-silk, or herb and the wings tied as before. This set includes, among a vast variety of flies, the May-fly, green drake, stone-fly, March-brown, red spinner, &c.

The Green Drake or May Fly, *fig.* 11.—Body made of yellow floss-silk or mohair, dyed a pale yellowish green, and ribbed with bright yellow silk; tail of two or three hairs of the sable or fitchet, or of fine horse-hair from the mane; legs of a gray cock's hackle, dyed the same color as the mohair, or of a ginger pile undyed; wings from the mallard's back-feather, dyed of the same yellowish green. Hook No. 6 or T.

The Gray Drake, *fig.* 12, is made as follows:—Body of pale dun-colored mohair; tail of two fibres from the feather of the mallard's back; legs of a brown or ginger cock's hackle; wings from the gray feather of the mal-lard's back, undyed. Hook No. 6.

The Stone-Fly, *fig.* 13.—Body of red mohair, ribbed with gold or yellow silk; tail of two long fibres from a coarse red cock's hackle; legs a reel cock's hackle, carried down over all the body; wings of the hen-pheasant's tail-feather, or of the gray goose wing-feather. Hook No. 6.

The March-Brown, *fig.* 14.—This fly is made of two

sizes; one on hook No. 7, the other on No. 11 or 12. The body is of brown floss-silk; tail of two long fibres of the red cock's hackle: legs of brown cock's hackle; wings of a woodcock's feather.

The Red Spinner, *fig*. 15, is tied on hook No. 7. Body of red mohair, sometimes ribbed with gold; tail of two fibres of a red cock's hackle; legs of the same hackle; wings of a brown mallard's feather.

The Winged-Larva of Mr. Blacker, *fig*. 16, resembles the green drake in all but the body, which is prolonged separately from the hook by means of a couple of hog's bristles, which are tied in with it and the tail-hairs, and extend about a quarter of an inch beyond the bend. The silk or dubbing is then carried from the shank to the bristles; and thus the fly has the appearance of a long body. The legs are often made with a dyed feather of the mallard's back, used as a hackle.

Extra Trout-Flies.—Those given in the preceding paragraphs will suffice for all common purposes; but they may be varied *ad infinitum* by the angler to suit particular localities. If, however, he makes himself perfect in the manufacture and use of these, and has the stock of materials necessary for fly-making, it will be at all times easy for him to extend his list, either by imitating the prevalent natural fly, or that which is successfully employed by the anglers familiar with the district. Mr. Stoddart is of opinion that, for the trout, the red, brown, and black hackles, with or without wings, and the hare-lug, are sufficient for all ordinary purposes. This is perhaps carrying simplicity to an extreme length; but there can be no doubt that the young angler is often overwhelmed with useless flies, as well as other complicated forms of fishing-tackle, in order to suit the trading propensities of the tackle-makers. No doubt in Mr. Stoddart's case the above flies would be more successful than others attached to the line of a beginner; but even the above celebrated *piscator* does not maintain that no others will be more successful at times than the three he has selected, but that there is no absolute necessity for them. This certainly is in accordance with my own experience, as I have known a very successful angler, who never possessed any fly but the red and black palmer and the black gnat. Still I have no doubt that at least as great a variety as I have enumerated will at certain times be useful, though some of them will only suit particular months. The following list will perhaps be some little aid to the young angler who is anxious to try a greater variety.

The Wren's Tail.—Body of sable-fur and gold-colored mohair mixed. No wings; legs of a wren's tail-feather, used as a hackle. Hook No. 8.

The Grouse-Hackle.—Body of gold-colored mohair mixed with the dark fur from the hare's ear. No wings; legs made with a reddish-brown grouse feather, used as a hackle. Hook No. 7.

The Dark Claret.—Body of claret mohair, fine towards the tail, and full towards the shank. Wings four, two below from the starling's wing, and the upper two from the partridge's tail.

The Spider-Fly.—Body of lead-colored floss-silk; legs of a small black cock's hackle below and above, with a hackle made from the woodcock's feather, taken from near the butt-end of the wing. Hook No. 7.

The Little Iron-Blue.—Body of slate-colored mohair; tail of two fine hairs from a dark sable; legs of a fine dun cock's hackle; wings of the coot's or starling's wing-feather. Hook No. 9 or 10.

The Blue-Blow.—Body of mole's fur; wings of the tomtit's tail-feather. Hook No. 14.

The Hare's Ear and Yellow.—Body the dark fur of a hare's ear, mixed with a little yellow mohair; wings of a starling's feather. Hook No. 8.

The Ant-Flies are of four kinds—the large and small red, and the large and small black. The red are tied on Nos. 7 and 12. Body of amber mohair, made large towards the tail; legs of a red cock's hackle; wings of a starling's feather. The black have a body of black ostrich herl, with a black hackle for legs; wings of the blue feather of the jay's wing.

The Mealy-White Night-Fly.—Body white rabbit-fur, made fully as large as a straw on a No. 5 hook; legs of a downy white hackle; wings of the soft mealy feathers of the white-owl.

The Mealy-Brown Night-Fly.—Body of the same size as the preceding, made of the fur of a tabby-rabbit; legs of a bittern's hackle, or a gray cock's; wings the brown feathers of a white owl. Hook Ho. 5 or 6.

Salmon-flies are made on the same principle as the trout-flies, but as they are larger, so they are capable of being tied with greater exactness and finish. They are generally of much more gaudy materials than the trout-flies, and in this respect they have latterly been used still more richly colored than was formerly the case, even in Ireland. Until lately, very sober salmon-flies were ordinarily used in Scotland, the prevailing colors being gray, brown, buff, and brick-dust; but now it is found that a much more brilliant set of colors will answer far better, and the Irish favorites, viz., scarlet, bright yellow, blue, and green, are the fashion, united with less bright toppings—as, for instance, the tail-feather of the pheasant, or the back or breast of the bittern or turkey. In Wales more sober flies are still in vogue; straw colors, natural mottles and pheasant or turkey feathers being considered the most killing. Tinsels are however approved of in all three localities, and are used more or less in almost every salmon-fly. In nearly all cases this fly consists of a body, a head, legs, and tail, and wings of a very compound nature; but the mode of tying is very similar to that adopted in trout fly-making. Most salmon-flies are tied with a small loop of gut attached to the shank, instead of, as in the trout-fly, a full length of that material; sometimes a bristle or a piece of wire is bent for the purpose, and again in some cases the gut, either plain or twisted, is tied on as in the trout-fly. Whichever mode is adopted, the end or ends of the gut or bristle must be shaved off, and moulded with the teeth into slight ridges, so as neither to present an abrupt and unsightly edge where they leave off, nor to be so smooth as to be liable to slip from the hook. This eye or length of gut is to be first whipped on to the hook in the usual way with strong waxed silk, which is then to be fastened off and removed; and for the subsequent tying, a finer and generally a bright-colored silk adapted to the particular fly, is to be employed. For American fishing, the gaudy flies seem generally to find the most favor; and the fish are so bold and little used to the angler's tricks, that coarser tackle and less finely finished flies will be found to succeed with them.

Sea trout-flies may be made of sizes and colors intermediate between the trout and salmon-flies. They are tied of all colors, and with or without the addition of a gaudy tail of golden pheasant fibres, and tinsel wound round the body. The following size and form, however, will suit the trout in lakes, and the average size of the sea-trout when ascending from the sea. The body is of brown mohair; legs of a black cock's hackle; wings of a brown mallard's feather; head of plain waxed silk. Hook No. 5 or 8. A good variation consists in using purple or scarlet dubbing for the body; red or lilac-dyed hackle, and the green-dyed feather generally used for the May-fly for the wings; with a tail of a few fibres of the common pheasant's tail-feather. Numberless variations of these flies are made and sold, but the whole of them are fanciful creations of the maker's brain, and not imitations of any living insect. The fisherman, therefore, may please his own fancy, and try his skill in any way that strikes him, and perhaps the more novel the fly, the better it may succeed, though there is still a considerable section of good anglers who adhere to the old-fashioned flies called the butcher, the doctor, &c.; but I fully believe that any slight variation or alteration from the annexed models, according to the contents of the angler's stock of materials, will be just as likely to succeed as the celebrated "ondine" of Ephemera, or the new "spirit-flies" of Mr. Blacker. These flies are serviceable for large brook trout in the larger American streams and lakes.

The landing-net is merely a hoop with a handle to it, and armed with a net for the purpose of taking the hooked fish out of the water, without danger to the tackle or of losing the fish. It is generally now made with a hollow handle, to take the top joints of the rod, and this handle screws off the ring, which is also jointed, for the convenience of carriage.

The gaff and landing-hook are constructed for the same purpose. The simple hook now used, attached to a firm handle, inflicts the least severe wound, and is more manageable than the gaff.

The basket or creel is slung over the shoulder by a belt, and is made of various sizes, to suit the probable amount or weight of fish expected by the angler.

Fish-bait kettles are made of tin, with a perforated lid, and a handle to carry them by.

The drag-hook is: a long line of strong whipcord wound on a thumb-reel, and armed with a three-hooked blunt drag weighted with lead, so that when a hook is caught in weeds or other impediment, the drag may be thrown on to the same spot, and the weed dragged away with the hook, or at all events the greater portion of the line may be saved.

The clearing-ring is intended for the same purpose, and is a jointed ring of heavy metal which opens and closes again with a catch. It is attached to a long line like the last, and is passed upon the end of the rod open, and when closed is slipped down the reel-line as low as possible, and then drawn to land, bringing sometimes the hook and obstacle with it, but generally breaking the casting-line near the hook or about the shot. This does not act so well as the drag-hook when a float is used.

The bait-box is merely a flat box perforated with small holes in the lid, for containing worms, or gentles, or dead minnows, in bran.

The disgorger is an instrument for removing the hook from the throat of those fish which swallow their bait, and is made of various forms. One end should be forked, and the other perforated with a hole, and ending with a sharp-cutting, round surface, like a spatula.

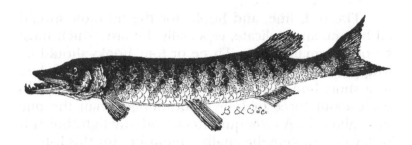

BAIT FISHING.

Every fish enumerated in the first section may be taken by this mode of angling; even the noble salmon and the wary trout may thus be captured. But almost all require some slight modification of the apparatus or bait employed, and of the mode of using them; and therefore each must form a subject to be studied by itself. Commencing with the smaller varieties of fish, and those most easily caught, I shall take all in the order of their usual presentation to the young angler. With each variety it will be my purpose to specify—first, the kind of rod, hook and line, to be used; secondly, the best bait; thirdly, the time and place best suited for each kind of fish; and fourthly, the mode of fishing.

The rod, line, and hooks for the minnow should all be fine and delicate, especially the last, which must be of the smallest size. Three or four hooks should be whipped on fine gut or strong horse-hair, and attached to a short line of horse-hair or silk, leaving the hooks each about three or four inches longer than the one next above it. A crow-quill float, and any light but stiff rod, will complete the angling requisites for this fish.

The bait should be of very small red worms, or pieces of them.

The lowest hook and bait should be suffered to float tolerably near the ground, and the highest at mid-water, above which these fish seldom feed. At the slightest indication of a bite the rod should be rapidly raised, as by this means many minnows which would otherwise be lost will be taken, while the worm is only partially in the mouth.

The tackle for these fish should be as follows:—Rod, an ordinary bottom-rod—the general one described at page 299 will suffice; line of plaited silk or twisted hair, with a good length of stout gut; float of cork or swan-quill; hook, No. 6 or 7. A plummet will always be required. Sometimes, as in fishing for chub, *sinking* and *drawing* are practised exactly as they are described.

Ground-baiting over night is always to be practised for carp or tench if the boat is to be used; and if the angler fishes from the bank, he should cast in a little of this useful accessory every few minutes.

The best baits are a couple of red worms or gentles; sometimes one of each will take the fancy of the carp, which is a very fickle and cautious fish, and very difficult to bring to hand. Taylor advocates green peas, which are said by him to be very efficacious; but all sorts of baits succeed at times and fail at others. The angler, therefore, who is anxious to take carp, may try caddies, bees, grasshoppers, and in fact the whole range of baits described at pages 299–302.

Carp are in season from February to September. They take a bait better after rain than at any other time. The deepest and stillest parts of the river or pond are those where these fish are the most likely to be found, but in summer they are very fond of basking near the surface, among the weeds, and it is then extremely difficult to persuade them to take any bait,

In fishing for carp, great care must be taken by the angler to keep well out of sight, as they are so cautious as to refuse all baits when alarmed by the sight of man. The line must also be very carefully and lightly dropped into the water, and not even the shadow of the rod allowed to fall over their haunts. For the carp, two or three rods may be used, as the bait must be left for a long time quietly in one spot, where the carp will often watch it most jealously for some time, and then, when perfectly satisfied of its freedom from guile, he will at last take it. Even with half a dozen rods there is no danger of the angler being overdone with more than one fish at a time. The bait should be suspended about a foot from the bottom.

For small perch, such as are most commonly met with. a "general rod" will suffice; and the common line with *good*-sized gut, and a No.4 or 5 hook, baited with lob-worms, or almost any other worm, or with the caddis, cater-pillar, or wasp-grub. These baits must be varied till some one is successful; or if it is known beforehand what bait suits the particular locality, that one should be selected. The paternoster-line, armed with various baits, may be used if the angler is not in possession of the above kind of information; and as the perch swims and feels at all depths, it is the best kind of tackle in deep water. In rivers where may weeds exist, or where there are piles, or roots, or trees, this tackle is not so manageable, and the sinking and drawing plan must be adopted.

For large perch, the minnow, either dead or alive, is the best bait; and both may be used at discretion. For open and clear water, or in running streams, the dead minnow, with the spinning-tackle as described at page

307, is the most killing bait; or the shiner may be used according to the plan described in the same page, with the parr-tail; and which, with the perch, I have known a most efficient lure; shrimp is also an undeniable bait, especially in tide streams. the gorge-hook is also successful, and is particularly serviceable in awkward and weedy rivers where the spinning-tackle can scarcely be used.

The season for perch is from March till December, during which long period they bite with varying degrees of readiness, and almost at all hours of the day. It is generally supposed that windy weather is the most likely to tempt these fish, of at all events, that they are as free to take the bait then as at other times. Such, however, is not the result of my own experience, as I have always found a marked difference in perch, as well as other fish, in connection with strong winds, and also with the time of day. Young anglers, therefore, should take this *dictum* with some caution.

Little difference in the mode of using the bait need be made from those recommended for other river fish, if the perch sought for are small; but in localities where large perch may be expected, and where the live or dead fish-bait is used, some considerable variation must be practised. Hitherto I have not had occasion to describe the mode of using the live and dead fish-baits; but as we now are considering their adoption in taking perch, it will be proper here to enter upon the subject. I have already alluded to the mode of applying the live minnow to the hook, or rather of inserting the latter in the hack of the fish close to its fin. When this has been done, and the gut is properly shotted with about two or three No. 1 shot, quietly enter the fish at some distance from the shore, and let if take its own course, swimming where it chooses. A float is only a hindrance to the live bait; and as it is dragged about on the surface of the water, it serves to attract, the attention of the perch, and is very apt to scare them away. As soon as the perch is seen or felt to take the halt, strike pretty firmly, though not with much force. Live frogs may be used in the same way, as well as newts.

Spinning for perch is practised as follows:—The bait being applied according to either of the methods described on page 308, the angler should use the general rod with the short top; a reel and reel-line of plaited-silk or twisted hair and silk will be necessary, and a good length of strong gut, or, when pike are likely to be met with, of gimp, armed with one or two box-swivels. With this apparatus the angler proceeds as follows:—He first casts or throws the minnow down the stream, if there is any, or, if in still water, as far out as he can; then, pulling the bait gently yet firmly to him for a yard or so, it revolves rapidly on its axis, and must be allowed to sink for a few inches at the end of that distance by his ceasing to draw in. The angler then repeats the operation till he brings the bait out of the water, when a cast in a fresh direction must be made, but exactly as before in principle. It is obvious, that for this purpose a long rod is required to command a greater extent of water, and a more numerous series of spins, and that running water materially assists the spinning: still, in dead water a well mounted minnow or shiner may be spun with great effect, and will kill there in preference to any other bait, except perhaps a live one of the same species.

The gorge-hook is used with the full-sized trolling-rod and a long line, a yard or two of which is pulled out in a loop clear of the reel, and held loose in the left hand. Cast as gently as possible the minnow from you downstream, or out into the water, if it is still. In thus casting, the loose portion of the line is expended, and the bait is thrown considerably further than it otherwise would be. Then begin to wind up a little at a time, stop, and wind again; thus imitating the actions of the living small fish represented by the dead bait. When the length of the line is reduced to a manageable amount, the action may be varied a little, and the fish may be eased downward or upward, or among piles or other likely places; but in all cases proceeding by slight jerks, and at the same time not too rapidly. When the bait is thus brought to hand again, repeat as before, and try all likely spots—first easting and drawing over and through the nearest places, and then extending the reach to the most distant ones. The expert angler will always study the actions of living fish, and endeavor to imitate them, which example is far better than any precept that can be given in print.

As these fish are strong, and often of good size, and are furnished with sharp teeth, the tackle must be in proportion. The rod is necessarily longer and stronger than that known as the "general rod," and must be of the kind known as the "trolling rod," which may be described as follows:—It should be here mentioned that pickerel are taken with the minnow or shiner, in three different ways—first, with live bait, secondly, with dead bait, in a way called "snap-fishing;" and thirdly, with the gorge-hook, on principles similar to those already described. The first and last of these modes require a long and tolerably stiff rod, while snap-fishing must be practised with the top-joints of the rod reduced in length, and of greater stiffness. This will serve to make the following account more intelligible. The angler who is very *exigeant* in his desires for the most perfect implements of his craft, will perhaps require two separate rods of varying sizes for each purpose, so as to suit broad and narrow rivers, as well as large and small fish; but the more easily satisfied fisherman will make one rod of the following dimensions serve every purpose. A bamboo rod is the lightest, and is yet strong and stiff enough for any practised fisherman; it will not, however, bear very rough usage, and for very large pickerel the butt and second joint should be of some light yet tough wood, such as holly, which may be bored for the sake of diminishing its weight, and also to accommodate within its cavity, as in a place of security, the small top joints. Of these it should have three—one short and stiff, and two others similar to one another, longer and more elastic than the first. The short one is made entirely of whalebone, and is not more than 12 or 18 inches long; the longer tops are made two thirds of hickory or lancewood, and the remainder of whalebone. These rods are generally made in five joints of nearly equal length; the first, second, and last as above described, and the intermediate two joints of bamboo. They are united by the ordinary brass ferules in the usual way, but sometimes other methods are practised; but there is so little occasion for any alteration, that it is unnecessary to take up the reader's time by any further description of them. Almost all trolling-rods used generally are furnished with rings, which are made to stand up from the rod, in order to allow the line to traverse their opening with greater facility. These are usually made of broad

brass ferules encircling the rod, and having lesser rings
of wire riveted into them; but a much lighter and cheaper plan answers perfectly well, and may be described as
follows Take a piece of wire of sufficient strength, and
bend it into a ring of the usual size, leaving a short tail on
each side; turn these tails to a right angle each wary, and
flatten the ends so that they will lie along the side of the
rod, when they may be whipped in the usual way. They
thus form stand-up rings, easily removable by cutting the
whipping-silk, and very capable of being restored, if by
any accident they are injured. One of these to the head
of each joint, and a second to the middle of the last, are
about the proper number. Some anglers, including that
high authority, Mr. Stoddart, approve of the same kind
of ring as is used in ordinary rods, but I confess that,
though I have the highest opinion of Mr. Stoddart's
judgment in general, yet in this instance I cannot agree
with him, as there can be no doubt in my mind that
the fixed and upright ring allows the line to run more
freely than the ordinary one. But the best of all are the
new patent railroad guides, which is stationary and flat
to the rod. A large reel is wanted, capable of holding
from 35 to 70 yards of line, according to the nature of
the fish and extent of water intended to be fished. This
reel should have a simple large barrel without multipliers. Floats may or may not be used, they are by no means
required. The reel-line must be strong, and the plaited
silk is that form now usually adopted, as it is found to be
more free from "kinking" than any other. An essential
accessory to pickerel-fishing is the swivel, which may be
either the box-swivel or the hook-swivel; the latter differing from the former only in having a small hook at one
end. These are attached to lengths of *gut,* or more usually *gimp,* forming with their help what are called double
or single swivel-traces.

The single swivel-trace consists of about 12 inches

of gut or gimp, with a hook-swivel at one end, and a loop of its own substance at the other, which attaches it to the reel-line by the usual draw bow-knot. The double swivel-trace has, in addition, an extra length of gut or gimp, ending also in a loop, and between the two a box-swivel, by which the tendency to twist in spinning is still further diminished. In both cases the hook-swivel receives the loop of the hook-length of gut or gimp *after it is baited;* and in both instances, also, swan-shot or lead, in some form, is required to sink the bait; and it is attached in greater or less weight, according to circumstances, to the gimp close to the hook-swivel.

The hooks will be more particularly described under each mode of fishing; and for their application to the bait a needle, called a baiting-needle, is required.

A landing-net or hook will be required, as pickerel are sometimes of such a size as to demand their assistance. The former is merely a circle of iron, either plain or jointed, with a handle which may be made to take on and off for the sake of convenience; and armed with a deep net, which receives the fish. The hook is intended to supply the place of the net, but is a clumsy substitute.

The baits used for pickerel are exceedingly various, reaching from the common lob-worm and ordinary hook—which will often take the small-sized fish—through all the degrees of live minnows and other fish, as well as frogs and newts, dead minnows and shiners, artificial minnows and shiners, and even the artificial fly. These various baits are used also in almost as many different ways, of which three have been already described in the list of baits, under the heads of "The live Minnow-bait," "The Spinning-minnow," and the "Gorge-hook bait." But besides these, the snap-hook bait is employed at those times when pickerel are shy of gorging, and inclined to eject the bait, or *blow* it out, as the angler denominates this act. The snap-hook is either the plain or the spring snap-hook, and they are both used for live, as well as dead fish baits; though the spring snap-hook is very apt to destroy the life of the fish very rapidly, and is a very cruel mode of baiting. The plain snap is made in several ways as follows:—First plan—two hooks, No. 4, should be tied back to back, then to these tie another smaller hook, No. 8, together with a piece of wire ending in an eye. To the eye is whipped a piece of gimp, and the other end of this has a loop by which it is attached to the hook-swivel in the usual way. In fixing on the bait proceed as follows: Take a good sized shiner, or small roach, or a perch with the back fin removed, arm the gimp with a baiting-needle and insert it behind the back fin, bringing it out again at the mouth and drawing the gimp after it, so that the short hook stands with the point rising out of the back, and the others are one on each side the belly; this bait ought to spin well. Second plan—exactly similar to the mode recommended by Mr. Stoddart of applying three hooks to the parr-tail, only that in England it is used with a whole fish, and the hooks point towards the head. Mr. Stoddart's plan is no doubt the best, and with a tail of the roach, dace, or perch, is admirably adapted to pickerel-fishing. Third plan—in this mode four hooks are used, which are separately whipped on to two pieces of gimp, looped at the other ends; one about three quarters of an inch in length, the other about three times as long. After arming them with the baiting-needle, they are each passed through the fish, the short one at the shoulder, the other near the tail, and both the loops being brought out at the mouth are attached to a hook-swivel, after which the mouth is sewn up and the bait is finished and ready for use, though sometimes, in addition, a leaden weight is sewn up in the mouth to sink the bait. The spring-snap bait is a more complicated machine, and is composed of a case which connects and keeps in place the shanks of the hooks, which, when in the case, resemble the common snap-hook, but which, when drawn out, expand by their own elasticity, and strike the fish in the act of so doing. This is sometimes applied to a live fish, but usually to a dead roach or shiner, or to a small bream. The bait should be about six ounces in weight, for a smaller one will not effectually conceal the hooks. In baiting the hooks, insert the small hook in the hack of the fish, near the back fin, taking a good hold of the flesh, and allowing the point to project a little way out of the skin, and the other two hooks to lie one on each side of the belly. The mode in which this acts is as follows: As soon as the pickerel seizes the fish in its mouth, he pulls slightly on the line, which causes the angler to strike, and this action draws the case from the shanks of the hooks and allows them to expand themselves, and thus prevent the pickerel from blowing the bait out of his mouth.

Pickerel are in season from May to February, but the best time for the sport of taking them with the hook is the period immediately before the weeds shoot, and again in October when they have rotted. The latter is the true pickerel season, as they are then firm and fleshy, and also voracious, so as to afford good sport. This fish is usually taken of good size in artificial waters, or in deep alluvial rivers. In these situations there are almost always great quantities of weeds, and when they exist in full vigor, it is almost impossible to land large pickerel, even if they are hooked. The bait also can scarcely, at such times and situations, be properly manoeuvred; and hence, it is by common consent considered that pickerel, though perfectly edible, should not be angled for till after Michaelmas, from which time till February the water is in good order for their capture. This rule applies only to weedy streams.

The mode of fishing for pickerel varies with the particular hook and bait employed. If the live bait is used with the ordinary hook, it can only be successful at times when the fish are voracious and ready for any bait, which, indeed, they often are. If this happens to be the case, the bait must be gently passed into the water, and will be more easily managed with a float, as with the length of line required in pickerel-fishing it is impossible otherwise to maintain a proper depth for the halt, which should, as far as possible, be made to swim at mid-water. This is effected by the float keeping the bait up, and the shotted line preventing its rising to the surface. If the bait seeks the weeds or other shelter it must be stopped, and if dull and sluggish, it must be stimulated by a gentle shaking of the rod. When removing the bait for a fresh throw, great care should be taken to do this gently, as a very little extra force will make a great difference in the duration of the life of the fish; and not only so, but the gentle mode will give the bait less pain than any other. The use of live baits is always more or less cruel, and surely every unnecessary degree of pain should be avoided. When the bait is seized by the pickerel, which may be known by the float disappearing under the water, be very careful to allow him to carry it off without restraint, and for this purpose draw off the line with the hand, and let it run loosely through the rings. If the slightest impediment occurs he will be sure to blow it out, and your hopes are blasted. After a short time, during which he has been quietly gorging the bait, he will again move off, and then is the time to strike, which you may do sharply, but not roughly. If this is cleverly done, the fish is firmly attached to the line, which, if of good materials and the hooks equally efficient, will land your fish for you with the aid of a little skilful management. Pickerel may be played with great advantage, and a considerable increase to the interest of the sport. The principle consists in yielding to him for a time, by letting out the line as far as is prudent, and the absence of weeds, &c., will allow; and when otherwise, making the elastic power of the rod withstand his progress by advancing the butt. In this way he will at last be tired out, and may then be landed with safety by means of the landing-net.

The snap-bait is employed only when the fish are wary and inclined to eject the ordinary kind, and it is used as follows:—I have already (on pages 330-331) described the mode of arming the hook with the bait, and also the peculiarly short and stiff top to the rod which is required. This last is necessary in order to give increased quickness to the stroke. The chief difference in this mode from that last described consists in the striking, which should be done the moment the pickerel seizes the bait, when, if successful, he may be landed or played according to circumstances, as before described, or if not too large, pulled out at once over the shoulder. Trolling, however, by means of the gorge-hook, is the most common mode of taking pickerel, and is also the most sportsmanlike, inasmuch as it is deprived of the stain of cruelty which attends upon live-bait fishing. It requires, as I have already observed, the full-sized trolling-rod, with long and strong line, a good-sized reel, free from multipliers, and all the apparatus peculiar to the gorge-hook—viz., cork-float, swivel-traces, gorge-hooks, and bait. When these are all artistically adjusted, the bait must be manoeuvred in the manner already described for perch, and it will generally be successful where good fish abound, and the fishing for them is attempted at the proper season. The butt of the rod should be rested against the thigh or groin, and it should be grasped by the hand about 18 inches higher up, which will give the angler great power over his rod, and also leave the left hand at liberty to manage the line, a loop or two of which should be held in that hand, ready to "pay out," as the sailors say, when the bait is cast. When a pickerel has

seized the bait, wait patiently, as already recommended, and the average time necessary for this exercise of
patience will be about six minutes; then strike, and play,
or not, as before mentioned.

In removing the bait from the mouth of the pickerel after landing him, be careful of his jaws and teeth,
which sometimes inflict severe wounds. The first thing
to be done is to knock him on the head, which will enable you to recover your hooks and gimp at your leisure,
whereas by attempting, by means of the disgorger, to
remove them while he is alive, great risk is incurred not
only to them, but to your own fingers. After he is quite
dead, open the mouth, and if the bait is still there, after
propping the mouth open, liberate the hooks with the
knife, and remove the bait; but if this has been swal-
lowed, make an incision into the stomach, and remove
them through it. Very often the process is a delicate and
tedious one, and many fish will require to be slit open
from the mouth to the stomach before the hooks can
be removed. An implement called the *spoon* is sold at all
tackle shops, which supersedes the use of bait, but it is
so deadly that it is held by sportsmen mere poaching to
use it.

All the varieties of bass may be taken either by fly-
fishing, or trolling, and also by bottom-fishing with live
bait, dead bait, or various pastes.

The striped bass in sea-ways is ordinarily taken,
either by squidding with a bright piece of bone ivory
or tin provided with hooks, or with the real squid on a
dropline.

He will rise freely in swift clear rivers above the
influence of tide to a large gaudy salmon-fly, and must

be fished for, precisely as the salmon, with a two-headed rod and salmon tackle. Being a bold strong fish, he fights hard, and requires skill and patience to land him.

He may also be trolled for successfully with dead bait, or spinning tackle, as the pickerel, or taken at the bottom with crab or shrimp. In the spring, and in rivers where shad run, there is no more killing bait than shad roe, prepared as described above.

The black bass and rock bass of the lakes will rise freely and afford good sport to a large fly made of scarlet ibis and silver pheasant feathers, four wings, two of each, with a body of scarlet chenil. They can also be trolled for successfully, as described above, or taken with a live bait on roving tackle, or with the deadly *spoon*. For the rock bass, the growler, and the pike perch, which two latter-named fish are taken precisely in the same manner, except that they will not rise to the fly, the common crawfish of the western waters, *Astacus Barioni*, is a favorite and killing bait.

The apparatus which is used for taking eels is exceedingly various, inasmuch as almost every kind of hook is occasionally adopted. Some of the different modes and tackle have been already described, such as the ledger-line, the common drop-line, the ordinary float-angling, &c. These may be used with eel-hooks and strong tackle; and the eel should be landed as quickly as possible after he is hooked, for the reason that he is otherwise sure to coil himself round some weed or pile, or other fixed object, and so set at defiance the efforts of the angler. Usually, however, these fish are taken at night, and the ledger-line answers very well for that purpose, the hook being mounted on strong whipcord or on gimp. The regular night line consists of a long and tolerably stout cord, to each end of which a brick or stone is attached weighing three or four pounds. At intervals of two or three feet a piece of whipcord or gimp 18 inches long should be firmly tied, and armed with an ordinary eel-hook. When all are baited, drop one brick or stone gently into the water, then, with a long pole or a boat, drop the other at the full length of the line, and leave the whole apparatus sunk till the next morning, when at early dawn they may be taken up again with a boat-hook, and the eels, if caught, removed. They should be set the last thing at night, that the bait may be fresh, and taken up at very early dawn.

Bobbing for eels is practised with a common darning-needle and worsted, several lengths of which are strung with worms, and then, after being gathered into loops, they are united by a strong line to a piece of lead weighing nearly a pound, and pierced with a hole for the purpose of attachment to the line. The eels are taken by their teeth catching in the worsted.

Trimmers are set for eels exactly as for pickerel, except that the hooks should be eel-hooks.

Sniggling is another mode of taking eels, which is carried on during the day, and the apparatus consists in a strong needle about two inches long, a stout whipcord-line, which is whipped to the needle from the eye to the middle, from which part it is suspended, and a short rod with a notch at the end, and capable of being set at any angle or curve, for which purpose it is either made of flexible wire or with hinged joints. The needle is baited with the worm, which is drawn over both needle and line, and when the angler strikes, he fixes the needle across the eel's throat.

The eel-spear is the most common of all the implements used in taking eels; but as it requires very little art, it is scarcely fitted for the sportsman's use, and is solely intended to be employed by those who take fish for profit. But the great bulk of the eels caught in this country are taken in traps set in the weirs of the rivers, when they run in the floods which are so constantly occurring.

The best baits for eels are either live fish or lobworms. Bead bait are not so readily taken, as there is no means during the night of simulating the motions of the living fish, as can be done with perch, trout, and pickerel, which take their food by day. Lob-worms, therefore, as being the most readily procured, and remaining alive on the hook for a considerable time, are the most common bait. The lampern is used in those rivers where it is met with, and is a very deadly bait. It requires care in its application not to injure the nine-eyes or gills, for if they are destroyed, the fish soon dies, and lies motionless and unattractive. The hook, therefore, should be entered below them, leaving the head and these openings hanging free. It is too large a bait for any but fullsized eels, as the small ones pull off the pendant portions without hooking themselves.

Eels may be taken during the spring, summer, and autumn. They haunt the recesses of the banks, or lie in the mud and weeds during the day, leaving these places only at night for food. Ponds, canals, and alluvial rivers are the chief localities for this fish, but few rivers are totally free from them. In some, however, they absolutely swarm, and even in small brooks they may be taken in quantities amounting to many hundredweight during their runs or migrations.

The modes of taking these fish vary with the apparatus employed. During the day, sniggling, bobbing, or ledger-line fishing will be the most successful. The first is practised as follows;—Take the needle, armed and suspended as already described, and draw on it a large lob-worm in the following manner. Enter the eye of the needle at the head of the worm, and run it down till the whole needle is covered except the point, which is inserted in the notch or slit at the end of the rod, leaving the worm free. In this way the head of the worm is presented to the eel, and is conducted into his hole or haunt by the bent end of the rod. As this end can be set at any angle, it may be guided round stumps or stones, and when it is gently insinuated as far as it will go, it is quietly left there. The line attached to the hook is held in the left hand, and as soon as the fish seizes the bait and has drawn it out of the cleft stick, slacken the line, and gently withdraw the stick give a little time for the eel to swallow the bait, and then strike, when the needle will cross his throat, and hold him securely. Do not attempt at once to draw him out, but let him tire himself first, and when he is exhausted, pull him out. Bobbing is practised with the worms strung on worsted, as already described, and gathered up in links, which are to be attached to a line of whipcord about two yards long, having a knot on it eight or ten inches from the worms, and the lead slipped down to that point. When the eels bite, their teeth stick in the worsted, and they may be gently pulled out before they disentangle them. This mode I have never seen practised, and I have great doubts of its efficiency with any but small eels. Boys, however, there is no doubt do thus succeed in taking large numbers of these. For the purpose of taking eels by night, the trimmers may be set as for pickerel, or the nightline as described above.

The bottom-rod for trouting should be at least 17 feet long, and should be, in fact, similar to that described above as the trolling-rod for pickerel. An ordinary trouting-reel and reel line are sufficient for the purpose; and the casting line should have six lengths of good single gut, slightly stained with brown or brownish green by means of common black or green tea. No silk should be used at the knots, but the simple angler's knot should be employed. The hook for trout best adapted for the worm is No. 3 or 4, and for the minnow, according to the kind of fishing adopted. When the hook is intended for the worm, it ought to be whipped on to the gut with crimson silk, as the dark silk usually employed alters the color of the transparent worm, and deters the trout from taking the bait. Shot, or lead in some form, is required, in order to sink the bait, and its weight should depend upon the strength of the current. Swan-shot answers best for this purpose, and, more or less, must be applied at the discretion of the angler, when by the water-side he ascertains the rate of the current. A float will sometimes, though not always, be needful, and may be either of cork or swan-quill, the latter being to be preferred. The hooks for spinning-tackle are similar to those described at page 307, and the gorge-hook will be found treated of at page 309.

The baits for trout used in bottom-fishing are chiefly worms and minnows, the latter either natural or artificial. Caddises, however, and caterpillars, with gentles and salmon-roe, are in some localities much prized. The worms which are the best for trout-fishing are the marsh-worm, the button-worm, and the brandling; the last being chiefly adapted to the smaller sizes of fish. They should be well scoured, and applied as follows:—Six or eight dozen worms will in all probability be required in a good day's fishing, and should be carried in some damp moss in an appropriate bait-box, or canvas bag. In putting the worms on the hook, take the latter in the right hand, between the finger and thumb, then taking a worm in the left finger and thumb, insert the point of the hook near the head of the worm, and run it along its body until the whole of the hook is concealed, and also a very short portion of the gut; in doing this, great care should be taken not to expose any part of the hook, and especially the barb, which should not on any account penetrate the side of the worm. If the worm is too small to conceal this quantity of the hook and line, and also to leave a portion, at least an inch long, hanging free from the end, two may be applied; and if, on the other hand, it is too long, the barbed end may be brought through and re-entered an inch or so lower down, so as to pucker up a coil of the worm's length, which adds to its allurement, and at the same time prevents too long a free portion from hanging from the end. The worm is thus injured as little as possible, and will live a considerable time if not roughly used in the water. It should be examined every now and then to see that it is not broken. Grubs, caterpillars, and gentles applied two or three at a time on the hooks—first one lengthwise, then one obliquely, so as to leave each end free, and finally one lengthwise to conceal the barb. The mode of applying the dead minnow and parr-tail has been described under the head of "Baits," as well as the other ordinary methods of baiting the gorge-hook and the live minnow-tackle.

The artificial minnow, in all its varieties, may be tried, and in some rivers and states of water will do great execution. In none, however, will it take equally well with a good and well-baited real minnow; and if these can be obtained, it is useless to attempt to take fish with an inferior article. The devil-bait is also sometimes successful; indeed trout are so capricious, that it is difficult at all times to say beforehand what they will take, and what refuse. I have already mentioned and described Mr. Blacker's modification of this bait.

The common trout is found in almost all the clear, gravelly, and quick running streams throughout the Northern and Middle States, and sometimes, though not in the same perfection, in streams of an opposite character. They spawn in the autumn, the exact time varying in different localities; and they come into season in the spring, when, also, their time of perfection will be early or late, in accordance with the nature of their *habitat,* A low temperature seems rather to accelerate than retard their condition. After August, trout are not fit for the sport, being full of roe, or else spent from the operation of spawning. For bottom-fishing, the deeper and stiller parts of the stream answer better than the very rough freshes, though even for this kind of fishing perfectly still water is not so well calculated as that rate of stream, which will move the bait without destroying its form or texture.

The various modes of taking trout will be now entered upon. First, fishing with the worm is practised by obtaining all the apparatus and bait described above; the angler then, with his wading-boots on, if he uses them, quietly wades into a part of the river which will command an extensive sweep of likely water; or, if preferring *terra firma,* he keeps as much as possible out of sight of the fish upon a part of the bank suitable for his purpose, and below the water to be fished. It must be known, that the worm should in all cases be cast up stream, and suffered to float down again, for reasons which will be clear enough when explained, as follows first, the trout always lie head up stream, and therefore do not see the angler so well below them as above; secondly, the bait floats gently down without injury, which must be done to it if dragged against stream; thirdly, in hooking the fish, the barb is much more likely to lay hold in this way than if he is struck in the line of the axis of his body; and fourthly, the water is not disturbed by the wader till it has been already fished. The angler swings or casts his worm gently as far up-stream as he can, using as long a line as he can easily manage, and no more, and suffering it to float down with the stream till within a short distance of the place where he is standing, when it should be lifted and re-cast. When a fish is felt to bite or lay hold of the worm, wait a few seconds till he has done nibbling, and the moment he is running off with it strike it smartly but tenderly with the wrist, not with the whole power of the arm, and proceed to land your fish with as little delay as possible.

Grub, caterpillars, gentles, &c., are all used in the same way, and will serve the angler well in many localities, but as a general bait for trout they are not equal to the worm. Fishing with the salmon-roe will be found more particularly described at the end of this section.

In using the live bait, the hook, of size No. 3, should be entered at the back-fin, and the barb should stand up a little above the surface; the line then being shotted, and a swan-quill float applied at about three feet from the hook, the bait is suffered to swim about in any direction but that of weeds, or other dangerous spots in the bed of the river. As, however, trout are chiefly found in strong running streams, and as in such situations some force must be exerted upon the minnow in keeping it from running with the stream, its life is soon destroyed, and therefore the live minnow is not so well adapted for trout-fishing as for perch or pickerel.

The dead minnow used with spinning-tackle, according to one or other of the modes recommended at page 306, is most suited for taking large trout; and the precise style of fishing with these baits is as follows:— but the angler should understand that the principle on which he conducts his operations is not that of a slavish imitation of the motions of the natural live minnow, such as will answer, to a certain extent, with the pickerel and perch, which are less wary than the trout, but rather to produce such a quick and constant spin of the bait as shall conceal the hooks from the fish to be caught. The principal point, therefore, is to fix the bait on the hooks so as to spin well, and to last in this state a long time; and thus to avoid as much as possible the renewing of the bait, by which time is lost, and generally just at the most valuable period of the day. No bait comes so near perfection in these several points as the parr-tail, and it will, I am persuaded, as far as a limited trial will allow of an opinion, be found to be better suited than any other to spinning for trout, in all streams where the current is strong. I have already remarked that shiners, or other fish of the same size, in the absence of the parr, will be large enough for this purpose. When the bait is properly applied, according to the mode recommended at page 308, the line should be cast as gently as possible by means of the trolling-rod, taking care not to injure the texture of the fish-bait by jerking it violently, and therefore avoiding too long a line and too forcible a throw. Underhand casting does less damage than when the bait is thrown overhand, and by its adoption the splash in its fall into the water is also much less considerable. In working the bait, everything depends upon the strength of the stream; but the rule always is to make the minnow spin as fast as possible without injury to its texture. Thus, when it is drawn against the stream, it may be steadily brought towards the hand and made to revolve chiefly by the action of the current. If, however, it is drawn down stream, a series of jerks must be given, or it will not spin sufficiently fast; and yet, if the pull is maintained so as to keep up the spinning at the same rate throughout, the casting-line itself makes a very prominent ripple, and by the overdoing of the attempt serves to scare away the fish. The line should always be well shotted, as the minnow will otherwise rise too near the surface, and no float will be required, inasmuch as the bait is always at the end of a "taut" line. Mr. Stoddart also recommends the adoption of a plain hook, baited with a minnow as when using a worm, running it in at the tail and bringing it out at the mouth; after which he hitches the gut over the tail to suit the bait in its proper position. With this he fishes as with a worm in low and clear states of the water; but as I have never seen this bait used, I cannot speak as to its efficiency. It is exactly the reverse of Izaak Walton's mode of entering the hook, and, according to Mr. Stoddart's practice and theory, is much to be preferred to it. Colonel Hawker's mode of baiting the hook, with the addition of side hooks, is used in the same way as ordinary spinning-tackle, and the minnow baited as he recommends will be found tolerably serviceable. It is merely the addition of the side hooks to Izaak Walton's method of applying the hook, which has the objection of offering the wrong end to the trout, having the barb at the tail instead of the head. It is, therefore, no wonder that trout so often are missed when rushing at it, since they almost invariably endeavor to seize the head. This is the case with most predacious animals, which are instinctively made aware that this part is the most vital organ, and they almost always begin by eating the brain where such an organ exists. When fishing with the minnow well leaded and in deep water, the angler seldom sees the trout rush at his bait, but is warned be the sense of touch, rather than by his eyes, that the trout is at it. At this moment the angler slackens his line gently for a couple of seconds, and then strikes with his wrist, using only a slight jerk. The trout is now either hooked or alarmed, but generally the former is the case, unless he is a very shy, wary old fox; in which case he is not likely to be again tempted on that day. If, however, the trout is seen approaching the minnow, the angler ought to endeavor, as far as his nerves will allow him, to continue the precise kind of motion which attracted the fish, until he not only *sees* him at the bait, but *feels* his pull, when he should proceed exactly as if all was out of sight. This, however, is a difficult task, and few young fishermen have sufficient command over themselves to avoid the mistake to which their attention is here directed. Every one who has hooked fish of any size with fine tackle, must be aware how difficult it is, when commencing trout-fishing, to carry out in practice the theory which he has been endeavoring to realize for some time past; and each, in his turn, must have been made painfully conscious of the danger not only of striking too soon and too hard, but of attempting to land a large fish with fine gut before he is tired.

The following instructions on fishing for the great lake trout were furnished for my work on Fish and Fishing, by an old and experienced angler, of high repute for science and skill, and much accustomed to the lakes. They are admitted to be the best ever published, and I have therefore no hesitation in quoting them here from my larger work.

I propose, in this connection, to treat of this fine
and exciting sport, describing

1st, The rod;

2d, The reel;

3d, The line;

4th, The leader, and train of hooks;

5th, The bait and flies;

6th, The bait-kettle;

7th, The boat and oarsman, or guide;

8th, The manner of striking the fish, when, the bait
is taken:

And lastly, 9th, How to play, and gaff the fish.

1st. The Rod.—A mutual friend, who writes occasionally for the "*Spirit*," and who is a most skilful troller,
wrote an article which appeared in the "*Spirit*" in the fall
of 1848, signed "M., Maspeth, Long Island," in which he
gave a capital description on most of the above heads.

The trolling-rod spoken of above, on page 298, will
answer all purposes. But the gentleman mentioned had
two of the most perfect trolling-rods I have seen; they
were made by Ben. Welch, of Cherry street, and are all
bamboo cane. I had one made by George Karr, of Grand
street, which I like very much; and I will describe it the
best way I can, although it is no easy matter to describe
on paper a rod of any kind:—Length from eleven to
thirteen feet; butt of ash, thoroughly seasoned, about
one and a quarter inches in diameter, or about as thick
as an ordinary bass-rod, The butt should be hollow, to
contain spare tips. The second, third and fourth joints
should be bamboo, so that when the rod is put together,
it will be about twelve feet.

The rod should have two spare tips; one should be
stronger and shorter than the other, to vary the fishing
according to the state of the weather, and circumstances.

The fourth, or last joint tip, should be about three

feet, thinner, and more pliant than the spare tops which fit in the bored butt. The first spare tip should be two feet long, stiffer and stronger than the original top. The second spare tip should be about fourteen inches long, strong and stiff; and in heavy weather, this strong, stiff tip will be the one to use.

Rod-making has been brought to such perfection, it would be a waste of time to give further instructions; but still I only know two men in this city who can make a true trolling-rod, viz.:—Ben. Welch, of Cherry street, and George Karr, of Grand street near Broadway.

Rings should never be used on rods of this character. The "railroad" through which the line travels, constitutes one of the peculiarities of this rod. Rings interfere with, and impede the line, and should not be used. The guides used by Welch are the only true ones—they are neat, light, with a thin flat shank, about one fourth of an inch in length, which is firmly secured on the different joints. There should be very few guides on the rod—five I consider sufficient, exclusive of the metal case at the top of each tip. This metal case should have a rounded surface, perfectly smooth, and sufficiently large to allow the line to run without the slightest obstruction or friction.

Let me give one hint before I take leave of the rod. I recommend that all trolling-rods should have guides on both sides—that is, a guide on the opposite side of the other: *not on the butt,* but on all joints from the butt to the end; and why? In this kind of fishing there is powerful pressure on the rod; and the very best will, from hard work, become bent, and remain bent, and thus lose its elasticity. To obviate this, turn round the joints, slip the line through the spare guides, and in a few hours the rod is "all straight."

2d. The Reel.—To give an explanation of this would be absurd. I will simply say, that No. 3 is about the proper size for a trolling-rod, without stop, click, or multiplier. The line cannot run off too free. According to my opinion, John Conroy can make the best reel in the world.

3d. The Line.—One hundred yards is abundant. Twisted silk is the best line for trolling. I know they kink, when new; but very little use will put an end to it—*id est* knock the kink out of it.

Plaited lines are very good and cheap, and do not kink: but they absorb the water, and do not run free from the rod.

A mixture of hair in lines is my abomination. It is the most dangerous and uncertain stuff a man can use. You can never depend on it; the hairs will give way with but little strain; and when you hook the heaviest fish, the greater danger is to be apprehended. I hate them.

4th. The Leader and Train of Hooks.—This word "leader" goes against my grain. The old familiar English-Irish sound of "casting-line," has a charm for my ear, equalled only by the still silent noise of

"Ballynahinch or Costello's flowing waters."

But let leader go for trolling.

Most Hollers use twisted gut for a leader, with a small swivel attached to one end. The other end is fastened to the reel-line, either by loop or knot, but a knot is by far preferable. The leader should be two yards long—some good and old hands use three yards. I never use twisted gut. I prefer a leader of good round salmon-gut.

The train of hooks is attached to the eye of the swivel, at the end of the leader. The train is made of five hooks, and made on the very best and most perfect gut, single. The strand upon which the hooks are tied, is fastened by a knot to another equally strong and perfect strand, which is fastened by a loop to a swivel at the end of the leader. Thus you have the rod, reel, line, leader, and train of hooks. Perhaps a sketch of the train of hooks will be better than an explanation. Here it is:

This train, it will be seen, is made of five hooks. The lip-hook should be a size or two smaller than the tail-hooks—say No. 5 for the tail, No. 6 for the middle, and No. 7 for the lip. These hooks are joined shank to shank, with the gut between them, and then firmly tied with waxed silk. But I procured from Ireland a set of hooks wedded or united together, and they are far superior to single hooks joined by tying together, for they frequently double up, and become very troublesome. George Karr, before named, can rig this kind of train better than any man in the city, as far as my experience goes.

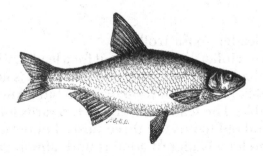

5th. The Bait and Plies.—The proper bait is the shiner, which can be plentifully procured in all the lakes of Hamilton County. They are taken with the smallest kind of hook, No, 12, with worm bait; and when secured, are put into the bait-kettle, and preserved until used. The mode of putting the shiner on the train is simple: put the lip or single hook through the lip, the middle hook in the belly, the end hook in the tail.

Unlike trout-fishing proper, I loop on my flies when trolling. About thirty-six inches from the shiner I loop on the leader—a large fly; and thirty inches from that fly I loop a smaller-sized one, and then I am rigged to "throw out."

6th. The Bait-Kettle.—This is a most indispensable article for the troller—he can't get along without it. It should be made of strong tin, painted green outside and white inside. The bottom should be wider than the top, but sloping gradually. Conroy has now in his store some very good and complete; but there is one great improvement, *to have the handle lie or fall inside the lid*. I recommend a small gauze ladle, with a short handle, to take the bait from the kettle when required; it will save much trouble, and injury, if not death, to the "dear little creatures."

The kettle should be replenished with water every hour; and one unerring sign that the shiner needs fresh waiter, is when he pokes his nose to the surface. "When the fishing is over, sink the kettle in the shoal water, and secure it, so that it cannot be tossed about by "wind or weather."

7th. The Boat and Oarsman, or Guide.—Here you must trust to luck—"first come, first served." But any person going to the house of John C. Holmes, at Lake Pleasant, will find good accommodation, and "honest John" will secure a good guide and a good boat; and from experience I can safely recommend Cowles, Batchellor, and Morrell, of Lake Pleasant, as faithful, honest, persevering, safe and skilful guides and oarsmen. Trolling is solely done from the boat. The troller with his face to the stern; the oarsman in the middle, or rather near the bow, and rows slowly and gently along the lake; about one and a half or two miles an hour is the proper speed.

8th. The Manner of Striking the Fish when the Bait is Taken.—Should there be much wind, thirty-five yards of line is sufficient to run out—if calm, say forty-five or fifty. When a fish is felt, the tip of the rod should he eased off, or given to the fish, in order that he have time to take hold; then give a good surge of the rod, and you will rarely miss striking him. Should you be fishing with two rods, which is almost always the case, pass the other rod to the oarsman. Never give the fish an inch, unless by actual compulsion; invariably keep him in hand— feel him at a distance, but still be kind and gentle, not rude or rough. Do not show the gaff until you know that the fish is "used up;" if a small fish, run the net *under* him; and if the fish is spent or exhausted, he will fall into it; but if he shows life, draw him *over* the net. If a large fish, use the guff, which pass under him, with the point downwards; then turn it up inside, and strike as near the *shoulder* as possible. I say *shoulder* instead of *tail*.

I believe that I have now done with this branch; but let me say, that no good troller uses lead or sinker of any kind. I have seen it used, but used to the destruction of sport and tackle. Sinkers carry the hooks to the bottom, and there you stick either to root or rock.

When trolling, you take, on the average, more fine brook trout than lake trout. I think that two to one is correct.

One word as to the sporting quality of the lake trout. The nine pound and a quarter trout, before mentioned, may perhaps be an exception; but I do affirm, that the lake trout is a fish of game, spirit, and endurance.

I have killed them from one to sixteen and a half pounds. The sixteen and a half pound lake trout was hooked by me, on a single gut leader; from the time I struck him, till his capture, was one hour and forty-five minutes. During the first half hour, he showed great bad temper, and kept the perspiration flowing off my head; he did sulk for half an hour, but it was a moving and a dragging sulk, unlike the salmon; and during this sulk he took me along the lake for about a mile; I became fatigued, and bore so heavy on him that I got him near the surface, and from that time until his death was one continued run and fight. He had not the vivacity of the nine and a quarter pound fish, but still I had "my hands full," and was effectually "used up" when he was gaffed by Cowles, my guide.

NATURAL AND ARTIFICIAL FLY-FISHING.

In the chapter on bottom-fishing, I have remarked that all fish may be taken by that mode; but now it must be explained, that the circle from which the victims of the fly-fisher's art are to be selected, is much more limited. He may, however, flatter himself that all, or nearly so, of the most prized varieties are included in his list, and this is the case not only in America and the British islands, but in almost all countries. In India, fly-fishing is practised to a great extent, and, indeed, wherever the *salmonidae* are found, it may be freely indulged in.

Natural fly-fishing consists in the use of the various living flies, grasshoppers, &c., which are found on the banks of rivers and lakes. It is practised by a process which is called dipping, but chiefly in such situations as are so much overhung with bushes as to preclude the use of the artificial fly. In these spots the water is generally still, and there is no possibility of offering the lure in any other position than a state of almost entire quiescence. Hence all imitations are easily discoverable; and the real fly and grasshopper, &c., are the only surface-baits which the fish will take.

Artificial fly-fishing, on the other hand, consists in the use of imitations of these flies, and also of other fancy flies, by means of an elastic rod and fine tackle, and by a process which is called whipping. All fish which will take the one will take the other kind of lure, but not always with an equal degree of avidity, as we shall hereafter find; but as the principle is the same in both cases, they are better treated of together, rather than to go over the same ground a second time.

The tackle for dipping is much more simple than that employed in whipping, and it consists of a moderately short and stiff rod; the spinning or trolling-rod, *minus* its butt joint, answers this purpose well,—of a short but strong reel-line of hand-twisted hair—of a single length—or two at most of gut—and a fine hook suited in size to the bait and fish. In dipping, it is usual to lengthen or shorten the line, which is used from a foot in length to two or three yards, by coiling it round the end of the top joint, and uncoiling it as the line is wished to be extended, and after the rod has been insinuated through the trees or bushes growing on the banks. Some anglers use a reel fixed upon the lower part of the second joint, and with a hair-line it acts pretty well; but with a plaited one, it is difficult to protrude the line from the end of the rod without so great a degree of disturbance as to alarm the fish. The uncoiling from the end of the rod is not unattended with this disadvantage; but it is less objectionable than doing so entirely from the reel; though I think, for the sake of convenience, that appendage may be added, taking care to have the lowest joint free, so as to be able to shorten the rod by that amount at pleasure.

For whipping, or fly-fishing as it is generally called—that is, for the use of the artificial fly—a rod, either single or two-handed, according to circumstances, is required, with a fine reel-line and large-barrelled reel; and also a long casting-line, with one, two, or three droppers, each armed with a fly.

The fly-rod is either a single-handed one, or, when used for the larger varieties of the trout, or for salmon, the two-handed rod. Both of these rods are usually made of the same materials, and they differ only in size, the single-handed varying from 11 to 13 feet in length, while the two-handed extends from 14 to 20 feet. They are both usually made in four or five lengths, but in Scotland they are, I believe, seldom in more than three pieces. The butt-end is generally an ash-sapling, sometimes solid, and at others hollowed out to receive the small joints. The middle joints are almost always made of hickory, and the top joint either of lancewood alone, or of that wood, spliced with the bamboo and strengthened with silk. Many of the best and lightest fly-rods are now made, except the butt-end, from rent and glued bamboo; and none are more beautiful and efficient than these if properly used; but they are very fragile in careless hands, and therefore scarcely fitted for the young angler. The reel is either simple, with a large drum or central barrel, or otherwise. The multiplier is made with a series of wheels, which are intended to give out and take in the line more rapidly than the simple machine. In this desirable point, I am satisfied that the object is attained much more completely by the simple large drum; for though the multiplier is very pretty in theory, yet in practice it is constantly failing in its powers when tested by a strong fish. Besides this, the large drum actually gives out line much faster than the multiplier, and has therefore that point in its favor; while in taking it in, he must be a bungler indeed who cannot wind the winch or handle rapidly enough to do all which he wishes to effect; and it is quite certain, that what is done is better and more smoothly done in this way than by the aid of wheels and cogs, which are liable to jerks and interruptions. Upon this reel is wound from 30 to 80 yards of line, varying with the rod and the fish, for which it is to be used. Thus the smaller fish, including the ordinary run of common trout and the grayling, will require only 80 or 35 yards, while the larger varieties of trout and the salmon should always have from 60 to 80 yards ready for their capture. The hairline should be regularly tapered, and should vary in strength from 24 hairs down to 14 for salmon, and from 18 down to 10 or 12 for trout. The tapering portion, however, should only extend in the trout line as far as it is clear of the reel, which may he estimated at about half the length of the line; and in the salmon line only for about 20 yards from the end. Plaited silk lines are now much used, especially for salmon, but I confess I have never seen, any line which could be thrown with as much certainty as the hand-made horse-hair line. It has just sufficient stiffness to carry itself smoothly through the air, with pliancy enough to adapt itself to all the varying evolutions of the angler's wrists and arms. The casting-line is composed of two, and sometimes of three portions; the first, or extreme portion consisting, in all cases, of several lengths of single gut carefully knotted together, with or without silk "lapping;" the next portion is usually of treble gut, twisted by the machine, or by quills and bobbins. To these some anglers add a third portion of twisted hair, which, however, is unnecessary if the reel-line is properly tapered, and is of hair also. The great principle to be carried out is to taper the line from the point of the rod to the end, so that in working it through the air it shall play smoothly, and obey the hand to the greatest nicety. In this respect it should imitate the four-in-hand whip, which is so graduated that it tapers all the way, and is hence capable of taking a fly off the leader's ear. The gut varies in strength and size, from that required for the salmon, to the finer sizes used in grayling or small trout-fishing. The single-gut portion is generally about two yards long, and terminates in a fly, which is called the stretcher, and which is either dressed on a length of gut, or has a fine loop left at its head, by which it may be attached to any fresh length of gut. About three or four feet from this stretcher another fly, called a dropper, is attached by means of a short length of gut, usually about three or four inches long; and at the junction of the single-gut with the twisted portion there is another dropper, with a somewhat longer length of gut. If more than two droppers are used, the single-gut length is increased to eight feet, and the third dropper is then introduced midway between the two already described, with a length of gut of about six inches, while that of the highest is increased to eight; by which gradual increase of length the stretcher and the droppers all ought to touch the water at the same time, while the foot length of the casting-line extends in a gentle sweep from the stretcher to the point of the rod. The mode of attaching these droppers to the casting-line is by opening the water-knots, and then introducing the dropper-gut between their two portions, after having previously knotted its end. This should be done as neatly as possible, to avoid making an unsightly projection. Most anglers whip the ends of the water-knots with white silk waxed with white wax, and also take a few turns round the dropper-gut to make all secure. The artificial flies have been already fully described above.

Whipping for small fish, as the dace, roach, or chub, where they exist, forms the best introduction to the use of the fly-rod, especially as these little fish may be met with in almost all our streams and rivers, and often in situations where there are no trees to interfere with the use of the line. Almost any small midge or gnat will take them; and the tackle throughout should be of the finest description, with a light single-handed rod of about 11 or 12 feet in length. The young angler should now take as much pains in throwing his fly as if he were intent upon the capture of the finest salmon. In watching the evolutions of the general run of fishermen, it is common enough to see two or three feet of line touching the water before the fly, whereas the contrary ought to be the case; and the fly should alight on the water as airily and gently as its natural prototype, with scarcely any portion of the line following its example by coining into contact with the water at all. If the angler will only endeavor to avoid jerking his line, and will coax his fly rather than force it forwards, he will soon see the difference. The cast or throw is effected as follows, when the rod is light and there is plenty of elbow-room. I am now supposing that the angler has a rod of 11 feet in length, and a line, altogether, of about 18, with either a single stretcher, or in addition one or two droppers, all very minute; he takes the casting-line in his left hand, at such a distance from the fly that it is quite clear of the ground, and with the rod pointing forward and to the left; then, at the moment when he looses the line, he, with a half-side, and half-backward movement of the arm, sweeps the line in a gentle curve till it is well behind and above him. It is at this point that the first mistake is likely to occur, as here the awkward hand generally jerks his fly, which is sometimes even whipped off with a snap, and after this jerk he can never regain that even and smooth flow which would otherwise follow its operation from the backward to the forward direction. When this movement is elegantly and effectively carried out, the line, without any abrupt change, is brought round the head from the backward to the forward movement without passing directly overhead, but in a line considerably above the level of the head of the angler; when it has passed before the body, it is thrown forwards *at the full length of the arm*, and, without the slightest hurry, to the point which it is intended the fly shall alight upon. If this is badly executed, and with any jerk, the line is doubled upon itself, and the loop thus made touches the water whilst the fly is two or three feet from its destination, and finally descends with a whole series of convolutions of gut or hair, enough to alarm all fish within sight. This is called throwing from the left shoulder, from which mode throwing from the right shoulder, or back-casting, differs in bringing the rod and arm, after they have achieved the backward movement, forward again by the side of the head, delivering the fly over the right shoulder, without making the complete circular sweep behind the body. Sometimes, when it is desirable to throw the fly with great delicacy, it is tried by waving the line from right to left over the head, in the form of a figure 8; but this can only be effectively done with a single fly, as the droppers interfere with the manoeuvre too much to allow of its being tried when they are used. The young angler should practise both methods, and should never consider that he has mastered the first great difficulty, until he has acquired the power of dropping his fly upon the water tolerably near a given snot by both the above methods, and without its being preceded by any portion of the line, or followed by more than a few inches of it. As soon as he has thus dropped his fly he begins to draw it more or less directly to him, and with a series of jerks, varying a good deal according to the fly and the fish to be taken. In whipping for small fry, very little more need be done than to bring the fly gently and steadily towards the bank, and then repeat the cast in a fresh direction. When hooked, they may be landed at once, even with a single hair-line. Dipping may be practised with the small fry, using the natural house-fly, or in fact any small fly; but it requires very little art, and I shall therefore postpone the description of this species of fishing until the paragraph treating of Chub-fishing.

Almost every species of fish, at some time or other, rises to fly in clear river waters; but the sea-trout is the only one which is ever known to take it in the open sea. This fish, however, affords great sport in the Gulf of St. Lawrence, even out of sight of land, with a large scarlet ibis fly, in a mackerel breeze. The pickerel, the bass, sometimes the perch, the smelt, and even the shad will rise to the fly, and all the small fry in the pools will take a midge on the smallest sized hook. Indeed, there is no prettier practice for a young hand, than whipping for smelt with the red fly, in large clear rivers.

Unlike the mere whipping for small fish, which I have dilated upon as forming an excellent introduction to trout-fishing, the latter requires great caution not to scare the fish, either by the too near presence of the angler, or by the awkward manipulation of his line and files. The management of the two-handed rod will more properly come tinder salmon and lake-trout fishing, for, although it is sometimes employed in fishing for common trout in large and wide rivers, yet it can scarcely even then be needed, and it certainly loses in delicacy of manipulation much more than it gains in its power of controlling a larger extent of water. Different men adopt various plans of throwing the fly, but it is of little consequence which mode of many is followed, so that the angler has only entire command of his rod and line, *and can do what he likes with his flies.* When this perfection of casting is arrived at, the angler may choose whether he will fish upstream or down, but he will soon find out by experience that the wind in his back is advantageous to him, and that he will scarcely succeed in any case in casting his fly in the face of a strong breeze, Beyond this, no rule will in all cases apply, and the fly-fisher must use his own discretion, founded in great measure upon practical observation, as to the precise mode in which he will reach and fish particular parts of the water that he believes to be the resort of good trout. Indeed, it is useless to attempt instructing the tyro by theoretical lessons in the details of an art in which it is certain that nothing but practice can give any degree of proficiency. This is constantly shown even in the professed fly-fisher of two or three seasons experience, who throws his fly with all the most approved motions, and is beforehand fully convinced that he is the equal of any angler, from Maine to Mississippi; but, when he sees fish after fish hooked and landed by some older hand following in his wake, and using the very same fly, with perhaps an inferior rod, he is obliged to confess that theory must succumb to delicacy of handling, and that fly-fishing is a practical art, rather than a science attainable in the closet. The various degrees of success mark the difference between the master and the scholar, and show that a lifetime may be spent in acquiring the power of deceiving this wary fish, and yet there may be room for improvement; hence it is that so many men of talent have been devotees to the fly-rod, and while they have enjoyed the beauties of nature displayed to them during the prosecution of their sport, they have nevertheless been much more deeply engaged in acquiring the art of fascinating a fish seldom of more than 20 ounces in weight. No one of these men would care for taking trout in any way unaccompanied by difficulty, and attainable without dexterity; but when it is found that by long practice, and careful observation, a feat can be accomplished which no other means will give, then the man who has mastered the power congratulates himself upon its possession, and is not unnaturally pleased in being enabled to display it, by showing what may be done after another's failure. Rivalry is the great zest in sport of all kinds, and the trout taken by an artist, in water which has been well flogged by his inferiors, are thought much more of than those landed where they rise to any bungler's throw. Rut to proceed to such a general description as may be of some little use to the tyro, I must first observe, that he should confine himself to a single-handed rod with a moderately long line—say, of from 15 to 18 feet, which he should at once draw off the reel, and of which he should hold the gut in his hand near the fly. With this he may proceed to fish the river which is the scat of his intended sport, and may walk quietly along its bank, throwing successively over every yard of likely water; but always fishing first the water nearest to him, and lengthening or shortening his line according to circumstances, such as the breadth of water, the freedom from trees, &c. He will find that he must not throw straight across the river, neither must he allow the fly or flies to be drawn too near his own bank, or he will not be able to lift them cleverly from the water, so as to get such a clear sweep as will enable him to re-cast them with precision and delicacy.

Hence, instead of fishing the water under his feet, he will throw his flies so as to take the edge next his own hank at the length of his line; and will thus successively throw over all on his side long before his person is seen; and when he brings his flies up to within 10 or 12 feet of where he is standing, he may lift them, because he has already well tried that portion of the water. But besides the excellence in throwing the fly, there is also a great art in striking and hooking the fish exactly at the right time, and with the proper degree of force. When the trout rises at the fly, which may always be seen by the angler, the rod should be raised with a motion upwards of the wrist only, avoiding, as far as the excitement of the moment will permit, all shoulder or elbow-work, and using just such a degree of wrist-action as may be judged will fasten so sharp an implement as the hook in so soft a substance as the mouth of the trout. Theoretically this may easily be estimated, but practically it will be found that the tyro generally jerks hard enough to strike a blunt hook deep into the jaws of a shark or dolphin. The object of striking at all, is to prevent the fish from having time to discover his mistake, the natural consequence of which would be to "blow out" the fly from his mouth. The fly-fisher, therefore, waits till the moment when the fly is actually within the lips of his victim, and then, with a gentle, yet rapid wrist-action, he fixes the hook there. This is much more easily done with a light single-handed rod than with one used by both hands, and hence it is advisable for this reason, as well as on account of the greater facilities in casting with it, to limit the young trout-fisher to its use. In playing trout when hooked, much depends upon their size; if small, they may be landed immediately; but if above half or three-quarters of a pound, according to the fineness of the tackle, and the gameness of the fish of that locality, it is necessary to yield to the powers for a tune, and to give him line for running; always taking care not to give him so much liberty as to enable him to reach adjacent weeds, or to rub his nose against the ground, and thus, in either way, get rid of his hook. When tolerably exhausted, by advancing the butt of the rod, and so using its flexibility as a safety-spring, the reel may be gradually wound up until the fish is brought near enough to be dropped quietly into the landing-net, after which it may be considered secure. But whoever has charge of the net, must keep well out of sight of the hooked fish until he is effectually exhausted, or he will be sure to make fresh straggles, and often to such an extent as to cause his loss. The fly may easily be cut out of the lip with a penknife, and is generally none the worse for the service it has performed.

Sea and lake-trout, when they take the fly, are to be managed in the same way as salmon, whose size and strength they approach much more nearly than those of the common trout.

For the salmon, tackle must be employed of a description much stronger than that used for trout; in principle, however, it is nearly similar; and a salmon-rod with its line may be compared, in all respects, to a trout-rod magnified with a slight power of the microscope.

The salmon-rod should be from 14 to 20 feet in length, and should be made of three or four lengths, at the discretion of the fisher. The butt is always of ash, the middle piece or pieces of hickory, perfectly free from flaw, and the top-piece of the best bamboo, ether rent and glued up or spliced in lengths, which of course only extend from joint to joint; this is better than lance-wood, which is apt to make the rod top-heavy. Angles of note differ as to the nature of the joints, which are sometime made to screw together; at others, with the bare wood of one joint dropping in to the brazed ferule terminating its next neighbor; and at others again, by having both ends brazed so as to oppose brass to brass. In both the latter cases the double pin, or bent wire and silk fastening are used, in order to prevent their becoming loose and unattached in the ardor of fishing. The rod should balance pretty evenly at the part where the upper hand grasps it above the reel, which is usually fixed at 18 or 20 inches from the but-end. These essential characteristics will suffice for the description of the salmon-rod. The reel-line has also been there described, and is of 80 to 100 yards in length, with the last 20 only tapered down to little more than half its regular size. To this is appended a casting-line made on the same plan as the trout-line, but one third longer in all its parts, and entirely of gut, which should be of the size called salmon-gut. The flies for salmon are described at page 402. When a dropper is used, it is generally appended at about four feet from the end.

These implements are used on a scale very different to trout-fishing and, generally speaking, with less delicacy in proportion to the increase of sweep, and the coarseness of the tackle; but in salmon-fishing, so much depends upon the extent of water covered in throwing the fly, that no pains should be spared to acquire this power as fully as possible. It must be remembered that in salmon-fishing, unlike trout-fishing, the river is often too broad for any line to reach nearly over all the good casts, and success is here often obtained solely by the power which some men have of sending their fly into parts which their weaker or less expert rivals cannot possibly cover. With the young angler, the first thing to be done is to secure the assistance of some resident guide well acquainted with the haunts of the fish, who will give him confidence, if he does nothing else. Without his aid the angler, if unsuccessful, will wander from point to point, and will be unable to do justice to himself, because he has no confidence that there are fish where he is trying for them. Indeed, even the experienced salmon-fisher is all the better for this assistance, if he is on strange water, as, though he may give a shrewd general guess as to the most probable casts for fish, he will often pass over good ones, and select those which are much inferior to his rejected localities. He will also get some information as to the probability of his flies suiting the particular river and time, and generally as to the fitness of his arrangements for that precise spot. This knowledge, once obtained, will serve as long as the river continues in the same state; but if rain, or the reverse, should alter the condition of the water, making it either much lower or much higher than before, the tyro will require additional aid from his *quondam* friend. This is known to all salmon-fishers, inasmuch as these fish frequent very different parts of the same river in a low, and again, in a high stage of the water; and the flies also will require considerable modification, according to these changing elements. There are, however, some general rules which may be of service, though they by no means apply in all cases. Thus, large rivers usually require larger flies than small streams, which latter will more often be successfully fished with a gaudy but comparatively small fly—that is, if the water is not too clear. The fish, generally lying at the bottom, will scarcely be attracted from the depth of a large river by a small fly, whilst if it is too gaudy, they are scared by its colors when they rise near the surface. Again, in small streams salmon seldom take any fly, except when the water is rather discolored, and in that state a dusky or dull one is not sufficiently attractive; and when the same condition of water exists in the large rivers a gaudy color will also be preferred. The size of the fly is of course an index to that of the hook, which is its foundation. Beyond these imperfect hints little aid can be given to the tyro, and he must learn by experience in his own person, or from that of others, the peculiar rules applicable to each locality.

The casting is generally from the left shoulder, backwards; after which the line is steadily and rather slowly brought over the right shoulder, with the rod held in both hands, and its point directed upwards and backwards. It is then brought forwards with an increase in speed and force, when, still accelerating the speed, the angler delivers his fly at the spot upon which he wishes it to alight. This throwing from the left shoulder is chiefly useful where there are low bushes, or other impediments near the ground behind the angler, under which circumstances the fly must be kept aloft; but sometimes the reverse is the case, and with impending trees and a bare background, the right shoulder or back-casting will avail much better than the rival mode above alluded to; but it is not so manageable with the two-handed rod as with the light singlehanded trout-rod, which may be used with as much certainty and facility as the four-in-hand whip. Mr. Stoddart lays it down as a rule that no man can manage properly, without the aid of the wind, a line more than four times the length of his rod, measuring from the fly to its point, and not including that part within the rings. This is certainly much within what is generally considered the extreme length of the salmon-line, and many professed fishers maintain that they can throw nearly twice as far as that length will command. But there is a vast difference between simply throwing a fly, and throwing it cleverly and effectually;

NATURAL AND ARTIFICIAL FLY-FISHING   369

still I cannot help thinking that Mr. Stoddart has a little underrated the power of the salmon-rod and line in good hands, when he limits the range to 35 yards from the spot where the angler stands. This I should say is about the average length of good fly-fishers, but I should think that some few tall and muscular men, who are also adepts, can command nearly 10 yards more, when the air is perfectly still, and the situation is favorable to the display of their power and skill. Much must depend upon the tackle, which should he very nicely graduated, and if the cast is intended to be very extensive, one fly only should be used; indeed in salmon-fishing it is seldom that much good is derived from a dropper in addition to the stretcher. When the fly is to be thrown in a wide river, of rather sluggish current, it may be directed nearly straight across, especially if the opposite bank can be reached; and the fly, after it has touched the water, may be brought back with a circular sweep, keeping the rod low until it is absolutely necessary to raise it in order to bring home the fly, and working it by gentle fits and starts so as to imitate the movements of a living insect, When, however, there is a considerable stream, the fly may be thrown obliquely downwards, as in trout-fishing, and is then brought back against the stream, and often without that attempt at jerking which must be made in comparatively still water. In all cases, the salmon-fisher should keep as much as possible out of sight; and when he has recourse to wading, he should only enter the water which he has already effectually tried; and when there, he should make as little disturbance in it as he can possibly avoid. In this respect, however, salmon are duller and less wary than common trout, or even than sea-trout; but still they are easily scared, and no one should incautiously run risks which are not absolutely required. The fly is worked very differently to the trout-fly, which must always be on the top of the water to be

effectual; whereas the salmon-fly should always be sufficiently under the water to avoid making any ripple as
it is drawn towards the thrower, and yet not so deep as
to be wholly out of sight. The young angler should not,
however, follow his lure too closely with his eye, or he
will be apt to strike when the fish rises at it; whereas, he
should always depend upon the sense of touch before
he raises his rod, which is the only motion to be adopted. Sharp striking, as in trout-fishing, is wholly repre-
hensible; and all that is required is the instinctive stand
which it is impossible to avoid making against the fish
as he seizes the fly, to run away with it. Sometimes, however, it is found difficult, or even impossible, to tempt
the salmon into actually seizing the fly; they will rise at
it again and again, but from some cause or other refuse
to take it into their jaws. In this case it must be changed
until one is found to suit their fancy, but the change
need not be made until the same fly has been tried two
or three times unsuccessfully. Patience and perseverance, with skill and science, will here be required, and
will always be served in the long run.

In playing the salmon, greater art is required than
in the corresponding department of trout-fishing; and,
in consequence, nearly one third of all the fish hooked
escape before they are landed. This arises generally
from imperfect hooking, but often also from defect in
the tackle, which has escaped the notice of the angler.
Besides these causes of danger, there are others depend-
ing upon the direction taken by the fish, which cannot
always be followed by the angler, either from the depth
of the water in large rivers, or from mechanical causes
in the shape of rocks, woods, &c., where the stream is
smaller. When hooked, the first thing to be done is to
raise the point of the rod, commonly called "giving the
fish the butt," which motion must be carried out with as
much power as the fisher considers his tackle will bear;

always remembering to give way by releasing the line, when the strain is too great for it to bear, and when the fish is resolutely bent upon running. But this exact calculation as to restraining or giving way is sometimes very difficult, especially as the size of the fish is no certain index to his power; nor can the size always be correctly estimated at the first commencement of the struggle, especially by the tyro at this kind of sport. A lively and fresh-run fish will appear twice as big as he really is whilst a large but dull one will sometimes deceive his pursuer into the belief that he is weak and powerless, and then, in a fit of desperation, he will show his real size and capabilities by breaking away with a long line towing astern. Mr. Stoddart's directions for playing the salmon are so good, that I am tempted to quote them in his own words:—"Always in running a fish, keep well up to, or, if possible, at right angles with its head. In the event of its taking across the current, instead of stemming or descending it, give the butt without reserve. In the case of a plunge or somerset, slacken line as quickly as possible, but lose no time in recovering it when the danger is over. When fish are plentiful, and in the humor to take the fly, it is better to risk the loss of an indifferent-sized individual which you happen to have hooked, than to allow a long range of unfished water to become disturbed through its capricious movements. In this case stint the line and hold on obdurately, but not beyond the presumed strength of your tackle. During the grilse season there are many portions of water, on Tweed especially, where it would be absolute folly in the angler were he to humor the fish to its heart's content. A lively nervous grilse may occasion more alarm among its kind than one is aware of, especially if the water be of the transparent hue it generally bears during the summer and autumnal months. In event, however, of the salmon being few or rising shyly, I would advise that some degree of care and ceremony be taken with what fortune brings to the hook; and that on such occasions more regard be paid to the management of the fish under control than to the non-disturbance of a few yards of stream, where the chances of adding to one's success are, at the least, extremely doubtful. In these circumstances avoid using undue violence. Should the fish escape, the consciousness of your having done so will only acid to the disappointment. There is one precaution particularly to be attended to in respect to a newly run fish, and that is, immediately on hooking it to use a moderate degree of pressure. The salmon will then brave or stem the current, and direct its course upwards; whereas, on tightening the reins, it will frequently do the reverse, and thus not only may a portion of the water in prospect become disturbed, but there is considerable chance, and in some places an absolute certainty, of the fish, if a large one, making its escape." Baggits generally descend the stream as a rule, when hooked, and no management will make them leave the current; but as they fight sluggishly, and as their loss is of little consequence, provided they do not run away with a good line, the butt may be shown them pretty early, and with a considerable degree of power.

The gaff is to be used in the following manner:— When the salmon has been thoroughly exhausted by his efforts to free himself from the boom in which he has been opposed by die elastic resistance offered by the rod, he is brought near the bank, still keeping the butt-end of die red evil advanced: and the assistant then proceeds to strike the gaff into the shoulder of the fish, or if he uses the single hook, to insert it into the gill-cover. The latter plan is the least injurious to the beauty of the fish, and in skilful hands will aim war every purpose. In all cases, however, the assistant, should keep out of tight until the angler is satisfied, by the yielding of the fish, that it is safe for him to approach, for a neglect of this precaution leads to the loss of many a fish. The assistant attempting to strike him before he is spent only makes him desperate; and the efforts to escape, which before this were within bounds, and under the control of the angler, are now rendered madly violent. This tries even good tackle too far, and either the hook itself or the gut gives way, or else the hold on the fish actually tears away. Tact and experience are the only safe guides in this delicate point, and without them apparent victory often ends in defeat. Instead of the gaff or hook, the landing-net is much used; and in the South, as well as in Wales, is perhaps more in vogue than the gaff. The only objection is its size; but as both must be carried by an assistant, since neither can be well managed by the angler himself, this is really of little consequence. If, however, the angler is either unable or unwilling to obtain an assistant, the hook with sliding stick is the best instrument for the purpose; but even with its aid he must wait until the fish is nearly spent, and must then draw near a low and shelving shore before he can venture to hook him under the gills. Most rivers, however, present these convenient spots at intervals, and the angler should play his fish until he reaches one, let the distance be what it may, if he wishes to run no unnecessary risk. In all cases when landed, the salmon should at once be knocked on the head, and the hook carefully removed with a penknife.

SEA FISHING.

Without descending to deep sea-fishing, with a drop-line and sinker of any given weight in many-fathom water, there is pretty fair sport to be had in the hays, and on most of the Atlantic sea-coasts in the spring, summer and autumn, with several varieties of fish, which are also excellent on the table.

The chief favorites are the following

The striped bass, *Labrax Lineatus.*

The king fish, *Umbrina Nebulosa.*

The weak fish, *Otolithus Regalis.* A variety of this fish, *Otolithus Carolinensis*, is frequent in the Southern rivers, and is known, improperly, as "the Trout."

The black fish, or Tautog, *Tautoga Americana.*

The sea bass, *Centropristes Nigricans.*

The sheep's head, *Sargus Ovis.*

The porgee, *Pagrus Argyrops.*

The sea perch, *Corvina Argyroleuca.*

The blue fish, *Temnodon Saliaior.*

It cannot be said, that there is any great skill or science in the taking of these fish; as there is, for instance, in fly-fishing, trolling or spinning with the dead bait; but it cannot be denied that there is much amusement, a good deal of excitement, and that this sort of fishing is, with an agreeable party, a pleasant way of passing a hot summer or sultry autumn day.

The best varieties of fish taken in the bays and estuaries of our rivers, are, of those above named especially; the weak fish, the king fish, the black fish, and the sheep's- head; the latter being the American epicure's prime boast, and the rival of the European turbot.

The weak fish is abundant in the vicinity of New York, and is angled for with much success in the inner bay. It is said to derive its name from the weakness of its mouth, which is so soft that it is often torn by the hook, so that the fish escapes. I have my doubts, however, whether this is not a misnomer for wheat fish, by which also it is known. It pulls fairly upon the hook, and, when struck of a considerable size, gives considerable play to the angler before it can be secured.

The best rod is a moderately stiff general fishing rod, with a reel, and from one hundred to one hundred and fifty yards of flax or hemp line; a No. 1 Kirby hook will probably be found, on the whole, the most successful; and the most killing baits are shrimp, shedder crabs, or clams. The weak fish occasionally runs up to eight or nine pounds, but the general average does not probably exceed two. When fresh out of the water, it is a good fish, somewhat resembling the trout in flavor, but it soon becomes soft and flaccid. It is not nearly so game a fish as the striped bass, or the king fish, yet it is not without its advocates and admirers.

Immediately around the Battery, and even from Castle Garden bridge, or the fiats off Communipaw, in

Buttermilk Channel, at Bergen Point, Elizabethtown Point, in the Kills, and in Newark bay, this fish frequently affords considerable sport.

The barb, or king fish, is a far superior fish to the last both in sporting qualities and in culinary excellence. He is to be caught with the same tackle described under the head of the weak fish, but he requires a smaller hook, as he has but a little mouth, and he takes the shedder crab more freely than any other bait. It is said that in 1827, a man and a boy in Jamaica bay, off Rockaway, killed four hundred and twenty-two king fish in six hours; but this, if it ever were done, is never like to be done again, as the king fish is said to be becoming very rare, some say in consequence of the persecution of the blue fish, which has recently become, in proportion as the barb has waxed scarce, largely abundant.

The king fish is a hold, sharp biter, and fights hard when he is first hooked. He is not, however, a heavy customer, running only from; a lb. to 2 lbs. at the utmost, a maximum which he rarely attains.

In New York harbor, the flats from Bergen Point to Jersey City, in the neighborhood of the rock known as Black Tom, and opposite Communipaw, are the best waters in this vicinity for the king fish; but they are also taken in the Passaic bay and the bays of Long Island.

The tautog, or black fish, is an ugly, leather-mouthed, spine-backed fish, but excellent in a barbecue, and a tolerably game fish on the hook, He comes into season early in spring, and it is said that the flowering of the dogwoods may be regarded as a sign that he is in condition.

His favorite grounds are the vicinity of submerged rocks, piles, or sunken wrecks, where there are strong whirls and eddies. He is always taken on the bottom.

A stout trolling-rod, with a strong flaxen line, a

reel, and two black-fish hooks of size to suit the angler's pleasure, each armed on foot lengths of trebly twisted gut, the one of twelve, the other of fifteen inches length, attached to a ring which is appended to the line below the sinker, constitute the best tackle.

The most killing bait is the little fiddler, or soldier crab; but the black fish also bites freely at the large finny worm of the salt-water beaches, *Nereis,* when baited on the proper hook.

He bites slowly, and likes to suck at the bait before swallowing it, but, when struck, he pulls well and fights hard, running for the most part downward. He runs in weight from one to ten or twelve pounds, and is famous for his tenacity of life.

The sheep's-head is usually taken with drop-lines of two hundred yards, a pound sinker, and a stout black-fish hook; but this is but a pull-baker, pull-devil kind of sport, and the only real way to fish for him is with a capital stiff trolling-rod, a large click reel, and a couple of hundred yards of stout flaxen line. The hook, a large sized one of the black-fish pattern, armed on gimp, should be buried to the arming in the neck of a whole, unbroken clam, which this ravenous and strong fish cracks shell and all, as his favorite bon bouche.

It is great joy to the angler who hooks one, great proof of skill and immense glory if he land him. For he is the king of salt-water game fish.

The blue fish is taken by squidding in swift tideways from a boat under sail in a stiffish breeze; and when one has the luck to come across a good shoal in the humor to bite, it is, beyond a doubt, great fun.

The following tables of time, tide, bait, depth, and tackle contain, it is believed, all that can be imparted by printed instruction to the learner. Patience, perseverance, good temper, and good luck must do the rest.

All of which, though it be not in the province to bestow, it is in the power earnestly to wish, for all his friends and readers, of their humble servant to command,

FRANK FORESTER.

The Cedars, *June* 30, 1856

NAME OF FISH.	DEPTH OF WATER.	HOW NEAR BOTTOM.	MOVING OR STILL BAIT.	HOW TO STRIKE.	HOW TO PLAY.
Striped Bass,	From 4 to 25 feet.	Within a foot or two of bottom.	Stationary, unless trolling for with rod, or squid.	Strike quickly.	Kill as quickly as he will let you.
Weak Fish,	"10 to 35 feet.	Within two feet of bottom.	Stationary.	Strike quickly.	Kill as quickly as he will let you.
King Fish,	"10 to 35 feet.	Not above a foot from bottom.	Stationary.	Strike quickly.	Kill as quickly as he will let you.
Sea Bass,	"5 to 50 fathom.	Three feet from bottom.	Stationary.	Strike quickly.	Pull by main force.
Black Fish,	"5 to 50 feet.	On the bottom.	Stationary.	Strike quickly.	Don't give an incb.
Sheep Fish,	16 feet.	On the bottom.	Stationary.	Let him run and strike himself.	Pull up by force, if you can.
Black Drum,	8 feet and over.	On the bottom.	Stationary.	Let him run and strike himself.	Kill, if you can.
Porgee,	25 to 100 feet.	Off the bottom.	Stationary.	Strike quickly.	Pull up immediately

NAME OF FISH.	WHAT ROD AND LINE.	WHAT SNOOD.	WHAT HOOK.	WHAT SINKER.	WHAT WEIGHT.
Striped Bass,	Trolling-rod, reel, and hemp line, or squidline without rod.	Gut.	No. 1 to 4 Kirby.	Enough to keep bait stationary, according to tide.	1 to 28 lbs., with rod, up to 50, with squid.
Weak Fish,	Trolling-rod, reel, and hemp line.	Gut.	No. 0 to 1 Kirby.	Do. do.	1/2 to 10 lbs., rod.
King Fish,	Trolling-rod, reel, and hemp line.	Gut.	No. 4. Kirby or Limerick.	Do. do.	1/2 to 2 lbs., rod.
Black Fish,	Trolling-rod, reel, and hemp line.	Gut.	No. 2 Black-fish.	Enough to keep bait stationary, *on bottom*	1 to 16 lbs.
Sea Bass,	Stout hemp drop-line.	None.	No. 2 Kirby.	Half pound.	1 to 10 lbs.
Sheep's-head,	Stout hemp drop-line, or stout rod, hemp line, and reel.	None, or Gimp.	No. 0 to 1 Black-fish.	Enough to keep bait on bottom.	5 to 15 lbs., average 10 lbs.
Porgee,	Drop-line.	None.	No. 0 to 1 Black-fish.	Half pound.	3/4 to 2 lbs.
Drum,	Drop-line, or strong rod and reel.	None, or Gut.	No. 0 to 1 Black-fish.	Enough to keep bait on bottom.	10 to 60 lbs.

NAME OF FISH.	BEST SPRING BAIT.	BEST SUMMER BAIT.	BEST AUTUMN BAIT.	TIME OF BAY.	TIME OF TIDE,
Striped Bass.	Shad Poe in rivers, Live Bait, Trolling, or Red Ibis Fly.	Shrimp, Shedder Crab, Soft Crab.	Shrimp, Shedder Crab, Soft Crab.	Personally, I believe one time is as good as another. But all men have their fancies.	Some persons prefer the turns of the tides; some high or low slack water. I think there is no choice except to keep the proper depth of water.
Weak Fish.	None.	Shrimp.	Shrimp.		
King Fish.	None.	Crab.	None.		
Black Fish.	Soft Clam, Crab, Shrimp, Fiddlers.	Soft Clam, Crab, Shrimp, Fiddlers.	Soft Clam, Crab, Shrimp, Fiddlers.		
Sea Bass.	Rockaway or Soft Clams, opened.	As in Spring.	As in Spring.		
Sheep's-Head.	Muscle or Clam, not opened.	As in Spring.	As in Spring.		
Porgees.	Hard Clam cut Bait.	As in Spring.	As in Spring.		
Sea Perch.	Shrimp.	As in Spring.	As in Spring.		

Be it observed, that I do not note Mackerel, because I do not regard him as game; and secondly, that no sportsman is presumed to catch Drum or Porgees, if he can help it.

APPENDIX.—A

Dear Sir:—

As you wished me to make out a list of the prices of my guns, I take the liberty of sending you this statement, as follows:—

Prices of Guns in General.

First quality of fine laminated steel barrels, with superfine bar-locks, steel case-hardened furniture, gold name plate, *pure* platina vents, with spare nipples, and wrench, and bore to order; with cover,   *only* $150 00

Second quality, same material, not so fine,   125 00

If mahogany case, and *finest* implements, and leather over-case suitable to first-mentioned gun be added, cost $25 00, or for all 175 00

Second class case for 2d class gun, with outfit as required,   from $15 00 to 20 00

Also double-barrel guns, *a good article*, of half and half, steel and iron, barrels. They shoot strong and keep clean; cost, according to finish,   from $60 00, to 100 00

The steel and twist guns, of various bores and lengths, such as you described; according to fineness, from $65 to 80 00 Plainer, from $40 00 to 50 00

All of which I will warrant to shoot strong, and regular in dispersion of shot; or I will alter them to suit purchaser, free of charge, if required after trial.

Of whatever price the gun is, I will have it shoot well, *when it leaves me,* but the finer stuff holds out the longer, resisting the affinity of lead to the barrels, as well as the corrosive qualities of gunpowder; hence my preference to steel barrels, or next to them, the steel mixture.

I have recently got word of a fellow in San Francisco, Cal., who has actually sold guns there, to friends of mine, as though they came from me, he pretending to act as my agent. I may here state to you, I have no agent, nor is any *new gun,* having my name on it, genuine, unless purchased of myself.

I have put the fellow in the hands of an attorney to settle with him, the same attorney being one of the men imposed on, by a sham gun, purporting to have come from me.

I herein send you a table of the comparative strength of gun-barrels, of various kinds of metals, as fully authenticated by experiments in proof.

You will perceive the laminated steel barrels stand first for strength, and stub and steel mixture next, and preserve their cleanliness.

	Equal to a pressure of	Pressure of proof charge.	Surplus strength.
Laminated steel,	6022 lbs.	1700 lbs.	4322 lbs.
Best stub and steel mixture,	5555	1700	3855
Wire twist,	5019 ⅓	1700	3319 ½
Stub twist,	4818	1700	3118
Charcoal iron,	4526	1700	2826
Threepenny skelp iron,	3841	1700	2141
Damascus iron,	3292	1700	1592
Twopenny skelp iron,	2840	1700	1140

I am, dear sir, yours respectfully,
John Mullin,
No. 16 Ann st., New York.

APPENDIX.—B

I have just learned that D. B. Trimble, Sportsman's Warehouse, No. 200 Baltimore st., Baltimore, has a lot of fine ducking guns of Westley Richards' best, made to order, of the Carroll's Island Club pattern, nearly similar in all respects to the guns recommended by me at p. 39.

These guns are of the best laminated steel.
Barrels 45 inch—6 gauge, will chamber 22 BB shot.
weight of barrels,...................8 lb.
"   stock,......................7 ½
"   entire gun,............ 15 ½

Platina vents. Bar-locks 5 ¼ inches, nipples military size, jointed loading-rod, spare nipples and cover, but no case. Price complete,.....................................$112 00

Mr. Trimble has guns of the same style by other makers, at 75 00

I have no hesitation in recommending the 112 dollar Westley Richards pieces as the best style of shoulder-duck-guns in the world, and very cheap at the price.

Guns of this fashion, and nearly of this size, were recommended by me. in 1850, to some gentlemen of Baltimore, to whom I showed one of the same kind, but somewhat larger, previous to which time they had not, I believe, been used in that section of the country.

APPENDIX.—C

Materials required for making artificial flies.

A complete fly-fisher will make his own flies, and will find much amusement in the practice of this delicate art. It will be necessary that he should provide himself with the following materials to enable him to imitate the flies described hereinbefore:

London, Kirby-sneck, and Limerick hooks, of all sizes. Of these the Limerick hook is in the greatest general estimation; but in the north of England, the Kirby-sneck hook is preferred for small hackle flies.

Feathers of the grouse, snipe, bittern, woodcock, partridge, landrail, golden plover, starling, and jay; hackles from cocks and peacocks.; furs of all colors, from the skins of squirrels, moles and water-rats; camel's hair; hare's ear and fur from its neck, and the yellow fur from the skin of the martin; mohairs of various shades, and camlets; black horse-hair; hog's down died various colors; gold, and silver twist; and sewing silk of various colors and thicknesses.

Silk twist, cobblers' and bees'-wax.

A pair of pliers, a pair of fine-pointed scissors,

a small hand slide-vice, and a fine-pointed strong dubbing-needle.

Silkworm gut, from the finest to the strongest, and Salmon gut, single and twisted.

Lengths of the white and sorrel hairs of stallions' tails.

There are other fancy materials, as monkey's fur; parrot's, kingfisher's, macaw's, gold and silver pheasant feathers, and, above all, the scarlet ibis.

Fancy flies often kill when no others will—witness the far-famed scarlet ibis wings, with gold twist body; no fly kills like it, year in and year out, on Long Island, and it is sure death to sea-trout in the gulf of St. Lawrence, and everywhere to smelt, which rise at it readily.